ALASKA,
ITS SOUTHERN COAST
AND THE SITKAN ARCHIPELAGO

LECTOR HOUSE PUBLIC DOMAIN WORKS

ALASKA,
ITS SOUTHERN COAST AND THE SITKAN ARCHIPELAGO

ELIZA RUHAMAH SCIDMORE

ISBN: 978-93-5344-833-2

Published: -

LECTOR HOUSE LLP
E-MAIL: lectorpublishing@gmail.com

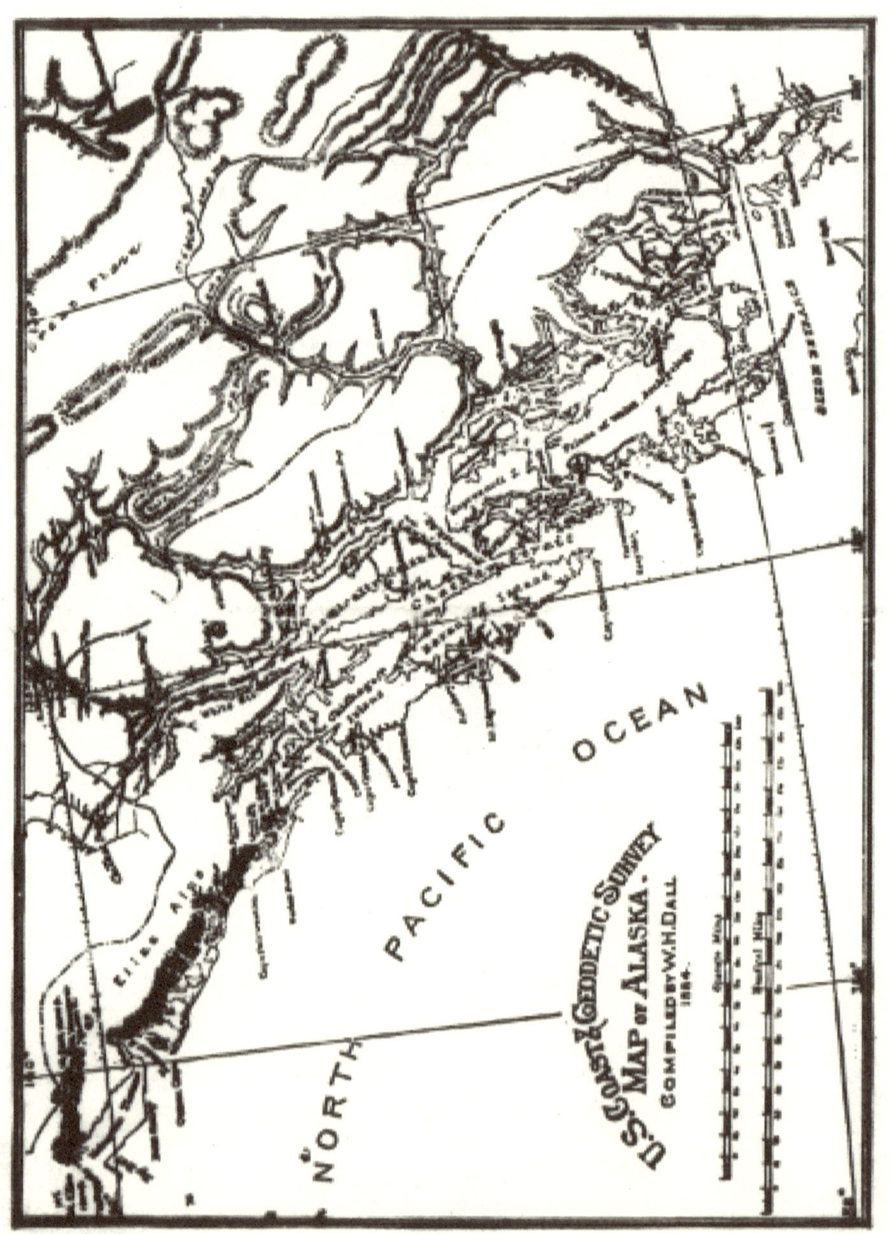

MAP OF ALASKA.

U.S. COAST & GEODETIC SURVEY
COMPILED BY W. H. DALL 1884.

ALASKA,

ITS SOUTHERN COAST AND THE SITKAN ARCHIPELAGO

BY

E. RUHAMAH SCIDMORE

WITH MAP AND ILLUSTRATIONS

"Berlin, Sept. 5.—We have seen of Germany enough to show that its climate is neither so genial, nor its soil so fertile, nor its resources of forests and mines so rich as those of Southern Alaska."—William H. Seward—Travels Around the World, Part VI. chap. v. page 708.

PREFACE.

These chapters are mainly a republication of the series of letters appearing in the columns of the *St. Louis Globe-Democrat* during the summer of 1883, and in the *St. Louis Globe-Democrat* and the *New York Times* during the summer of 1884. To readers of those journals, and to many exchange editors, who gave further circulation to the letters, they may carry familiar echoes. The only excuse for offering them in this permanent form is the wish that the comparatively unknown territory, with its matchless scenery and many attractions, may be better known, and a hope that those who visit it may find in this book information that will add to their interest and enjoyment of the trip.

In rearranging the original letters many errors have been corrected and new material incorporated. During brief summer visits it was impossible to make any serious study, solve the mysteries of the native people, or give other than fleeting sketches of their out-door life and daily customs. Elaborate resumés of the writings of Baron Wrangell and Bishop Veniaminoff have been given by Professor Dall in his work on "The Resources of Alaska," and by Ivan Petroff in the Census Report of 1880 (Vol. IX.), and have since been so often and so generally quoted as hardly to demand another introduction to those interested in ethnology. Such mention as I have made of the traditions and customs of the Thlinkets is condensed from many deck and table talks, and from conversations with teachers, traders, miners, and government officers in Alaska. Wherever possible, credit has been given to the original sources of information, and the "Pacific Coast Pilot" of 1883 and other government publications have been freely consulted. The nomenclature and spelling of the "Coast Pilot" have been followed, although to its exactness and phonetic severity much picturesqueness and euphony have been sacrificed.

The map accompanying the book is a reduced section of the last general chart of Alaska published by the United States Coast and Geodetic Survey, and is reproduced here by the permission of the compiler, Prof. William H. Dall.

Of the illustrations, the cut of the Indian grave at Fort Wrangell was one accompanying an article published in *Harper's Weekly*, August 30, 1884, and other pictures have been presented to readers of the *Wide Awake* magazine of March, 1885. For views of the Davidson glacier, the North River, and the top of the Muir glacier, and the interior of the Greek Church at Sitka, from which cuts were made, I am indebted to a daring and successful amateur photographer of San Francisco, to whom especial credit is due.

To the officers of the ship and agents of the company I have to express appreciation of the favors and courtesies extended by them to my friends and to myself.

Each summer I bought my long purple ticket, reading from Portland to Sitka and return, with pleasurable anticipations; and all of them—and more—being realized, I yielded up the last coupons with regret.

For information given and assistance rendered in the course of this work I am under obligations to many people. I would particularly make my acknowledgments in this place to Prof. WILLIAM H. DALL, Capt. JAMES C. CARROLL, Hon. FREDERIC W. SEWARD, Prof. JOHN MUIR, Prof. GEORGE DAVIDSON, Capt. R. W. MEADE, U.S.N., Capt. C. L. HOOPER, U.S.R.M., and Hon. J. G. SWAN.

E. R. S.

WASHINGTON, D. C., March 15, 1885.

CONTENTS

LIST OF ILLUSTRATIONS

SOUTHERN ALASKA
AND THE SITKAN ARCHIPELAGO.

CHAPTER I.

THE START—PORT TOWNSEND—VICTORIA— NANAIMO.

Although Alaska is nine times as large as the group of New England States, twice the size of Texas, and three times that of California, a false impression prevails that it is all one barren, inhospitable region, wrapped in snow and ice the year round. The fact is overlooked that a territory stretching more than a thousand miles from north to south, and washed by the warm currents of the Pacific Ocean, may have a great25 range and diversity of climate within its borders. The jokes and exaggerations that passed current at the time of the Alaska purchase, in 1867, have fastened themselves upon the public mind, and by constant repetition been accepted as facts. For this reason the uninitiated view the country as a vast ice reservation, and appear to believe that even the summer tourist must undergo the perils of the Franklin Search and the Greeley Relief Expeditions to reach any part of Alaska. The official records can hardly convince them that the winters at Sitka are milder than at New York, and the summers delightfully cool and temperate.

In the eastern States less has been heard of the Yukon than of the country of the Congo, and the wonders of the Stikine, Taku, and Chilkat rivers are unknown to those who have travelled far to view the less impressive scenery of the Scandinavian coast. Americans climb the well-worn route to Alpine summits every year, while the highest mountain in North America is unsurveyed, and only approximate estimates have been made of its heights. The whole 580,107 square miles of the territory are almost as good as unexplored, and among the islands of the archipelago over 7,000 miles of coast are untouched and primeval forests.

The Pribyloff or Seal Islands have usurped all interest in Alaska, and these two little fog-bound islands in Behring Sea, that are too small to be marked on an ordinary map, have had more attention drawn to them than any other part of the territory. The rental of the islands of St. Paul and St. George, and the taxes on the annual one hundred thousand sealskins, pays into the treasury each year more than four per cent interest on the $7,200,000 originally paid to Russia for its possessions in North America. This fact is unique in the history of our purchased territories, and justifies Secretary Seward's efforts in acquiring it.

The neglect of Congress to provide any form of civil government or protection for the inhabitants checked all progress and enterprise, and kept the country in the background for seventeen years. With the development of the Pacific northwest, settlements, mining-camps, and fisheries have been slowly growing, and increasing in numbers in the southeastern part of Alaska, adjoining British Columbia. The prospectors and the hardy pioneers, who seek the setting sun and follow the frontiers westward, were attracted there by the gold discoveries in 1880, and the impetus then given was not allowed to subside.

Pleasure-travellers have followed the prospectors' lead, as it became known that some of the grandest scenery of the continent is to be found along the Alaska coast, in the region of the Alexander or Sitkan Archipelago, and the monthly mail steamer is crowded with tourists during the summer season. It is one of the easiest and most delightful trips to go up the coast by the inside passage and cruise through the archipelago; and in voyaging past the unbroken wilderness of the island shores, the tourist feels quite like an explorer penetrating unknown lands. The mountain range that walls the Pacific coast from the Antarctic to the Arctic gives a bold and broken front to the mainland, and everyone of the eleven hundred islands of the archipelago is but a submerged spur or peak of the great range. Many of the islands are larger than Massachusetts or New Jersey, but none of them have been wholly explored, nor is the survey of their shores completed. The Yosemite walls and cascades are repeated in mile after mile of deep salt-water channels, and from the deck of an ocean steamer one views scenes not paralleled after long rides and climbs in the heart of the Sierras. The gorges and cañons of Colorado are surpassed; mountains that tower above Pike's Peak rise in steep incline from the still level of the sea; and the shores are clothed with forests and undergrowth dense and impassable as the tangle of a Florida swamp. On these summer trips the ship runs into the famous inlets on the mainland shore and anchors before vast glaciers that push their icy fronts down into the sea. The still waters of the inside passage give smooth sailing nearly all of the way; and, living on an ocean steamer for three and four weeks, one only feels the heaving of the Pacific swells while crossing the short stretches of Queen Charlotte Sound and Dixon Entrance.

The Alaska steamer, however, is a perfect will o' the wisp for a landsman to pursue, starting sometimes from Portland and sometimes from San Francisco, adapting its schedule to emergencies and going as the exigencies of the cargo demand. It clears from Puget Sound ports generally during the first days of each month, but in midwinter it arranges its departure so as to have the light of the full moon in the northern ports, where the sun sets at three and four o'clock on December afternoons.

When the steamer leaves Portland for Alaska, it goes down the Columbia River, up the coast of Washington Territory, and, reaching Victoria and Port Townsend three days later, takes on the mails, and the freight shipped from San Francisco, and then clears for the north. The traveller who dreads the Columbia River bar and the open ocean can go across overland to Puget Sound, and thence by the Sound steamers to whichever port the Alaska steamer may please to anchor in.

The first time that I essayed the Alaska trip, the steamship *Idaho* with its shining black hull, its trim spars, and row of white cabins on deck, slipped down the Columbia River one Friday night, and on Monday morning we left Portland to overtake it. It was a time of forest fires, and a cloud of ignorance brooded over Puget Sound, only equalled in density by the clouds of smoke that rolled from the burning forests on shore, and there was an appalling scarcity of shipping news. The telegraph lines were down between the most important points, and the Fourth of July fever was burning so fiercely in patriotic veins that no man had a clear enough brain to tell us where the ship *Idaho* was, had gone to, or was going to. For two restless and uncertain days we see-sawed from British to American soil, going back and forth from Victoria to Port Townsend as we were in turn assured that the ship lay at anchor at one place, would not go to the other, and that we ran the risk of losing the whole trip if we did not immediately embark for the opposite shore. The dock hands came to know us, the pilots touched their hats to us, the agents fled from their ticket-offices at sight of us, and I think even the custom-house officers must have watched suspiciously, when the same two women and one small boy paced impatiently up and down the various wharves at that end of Puget Sound. We saw the Union Jack float and heard the American eagle scream on the Fourth of July, and after a night of fire-crackers, bombs, and inebriate chorus-singing, the *Idaho* came slipping into the harbor of Port Townsend as innocently as a messenger of peace, and fired a shot from a wicked little cannon, that started the very foundations of the town with its echoes.

Port Townsend, at the entrance of Puget Sound, is the last port of entry and custom-house in the United States, and the real point of departure for the Alaska steamers. It was named by Vancouver in 1792 for his friend, "the most noble Marquis of Townsend," and scorning the rivalry of the new towns at the head of Puget Sound, believes itself destined to be the final railway terminus and the future great city of this extreme northwest. The busy and thriving little town lies at the foot of a steep bluff, and an outlying suburb of residences stretches along the grassy heights above. A steep stairway, and several zig-zag walks and roads connect the business part of Port Townsend with the upper town, and it argues strong lungs and a goat-like capacity for climbing on the part of the residents, who go up and down the stairway several times a day. A marine hospital flies the national flag from a point on the bluff, and four miles west on the curve of the bay lies Fort Townsend, where a handful of United States troops keep up the traditions of an army and a military post. Near the fort is the small settlement of Irondale, where the crude bog ore of the spot is successfully melted with Texada iron ore, brought from a small island in the Gulf of Georgia. The sand spit on which Port Townsend society holds its summer clam-bakes, and the home of the "Duke of York," the venerable chief of the Clallam tribe, are points of interest about the shores.

Across the Straits of Fuca there is the pretty English town of Victoria, that has as solid mansions, as well-built roads, and as many country homes around it, as any little town on the home island. It has an intricate land-locked harbor, where the tides rush in and out in a way that defies reason, and none have ever yet been able to solve the puzzle and make out a tide-table for that harbor. All Victoria breathes the atmosphere of a past and greater grandeur, and the citizens feelingly revert to the time when British Columbia was a separate colony by itself, and Victoria the seat of the miniature court of the Governor-General and commander-in-chief of its forces. There is no real joy in the celebration of "Dominion Day," which reminds them of how British Columbia and the two provinces of Canada were made one under the specious promise of a connecting railway. Recent visits of Lord Dufferin and the Marquis of Lorne stilled some of the disaffection, and threats of annexation to the United States are less frequent now.

Victoria has "the perfect climate," according to the Princess Louise and other sojourners, and there is a peace and rest in the atmosphere that charms the briefest visitor. Every one takes life easily, and things move in a slow and accustomed groove, as if sanctioned by the custom of centuries on the same spot. Business men hardly get down town before ten o'clock in the morning, and by four in the afternoon they are striding and riding off to their homes, as if the fever and activity of American trade and competition were far away and unheard of. The clerk at the post-office window turns a look of surprise upon the stranger, and bids him go across the street, or down a block, and buy his postage-stamps at a stationer's shop, to be sure.

The second summer that my compass was set for the nor'-norwest, our party of three spent a week at Victoria before the steamer came in from San Francisco, and the charm of the place grew upon us every day. The drives about the town, along the island shores, and through the woods, are beautiful, and the heavy, London-built carriages roll over hard and perfect English highways. Ferns, growing ten and twelve feet high by the roadside, amazed us beyond expression, until a loyal and veracious citizen of Oregon assured us that ferns eighteen feet high could be found anywhere in the woods back of Astoria; and that he had often been lost in fern prairies among the Cascade mountains, where the fronds arched far above his head when he was mounted on a horse. Wild rose-bushes are matted together by the acre in the clearings about the town, and in June they weight the air with their perfume, as they did a century ago, when Marchand, the old French voyager, compared the region to the rose-covered slopes of Bulgaria. The honeysuckle attains the greatest perfection in this climate, and covers and smothers the cottages and trellises with thickly-set blossoms. Even the currant-bushes grow to unusual height, and in many gardens they are trained on arbors and hang their red, ripe clusters high overhead.

For a few days we watched anxiously every trail of smoke in the Straits of Fuca, and at last welcomed the ship, one sunny morning, when the whole Olympic range stood like a sapphire wall across the Straits, and the Angels' Gate gave a clear view of more azure slopes and snow-tipped summits through that gap in the mountain front. Instead of the trim propeller *Idaho*, the old side-wheeler, the *Ancon*, was put on the Alaska route for the summer months, and the fact of its having taken five days for the trip up from San Francisco did not prepossess us with any false notions of its speed. The same captain and officers from the *Idaho* were on board, and after making the tour of Puget Sound again, we were quite resigned to the change of ships by the time we finally left Victoria.

At Victoria the steward buys his last supplies for the coming weeks of great appetites; for with smooth water and the tonic of sea and mountain air both, the passengers make great inroads on the ship's stores. The captain often affects dismay at the way the provisions disappear, and threatens to take an account of stores at Sitka and bring the ship down by the outside passage in order to save some profit for the company. During the last hours at the Victoria wharf, several wagon-loads of meat had been put in the ice-boxes of the *Ancon*, when some live beef came thundering down the wharf, driven by hallooing horsemen. Each month the ship takes up these live cattle and sheep, and leaving them to fatten on the luxurious grasses of Sitka, insures a fresh supply of fresh beef for the return voyage. It was within half an hour of sailing-time when the herders drove the sleek fellows down to the wharf, and for an hour there was a scene that surpassed anything under a circus tent or within a Spanish arena. The sailors and stevedores had a proper respect for the bellowing beasts, and kept their distance, as they barricaded them into a corner of the wharf. The ship's officer who had charge of loading the cargo is "a salt, salt sailor," with a florid complexion; and it was his brave part to advance, flap his arms, and say "Shoo!" and then fly behind the first man or barrel, or dodge into the warehouse door. The crowd gathered and increased, the eighty passengers, disregarding all signs and rules, mounted on the paddle-boxes and clung to the ratlines forward, applauded the picador and the matador, and hummed suggestive airs from *Carmen*. When the lasso was fastened round one creature's horns, and his head was drawn down close to a pile, there were nervous moments when we waited to see the herder tossed on high, or else voluntarily leaping into the water to escape the savage prods of the enraged beast. There was great delay in getting the belts ready to put round the animals so that they could be swung over into the ship, and while the great bull-fight was in progress and the hour of sailing had come, the captain rode down the wharf in a carriage, strode on to the ship and demanded, in a stiff, official tone, "How long have these cattle been here?" "More than an hour, sir," replied the mate. "Turn those cattle loose and draw in the gang-plank," was the brief order from the bridge, and the one warning shriek of the whistle scattered the spectators and sent the excited beasts galloping up the wharf. While the gang-plank was being withdrawn, two Chinamen came down on a dog trot, hidden under bundles of blankets, with balanced baskets across their shoulders, and pickaxes, pans, and mining tools in their arms. Without a tremor the two Johns walked out on the swaying plank, and, stepping across a gap of more than two feet, landed safely on deck, bound and equipped for the deserted placer mines on Stikine River.

We left Victoria at noon, and all the afternoon the passengers gave their preliminary ohs! and ahs! strewed the decks with exclamation points, and buried their heads in their pink-covered maps of British Columbia, while the ship ran through narrow channels and turned sharp curves around the picturesque islands for the possession of which England and America nearly went to war. San Juan Island, with its limekilns, its gardens, meadows, and browsing sheep, was as pretty and pastoral a spot as nations ever wrangled about, and the Emperor of Germany did just the right thing when he drew his imperial pencil across the maps and gave this garden spot of San Juan to the United States. The beautiful scenery of the lower end of the Gulf of Georgia fitly introduces one to the beauties of the inland passage which winds for nearly a thousand miles between the islands that fringe this northwest coast, and even the most captious travellers forgot fancied grievances over staterooms, table seats, and baggage regulations. The exhausted purser, who had been persecuted all day by clamoring passengers and anxious shippers, was given a respite, and all was peace, satisfaction, and joy on board. In the nine o'clock gloaming we rounded the most northern lighthouse that gleams on this shore of the Pacific, and, winding in and through the harbor of Nanaimo, dropped anchor in Departure Bay.

The coal mines of Nanaimo have given it a commercial importance upon which it bases hopes of a great future; but it has no bustling air to it, to impress the stranger from over the border with that prospect. In early days it was an important trading-post of the Hudson Bay Company, and a quaint old block-house still stands as a relic of the times when the Indian canoes used to blacken the beach at the seasons of the great trades. The traders first opened the coal seams near Nanaimo, and thirty years ago used to pay the Indians one blanket for every eight barrels of coal brought out.

Geologists have hammered their way all up the Pacific Coast without finding a trace of true coal, and on account of the recent geological formation of the country they consider further search useless. The nearest to true coal that has been found was the coal seam on the Arctic shore of Alaska near Cape Lisburn. Captain Hooper, U.S.R.M., found the vein, and his vessel, the *Corwin*, was supplied with coal from it during an Arctic cruise in 1880. Otherwise, the lignite beds of Vancouver Island supply the best steaming coal that can be had on the coast, and a fleet of colliers ply between Nanaimo and the chief ports on the Pacific.

The mines nearest the town of Nanaimo were exhausted soon after they were worked systematically, and operations were transferred to Newcastle Island in the harbor opposite the town. A great fire in the Newcastle mine obliged the owners to close and abandon it, and the whole place stands as it was left, the cabins and works dropping slowly to decay. Even the quarry from which the fine stone was taken for the United States Mint at San Francisco is abandoned, and its broken derricks and refuse heaps make a forlorn break in the beauty of the mild shores of the island.

Richard Dunsmuir found the Wellington mines at Departure Bay by accident, his horse stumbling on a piece of lignite coal as he rode down through the woods one day. The admiral of the British fleet and one other partner ventured £1,000 each in developing the mine, and at the end of ten years the admiral withdrew with £50,000 as his share, and a year since the other partner sold out his interests to Mr. Dunsmuir for £150,000. At present the mines pay a monthly profit of £8,000, and Yankee engineers claim that that income might be doubled if the mines were worked on a larger scale, as, with duty included, this black lignite commands the highest price and is most in demand in all the cities of California and Oregon. Mr. Dunsmuir is the prime mover in building the Island railway, which is to connect Nanaimo with the naval harbor of Esquimault near Victoria. Charles Crocker and Leland Stanford of the Central Pacific road are connected with Mr. Dunsmuir in this undertaking, and to induce these capitalists to take hold of it the colonial government gave a land grant twenty-five miles wide along the whole seventy miles of the railroad, with all the timber and mineral included.

The great Wellington mines have had their strikes, and after the last one the white workmen were supplanted by Chinese, who, though wanting the brawn and muscle of the Irishmen, could work in the sulphur formations without injuring their eyes. By an explosion of fire-damp in May, 1884, many lives were lost, and gloom was cast over the little settlement on the sunny bay.

On this lee shore of Vancouver Island the climate is even softer and milder than at Victoria, and during my three visits Nanaimo has always been steeped in a golden calm of steady sunshine. While waiting for the three or four hundred tons of coal to be dropped into the hold, carload by carload, the passengers amuse themselves by visiting the quiet little town, stirring up the local trade, and busying the postmaster and the telegraph operator. A small boy steers and commands the comical little steam-tug that is omnibus and street car for the Nanaimo and Wellington people, and makes great profits while passenger steamers are coaling.

When all the anglers, the hunters, the botanists and the geologists had gone their several ways from the ship one coaling day, the captain made a diversion for the score of ladies left behind, by ordering out a lifeboat, and having the little tug tow us around the bay and over to Nanaimo. When the ladies had all scattered into the various shops, the captain made the tour of the town and found that there was not a trout to be had in that market. Then he arranged that if the returning fishermen came back to the ship in the evening and laid their strings of trout triumphantly on deck, a couple of Indians should force their way into the admiring crowd and demand pay for fish sold to the anglers. Can any one picture that scene and the effect of the joke, when it dawned upon the group?

A great bonfire on the beach in the evening rounded off that coaling day, and the captain declared the celebration to be in honor of Cleveland and Hendricks, who had that day been nominated at the National Democratic Convention in Chicago. Although the partisans of the other side declined to consider it a ratification meeting on British soil, they helped heap up the burning logs and drift-wood until the whole bay was lighted with the flames. With blue lights, fire-crackers, rockets and pistol-popping the fête continued, the Republicans deriding all boasts and prophecies of their opponents, until the commander threatened to drop them on some deserted island off the course until after the election. History has since set its seal upon the prophecies then made, and some of the modest participants of the Democratic faith think their international bonfire assisted in the result.

CHAPTER II.

THE BRITISH COLUMBIA COAST AND TONGASS.

If Claude Melnotte had wanted to paint a fairer picture to his lady, he should have told Pauline of this glorious northwest coast, fringed with islands, seamed with fathomless channels of clear, green, sea water, and basking in the soft, mellow radiance of this summer sunshine. The scenery gains everything from being translated through the medium of a soft, pearly atmosphere, where the light is as gray and evenly diffused as in Old England itself. The distant mountain ranges are lost in the blue vaporous shadows, and nearer at hand the masses and outlines show in their pure contour without the obtrusion of all the garish details that rob so many western mountain scenes of their grander effects. The calm of the brooding air, the shimmer of the opaline sea around one, and the ranges of green and russet hills, misty purple mountains, and snowy summits on the faint horizon, give a dream-like coloring to all one's thoughts. A member of the Canadian Parliament, in speaking of this coast country of British Columbia, called it the "sea of mountains" and the channels of the ocean through which one winds for days are but as endless valleys and steep cañons between the peaks and ranges that rise abruptly from the water's edge. Only the fiords and inlets of the coast of Norway, and the wooded islands in the Inland Sea of Japan, present anything like a counterpart to the wonderful scenery of these archipelagos of the North Pacific. From the head of Puget Sound to the mouth of the Chilkat River there are seven hundred and thirty-two miles of latitude, and the trend of the coast and the ship's windings between and around the islands make it an actual voyage of more than a thousand miles on inland waters.

The Strait or Gulf of Georgia, that separates Vancouver's Island from the mainland, although widening at times to forty miles, is for the most part like a broad river or lake, landlocked, walled by high mountain ranges on both sides, and choked at either end with groups of islands. The mighty current of the Frazer River rolls a pale green flood of fresh water into it at the southern entrance, and the river water, with its different density and temperature floating on the salt water, and cutting through it in a body, shows everywhere a sharply defined line of separation. In the broad channels schools of whales are often seen spouting and leaping, and on a lazy, sunny afternoon, while even the mountains seemed dozing in the waveless calm, the idlers on the after deck were roused by the cry of "Whales!" For an hour we watched the frolicking of the snorting monsters, as they spouted jets of water, arched their black backs and fins above the surface, and then disappeared with perpendicular whisks of their huge tails.

Toward the north end of Vancouver's Island, where Valdes Island is wedged in between it and the mainland shore, the ship enters Discovery Pass, in which are the dangerous tide rips of Seymour Narrows. The tides rushing in and out of the Strait of Georgia dash through this rocky gorge at the rate of four and eight knots an hour on the turn, and the navigators time their sailing hours so as to reach this perilous place in daylight and at the flood tide. Even at that time the water boils in smooth eddies and deep whirlpools, and a ship is whirled half round on its course as it threads the narrow pass between the reefs. At other times the water dashes over the rapids and raises great waves that beat back an opposing bow, and the dullest landsman on the largest ship appreciates the real dangers of the run through this wild ravine, where the wind races with the water and howls in the rigging after the most approved fashion for thrilling marine adventures. Nautical gossips tell one of vessels that, steaming against the furious tide, have had their paddle wheels reversed by its superior strength, and have been swept back to wait the favorable minutes of slack water. Others, caught by the opposing current, are said to have been slowly forced back, or, steaming at full speed, have not gained an inch of headway for two hours. The rise and fall of the tides is thirteen feet in these narrows, and although there are from twenty to sixty fathoms of water in the true channel, there is an ugly ledge and isolated rocks in the middle of the pass on which there are only two and a quarter fathoms. Long before Vancouver carried his victorious ensign through these unknown waters, the Indians had known and dreaded these rapids as the abode of an evil spirit, and for half a century the adventurous Hudson Bay traders went warily through the raging whirlpools.

Although the British Admiralty have made careful surveys, and the charts are in the main accurate, there have been serious wrecks on this part of the coast. The United States man-of-war *Saranac* was lost in Seymour Narrows on the 18th of June, 1875. The *Saranac* was an old side-wheel steamer of the second rate in naval classification, carrying eleven guns, and was making its third trip to Alaskan waters. There was an unusually low tide the morning the *Saranac* entered the pass, and the ship was soon caught in the wild current, and sent broadside on to the mid-rock. It swung off, and was headed for the Vancouver shore, and made fast with hawsers to the trees, but there was only time to lower a boat with provisions and the more important papers before the *Saranac* sunk, and not even the masts were left visible. The men camped on shore while a party went in the small boats to Nanaimo for help. No attempt was ever made to raise the ship, and in the investigation it was shown that the boilers were in such a condition when they reached Victoria, that striking the rock in Seymour Narrows was only one of the perils that awaited those on board. No lives were lost by this disaster, and Dr. Bessels, of the Smithsonian Institute, who was on his way up the coast to make a collection of Indian relics for the Centennial Exposition, showed a scientist's zeal in merely regretting the delay, and continuing on his journey by the first available craft. In April, 1883, the steamer *Grappler*, which plied between Victoria and the trading-posts on the west coast, took fire late at night, just as it was entering Seymour Narrows. The flames reached the hempen rudder-ropes, and the boat was soon helplessly drifting into the rapids. Flames and clouds of smoke made it difficult to launch the boats, and all but one were swamped. The frantic passengers leaped overboard while the ship was whirling and careening in the rapids, and the captain, with life-preserver on, was swept off, and disappeared in midstream. The *Grappler* finally drifted in to the Vancouver shore, and burned until daylight. Another United States war vessel, the *Suwanee* was lost a hundred miles beyond the Seymour Narrows by striking an unknown rock at the entrance to Queen Charlotte Sound.

In crossing this forty-mile stretch of Queen Charlotte Sound the voyager feels the swell, and touches the outer ocean for the first time. If the wind is strong there may be a chopping sea, but in general it is a stilled expanse on which fog and mist eternally brood. The Kuro Siwo, or Black Stream, or Japan Current, of the Pacific, which corresponds to the Gulf Stream of the Atlantic, touches the coast near this Sound, and the colder air from the land striking this warm river of the sea produces the heavy vapors which lie in impenetrable banks for miles, or float in filmy and downy clouds along the green mountain shores. It is this warm current which modifies the climate of the whole Pacific coast, bends the isothermal lines northward, and makes temperature depend upon the distance from the sea instead of upon distance from the equator. Bathed in perpetual fog, like the south coast of England and Ireland, there is a climatic resemblance in many ways between the islands of Great Britain and the islands of the British Columbia shore. The constant moisture and the long days force vegetation like a hothouse, and the density of the forests and the luxuriance of the undergrowth are equalled only in the tropics. The pine-trees cover the mountain slopes as thickly as the grass on a hillside, and as fires have never destroyed the forests, only the spring avalanches and land-slides break their continuity. There is an inside passage between the mountains from Queen Charlotte to Milbank Sound that gave us an afternoon and evening in the midst of fine scenery, but for another whole day we passed through the grandest of fiords on the British Columbia coast.

The sun rose at three o'clock on that rare summer morning, when the ship thrust her bow into the clear, mirror-like waters of the Finlayson Channel, and at four o'clock a dozen passengers were up in front watching the matchless panorama of mountain walls that slipped silently past us. The clear, soft light, the pure air, and the stillness of sky, and shore, and water, in the early morning, made it seem like the dawn of creation in some new paradise. The breath of the sea and the breath of the pine forest were blended in the air, and the silence and calm added to the inspiration of the surroundings. The eastern wall of the channel lay in pure shadow, the forest slopes were deep unbroken waves of green, with a narrow base-line of sandstone washed snowy white, and beneath that every tree and twig lay reflected in the still mirror of waters of a deeper, purer, and softer green than the emerald.

The marks of the spring avalanches were white scars on the face of the mountains, and the course of preceding landslides showed in the paler green of the ferns, bushes, and the dense growth of young trees that quickly cover these places. Cliffs of the color and boldness of the Yosemite walls shone in the sunlight on the opposite side, and wherever there were snowbanks on the summits, or lakes in the hollows and amphitheatres back of the mountain ridge, foaming white cataracts tumbled down the sheer walls into the green sea water. Eagles soared overhead in long, lazy sweeps, and hundreds of young ducks fluttered away from the ship's bow, and dived at the sharp echoes of a rifle shot. In this Finlayson Channel the soundings give from 50 to 130 fathoms, and from the surface of these still, deep waters the first timbered slopes of the mountains rise nearly perpendicularly for 1,500 feet, and their snow-crowned summits reach 3,000 feet above their perfect reflections. From a width of two miles at the entrance, the pass narrows one half, and then by a turn around an island the ship enters Tolmie and Fraser channels, which repeat the same wonders in bolder forms, and on deeper waters. At the end of that last fiord, where submerged mountain peaks stand as islands, six diverging channels appear, and the intricacy of the inside passage up the coast is as marvellous now, as when Vancouver dropped his anchor in this Wright Sound, puzzled as to which way he should turn to reach the ocean. Finer even than the three preceding fiords is the arrowy reach of Grenville Channel, which is a narrow cleft in the mountain range, forty-five miles long, and with scarcely a curve to break the bold palisade of its walls. In the narrowest part it is not a quarter of a mile in width; and the forest walls, and bold granite cliffs, rising there to their greatest height, give back an echo many times before it is lost in long reverberations.

Emerging from Grenville Channel, the church and houses of Metlakatlah, the one model missionary settlement on the coast, and an Arcadian village of civilized and Christianized Indians, were seen shining in the afternoon sun. At that point the water is tinged a paler green by the turbid currents of the Skeena River, and up that river the newest El Dorado has lately been found. Miners have gone up in canoes, and fishermen have dropped their lines and joined them in the hunt for gold, which is found in nuggets from the size of a pea to solid chunks worth $20 and $60. "Jerry," the first prospector, took out $600 in two days, and in the same week two miners panned out $680 in six hours. One nugget, taken from a crevice in a rock, was sent down to Victoria, and found to be pure gold and worth $26. Other consignments of treasure following, that quiet colonial town has been shaken by a gold fever that is sending all the adventurous spirits off to the Lorne Creek mines.

Before the sunset hour we crossed Dixon Entrance and the famous debatable line of 59° 40′, and the patriots who said the northern boundary of the United States should be "Fifty-nine Forty, or Fight," are best remembered now, when it is seen that the Alaska possessions begin at that line. We were within the Alaska boundaries and standing on United States soil again at the fishing station of Tongass, on Wales Island. It is a wild and picturesque little place, tucked away in the folds of the hills and islands, and the ship rounded many points before it dropped anchor in front of two new wooden houses on a rocky shore that constituted Tongass. A cluster of bark huts and tents further down the beach was the home of the Indians who catch, salt, and barrel the salmon. There was one white man as host at the fish house, a fur-capped, sad-eyed mortal, who wistfully said that he had not been "below" in seven years, and entertained us with the sight of his one hundred and forty barrels of salmon, and the vats and scow filled with split and salted or freshly caught fish. He showed us a string of fine trout that set the amateur fishermen wild, and then gallantly offered to weigh the ladies on his new scales. Over in the group of Tongass Indians, sitting stolidly in a row before their houses, there was a "one-moon-old" baby that gave but a look at the staring white people, and then sent up one pitiful little barbaric yawp. A clumsy, flat-bottomed scow was rowed slowly out to the steamer, and while the salt, the barrel hoops, barrel staves, and groceries were unloaded to it from the ship, a ball was begun on deck. A merry young miner bound for the Chilkat country gave rollicking old tunes on his violin, and a Juneau miner called off figures that convulsed the dancers and kept the four sets flying on the after deck. "The winnowing sound of dancers' feet" and the scrape of the fiddle brought a few Indian women out in canoes, and they paddled listlessly around the stern, talking in slow gutturals of the strange performances of the "Boston people," as all United States citizens have been termed by them since Captain Gray and John Jacob Astor's ships first came to the Northwest coast. At half-past ten o'clock daylight still lingered on the sky, and the Chicago man gravely read a page of a Lake Shore railroad time-table in fine print for a test, and then went solemnly to bed, six hundred miles away from the rest of the United States.

CHAPTER III.

CAPE FOX AND NAHA BAY.

From the Tongass fishery, which is some miles below the main village of the Tongass Indians and the deserted fort where United States troops were once stationed, the ship made its way by night to Cape Fox. At this point on the mainland shore, beyond Fort Tongass, the Kinneys, the great salmon packers of Astoria, have a cannery that is one of the model establishments up here. Two large buildings for the cannery, two houses, a store, and the scattered line of log houses, bark houses and tents of the Indian village, are all that one sees from the water. In the cannery most of the work is done by the Indians, but a few Chinamen perform the work which requires a certain amount of training and mechanical skill. The Indians cast the nets and bring in the shining silver fish with their deep moss-green backs and fierce mouths, and heap them in slippery piles in an outside shed overhanging the water. A Chinaman picks them up with a long hook, and, laying them in a row across a table, goes through a sleight-of-hand performance with a sharp knife, which in six minutes leaves twenty salmon shorn of their heads, tails, fins, and inwards. Experienced visitors to such places took out their watches and timed him, and in ten seconds a fish was put through his first rough process of trimming, and passed on to men who washed it, cleaned it more thoroughly, scraped off a few scales, and by a turn of revolving knives cut it in sections the length of a can. Indian women packed the tins, which were soldered, plunged into vats of boiling water, tested, resoldered, laquered, labelled, and packed in boxes in quick routine. There was the most perfect cleanliness about the cannery, and the salmon itself is only touched after the last washing by the fingers of the Indian women, who fill the cans with solid pieces of bright red flesh. In 1883 there were 3,784 cases of canned salmon shipped from this establishment as the result of the first season's venture. In the following year, 1,156 cases were shipped by the July steamer, and the total for the season was about double that of the preceding year.

Owing to the good salmon season and the steady employment given them at the cannery, the Indians held their things so high that even the most insatiate and abandoned curio-buyers made no purchases, although there has been regret ever since at the thought of the wide old bracelets and the finely-woven hats that they let escape them. At Cape Fox a shrewd Indian came aboard, and spied the amateur photographer taking groups on deck. Immediately he was eager to be taken as well, and followed the camera around, repeating, "How much Siwash picture?" He was not to be appeased by any statements about the photographer doing his work for his own amusement, and pleaded so hard that the artist finally relented and turned his camera upon him. The Indian stiffened himself into his most rigid attitude, when directed to a corner of the deck between two lifeboats, and when the process was over he could hardly be made to stir from his pose. When we pressed him to tell us what he wanted his picture for, he chuckled like any civilized swain, and confessed the whole sentimental story by the mahogany blush that mantled his broad cheeks.

Up Revillagigedo Channel the scenery is more like that of the Scotch lakes, broad expanses of water walled by forest ridges and mountains that in certain lights show a glow like blooming heather on their sides. The Tongass Narrows, which succeed this channel of the long name, give more views of cañons filled with water, winding between high bluffs and sloping summits. It was a radiant sunny morning when we steamed slowly through these beautiful waterways, and at noon the ship turned into a long green inlet on the Revillagigedo shore, and cast anchor at the head of Naha Bay. Of all the lovely spots in Alaska, commend me to this little landlocked bay, where the clear green waters are stirred with the leaping of thousands of salmon, and the shores are clothed with an enchanted forest of giant pines, and the undergrowth is a tangle of ferns and salmon-berry bushes, and the ground and every log are covered with wonderful mosses, into which the foot sinks at every step.

The splash of the leaping salmon was on every side and at every moment, and the sight of the large fish jumping above the surface and leaping through the air caused the excitable passenger at the stern to nearly capsize the small boat and steer wildly. As the sailors rowed the boat up the narrow bay, where the ship could barely swing round with the tide, the Chicago man pensively observed: "There's a thousand dollars jumping in the air every ten minutes!"

The anglers were maddened at the sight of these fish, for although these wild northern salmon can sometimes be deluded by trolling with a spoon-hook, they have no taste for such small things as flies, and are usually caught with seines or spears, except during those unusual salmon runs when the Indians wade in among the crowded fins and shovel the fish ashore with their canoe paddles.

At the head of Naha Bay, over a narrow point of land, lies a beautiful mountain lake, whose surface is a trifle below the high-water mark, and at low tide there is a fine cascade of fresh water foaming from between the rocks in the narrow outlet. During the run of salmon, the pool at the foot of the fall is crowded with the struggling fish; but the net is cast in the lake as often as in the bay, and the average catch is eighty barrels of salmon a day. The salmon are cleaned, salted, and barrelled in a long warehouse overhanging the falls, and a few bark houses belonging to the Indians who work in the fishery are perched picturesquely on the little wooded point between the two waters. Floating across this lovely lake in a slimy boat that the Indians had just emptied of its last catch of salmon, the beauty of its shores was more apparent, and the overhanging trees, the thickets of ferns, bushes, and wild grasses, the network of fallen logs hidden under their thick coating of moss, and the glinting of the sunshine on bark and moss and lichens, excited our wildest enthusiasm. In Alaska one sees the greatest range of greens in nature, and it is an education of the eye in that one color to study the infinite shades, tints, tones, and suggestions of that primary color. Of all green and verdant woods, I know of none that so satisfy one with their rank luxuriance, their beauty and picturesqueness; and one feels a little sorrow for those people who, never having seen Alaska, are blindly worshipping the barren, burnt, dried-out, starved-out forests of the East. In still stretches of this lake at Naha there are mirrored the snow-capped summits whose melting snows fill its banks, and the echo from a single pistol-shot is flung back from side to side before it dies away in a roar. Beyond this lake there is a chain of lakes, reached by connecting creeks and short portages, and the few white men who have penetrated to the farthest tarn in the heart of Revillagigedo Island say that each lake is wilder and more lovely than the last one. A mile below the fishery, and back in the woods, there is a waterfall some forty feet in height; and a mountain stream, hurrying down from the clear pools and snow-banks on the upper heights, takes a leap over a ledge of rocks and covers it with foam and sparkling waters.

The fishery and trading-post at Naha Bay was established in 1883, and shipped 338 barrels of salted salmon that first season. In 1884 over 500 barrels were shipped, and throughout June and July the salmon were leaping in the bay so thickly that at the turn of the tide their splashing was like falling rain.

CHAPTER IV.

KASA-AN BAY.

Kasa-an, or Karta Bay opens from Clarence Strait directly west of Naha Bay, and the long inlet runs in from the eastern shore of the Prince of Wales island for twenty miles. There are villages of Kasa-an Indians in the smaller inlets and coves opening from the bay, and carved *totem* poles stand guard over the large square houses of these native settlements. The bay itself is as lovely a stretch of water as can be imagined, sheltered, sunny, and calm, with noble mountains outlining its curves, and wooded islands drifted in picturesque groups at the end. It was a Scotch loch glorified, on the radiant summer days that I spent there, and it recalled one's best memories of Lake George in the softer aspects of its shores.

Smaller inlets opening from the bay afford glimpses into shady recesses in the mountain-sides, and one little gap in the shores at last gave us a sight of the trader's store, the long row of lichen-covered and moss-grown sheds of the fishery, with the usual cluster of bark houses and tents above a shelving beach strewn with narrow, black canoes. A group of Indians gathered on shore, their gay blankets, dresses, and cotton kerchiefs adding a fine touch of color to the scene, and the men in the fishery, in their high rubber boots and aprons, flannel shirts and big hats, were heroic adjuncts to the picturesque and out-of-the-way scene.

There was a skurrying to and fro and great excitement when the big steamer rounded slowly up to the little wharf, and bow line, stern line, and breast lines were thrown out, fastened to the piles and to the trees on shore, and the slack hauled in at the stentorian commands of the mate. Karta, or Kasa-an Bay has been a famous place for salmon for a score of years, and is best known, locally, as the Baronovich fishery. Old Charles V. Baronovich was a relic of Russian days, and a character on the coast. He was a Slav, and gifted with all the cunning of that race, and after the transfer of the country to the United States, he disturbed the serenity of the customs officials by the steady smuggling that he kept up from over the British border. He would import all kinds of stores, but chiefly bales of English blankets, by canoe, and when the collector or special agent would penetrate to this fastness of his, they found no damaging proof in his store, and only a peppery, hot-headed old pirate, who swore at them roundly in a compound language of Russian, Indian, and English, and shook his crippled limbs with rage. He was also suspected of selling liquor to the Indians, and a revenue cutter once put into Kasa-an Bay, with a commander whom smugglers seldom baffled, and who was bound to uncover Baronovich's wickedness. The wily old Slav received the officers courteously. He listened to the formal announcement of the purpose of their visit, and bade them search the place and kindly do him the honor of dining with him when they finished. Baronovich dozed and smoked, and idled the afternoon away, while a watch kept a close eye upon him, and the officers and men searched the packing-house, the Indian houses and tents, and the canoes on the beach. They followed every trail and broken pathway into the woods, tapped hollow trees, dug under the logs, and peered down into the waters of the bay, and finally gave up the search, convinced that there was no liquor near the place. Baronovich gave them a good dinner, and towards the close a bottle of whiskey was set before each officer, and the host led with a toast to the captain of the cutter and the revenue marine.

This queer old fellow married one of the daughters of Skowl, the Haida chief who ruled the bay. She is said to have been a very comely maiden when Baronovich married her, and is now a stately, fine-looking woman, with good features and a creamy complexion. While Baronovich was cleaning his gun one day, it was accidentally discharged, and one of his children fell dead by his own hand. The Indians viewed this deed with horror, and demanded that Skowl should take his life in punishment. As it was proved an accident, Skowl defended his son-in-law from the charge of murder, and declared that he should go free. Ever after that the Indians viewed Baronovich with a certain fear, and ascribed to him that quality which the Italians call the "evil eye."

With the passion of his race for fine weapons and fine metal work, Baronovich possessed many old arms that are worthy of an art museum. A pair of duelling pistols covered with fine engraving and inlaying were bought of his widow by one of the naval officers in command of the man-of-war on this station, and an ancient double-barrelled flint-lock shot-gun lately passed into the hands of another officer. The shot-gun has the stock and barrels richly damascened with silver and gold, after the manner of the finest Spanish metal work, and the clear gray flints in the trigger give out a shower of sparks when struck. Gunnell of London was the maker of this fine fowling-piece, and it is now used in the field by its new owner, who prefers it to the latest Remington.

Baronovich was a man with a long and highly-colored history by all the signs, but he died a few years since with no biographer at hand, and his exploits, adventures, and oddities are now nearly forgotten. The widow Baronovich still lives at Kasa-an, unwilling to leave this peaceful sunny nook in the mountains, but the fishery is now leased to a ship captain, who has taken away the fine old flavor of piracy and smuggling, and substituted a *régime* of system, enterprise, and eternal cleanliness.

The wandering salmon that swarm on this coast by millions show clear instincts when they choose, without an exception, only the most picturesque and attractive nooks to jump in. They dart and leap up Kasa-an Bay to the mouths of all the little creeks at its head, and three times during the year the water is alive with them. The best salmon run in June and July, and in one day the seine brought in eighteen hundred salmon in a single haul. Two thousand and twenty-one hundred fish have weighted the net at different hauls, and the fish-house was overrunning with these royal salmon. Indian women do the most of the work in the fishery—cleaning and splitting the fish and taking out the backbones and the worthless parts with some very deft strokes from their murderous-looking knives. The salmon are washed thoroughly and spread between layers of dry salt in large vats. Brine is poured over them, and they are left for eight days in pickle. Boards and weights are laid on the top of the vats, and they are then barrelled and stored in a long covered shed and treated to more strong brine through the bung-hole until ready for shipment. Of all salt fish the salt salmon is the finest, and here, where salmon are so plentiful, a barrelled dainty is put up in the shape of salmon bellies, which saves only the fattest and most tender portions of these rich, bright red Kasa-an salmon.

Over fifteen hundred barrels were packed in 1884, and under the new *régime* the Kasa-an fishery has distanced its rivals in quantity, while the quality has a long-established fame.

These Kasa-an Indians are a branch of the Haidas, the finest of the Indian tribes of the coast. They are most intelligent and industrious people, and are skilled in many ways that render them superior to the other tribes of the island. Their permanent village is some miles below the fishery, and their square whitewashed houses, and the tomb and mortuary column of Skowl, their great chief, makes quite a pretty scene in a shady green inlet near Baronovich's old copper mine. A few of their houses at the fishery are of logs or rough-hewn planks, but the most of them are bark huts, with a rustic arbor hung full of drying salmon outside. These bits of bright-red salmon, against the slabs of rough hemlock bark, make a gay trimming for each house, and when a bronzed old hag, in a dun-colored gown, with yellow 'kerchief on her head, stirs up the fire of snapping fir boughs, and directs a column of smoke toward the drying fish, it is a bit of aborigine life to set an artist wild. Their bark houses are scattered irregularly along the beach above high-water mark, and a fleet of slender, black canoes, with high, carved bows, are drawn up on the sand and pebbles. The canoe is the only means of locomotion in this region of unexplored and impenetrable woods, and the Indian is even more at home in it than on shore. No horseman cares for his steed more faithfully than the Siwash tends and mends his graceful cedar canoe, hewn from a single log, and given its flare and graceful curves by being steamed with water and hot stones, and then braced to its intended width. The Haida canoe has the same high, double-beaked prow of the Chinook canoes of Puget Sound, but where the stern of the latter drops in a straight line to the keel, the Haida canoe has a deep convex curve. By universal fashion all of these canoes are painted black externally, with the thwarts and bows lined with red, and sometimes the interior brightened with that color. The black paint used to be made from a mixture of seal oil and bituminous coal, and the red paint was the natural clay found in places throughout all Indian countries. Latterly the natives have taken to depending on the traders' stores for paint, but civilization has never grasped them so firmly as to cause them to put seats or cross-pieces in their canoes. They squat or sit flat in the bottom of their dugouts for hours without changing position. It gives white men cramps and stiff joints to look at them, and sailors are no luckier than landsmen in their attempts to paddle and keep their balance in one of these canoes for the first time.

The Indians use a broad, short paddle, which they plunge straight down into the water like a knife, and they literally shovel the water astern with it. The woman, who has a good many rights up here that her sisters of the western plains know not, sits back of her liege, and with a waving motion, never taking the paddle out of the water once, steers and helps on the craft. Often she paddles steadily, while the man bales out the water with a wooden scoop. When the canoes are drawn up on the beach they are carefully filled with grass and branches, and covered with mats or blankets to keep them sound and firm. A row of these high-beaked canoes thus draped has a very singular effect, and on a gloomy day they are like so many catafalques or funeral gondolas. Baronovich's old schooner, the *Pioneer of Cazan*, lies stranded on the beach in the midst of the native boats, moss and lichens tenderly covering its timbers, and vagrant grasses springing up in the seams of the old wreck. The dark, cramped little cabin is just the place for ghosts of corsairs and the goblins of sailors' yarns, and although it has lain there many seasons, no Indian has yet pre-empted it as a home for his family and dogs.

THREE CARVED SPOONS AND SHAMAN'S RATTLE.

The thrifty Siwash, which is the generic and common name for these people, and a corruption of the old French voyagers' *sauvage*, keeps his valuables stored in heavy cedar chests, or gaudy red trunks studded with brass nails; the latter costly prizes with which the Russian traders used to tempt them. At the first sound of the steamer's paddle-wheels,—and they can be heard for miles in these fiords,—the Indians rummaged their houses and chests and sorted out their valuable things, and when the first ardent curio-seeker rushed through the packing-houses and out towards the bark huts, their wares were all displayed. The Haidas are famous as the best carvers, silversmiths, and workers on the coast; and there are some of their best artists in this little band on Kasa-an Bay. An old blind man, with a battered hat on his head and a dirty white blanket wrapped around him, sat before one bark hut, with a large wooden bowl filled with carved spoons made from the horns of the mountain goat. These spoons, once in common use among all these people, are now disappearing, as the rage for the tin and pewter utensils in the traders' stores increases, although many of them have the handles polished and the bowls worn by the daily usage of generations. The horn is naturally black, and constant handling and soaking in seal oil gives them a jetty lustre that adds much to the really fine carvings on the handles. Silver bracelets pounded out of coin, and ornamented with traceries and chasings by the hand of "Kasa-an John," the famous jeweller of the tribe, were the prizes eagerly sought and contended for by the ladies. The bangle mania rages among the Haida maids and matrons as fiercely as on civilized shores, and dusky wrists were outstretched on which from three to nine bracelets lay in shining lines like jointed mail. Anciently they pounded a single heavy bracelet from a silver dollar piece, and ornamented the broad two-inch band with heraldic carvings of the crow, the bear, the raven, the whale, and other emblematic beasts of their strangely mixed mythology. Latterly they have become corrupted by civilized fashions, and they have taken to narrow bands, hammered from half dollars and carved with scrolls, conventional eagles copied from coins, and geometrical designs. They have no fancy for gold ornaments, and they are very rarely seen; but the fancy for silver is universal, and their methodical way of converting every coin into a bracelet and stowing it away in their chests gives hope of there being one place where the surplus silver and the trade dollars may be legitimately made away with.

In one house an enlightened and non-skeptical Indian was driving sharp bargains in the sale of medicine-men's rattles and charms, and kindred relics of a departed faith. His scoffing and irreverent air would have made his ancestors' dust shake, but he pocketed the *chickamin*, or money, without even a superstitious shudder. The amateur curio-buyers found themselves worsted and outgeneralled on every side in this rich market of Kasa-an by a Juneau trader, who gathered up the things by wholesale, and, carrying them on board, disposed of them at a stupendous advance. "No more spoon," said the old blind chief as he jingled the thirteen dollars that he had received from this trader for his twenty beautifully carved spoons, and the tourists who had to pay two dollars a piece for these ancestral ladles echoed his refrain and began to see how profits might mount up in trading in the Indian country. Dance blankets from the Chilkat country, woven in curious designs in black, white, and yellow wool, spun from the fleece of the mountain goat, were paraded by the anxious owners, and the strangers elbowed one another, stepped on the dogs, and rubbed the oil from the dripping salmon overhead in the smoky huts, in order to see and buy all of these things.

Old Skowl bid defiance to the missionaries while he lived, and kept his people strictly to the faith and the ways of their fathers. If they fell sick, the *shaman* or medicine-man came with his rattles and charms, and with great *hocus-pocus* and *"Presto change"* drove away or propitiated the evil spirits that were tormenting the sufferer. If the patient did not immediately respond to the treatment, the doctor would accuse some one of bewitching his victim, and demand that he should be tortured or put to death in order to relieve the afflicted one. It thus became a serious matter for every one when the doctor was sent for, as not even the chiefs were safe from being denounced by these wizards. No slave could become a *shaman*, but the profession was open to any one else, regardless of rank or riches, and the medicine man was a self-made grandee, unless some great deformity marked him for that calling from birth. As preparation for his life-work he went off by himself, and fasted in the woods for many days. Returning, he danced in frenzy about the village, seizing and biting the flesh of live dogs, and eating the heads and tongues of frogs. This latter practice accounts for the image of the frog appearing on all the medicine men's rattles; and in the totemic carvings the frog is the symbol of the *shaman*, or speaks of some incident connected with him. Each *shaman* elected to himself a familiar spirit, either the whale, the bear, the eagle, or some one of the mythological beasts, and gifted with its qualities, and under the guidance of this totemic spirit, he performed his cures and miracles. This token was carved on his rattles, his masks, drums, spoons, canoes, and all his belongings. It was woven on his blankets, and after death it was carved on bits of fossil ivory, whale and walrus teeth, and sewed to his grave-clothes. The *shaman's* body was never burned, but was laid in state in the large grave boxes that are seen on the outskirts of every village. Columns capped with *totemic* animals and flags mark these little houses of the dead, and many of them have elaborately carved and painted walls. The *shaman's* hair was never cut nor touched by profane hands, and each hair was considered a sacred charm by the people. Captain Merriman, while in command of the U. S. S. *Adams*, repeatedly interfered with two *shamans*, who were denouncing and putting to torture the helpless women and children in a village where the black measles was raging. He found the victims of this witchcraft persecution with their ankles fastened to their wrists in dark, underground holes, or tied to the rocks at low tide that they might be slowly drowned by the returning waters. All threats failing, the two *shamans* were carried on the *Adams*, and the ship's barber sheared and shaved their heads. The matted hair was carried down to the boiler room and burned, for if it had been thrown overboard it would have been caught and preserved, and the *shamans* could have retained at least a vestige of authority. The Indians raised a great outcry at the prospect of harm or indignity being offered their medicine-men, but when the two shaved heads appeared at the gangway, the Indians set up shouts of derision, and there were none so poor as to do them honor after that. A few such salutary examples did much to break up these practices, and though their notions of our medicine are rather crude, they have implicit faith in the white, or "Boston doctors."

If these fish-eating, canoe-paddling Indians of the northwest coast are superior to the hunters and horsemen of the western plains, the Haidas are the most remarkable of the coast tribes, and offer a fascinating study to anyone interested in native races and fellow man. From Cape Fox to Mount St. Elias the Indians of the Alaska coast are known by the generic name of Thlinkets, but in the subdivision of the Thlinkets into tribes, or *kwans*, the Haidas are not included. The Thlinkets consider the Haidas as aliens, but, except in the language, they have many things in common, and it takes the ethnologist's eye to detect the differences. The greater part of the Haida tribe proper inhabit the Queen Charlotte Islands in the northern part of British Columbia, and the few bands living in villages in the southern part of Alaska are said to be malcontents and secessionists, who paddled away and found homes for themselves across Dixon Entrance. I have heard it stated, without much authority to sustain it, however, that old Skowl was a deserter of this kind, and, not approving of some of the political methods of the other chiefs in his native village, withdrew with his followers and founded a colony in Kasa-an Bay. This aboriginal "mugwump," as he would be rated in the slang of the day, was conservative in other things, and his people have the same old customs and traditions as the Haidas of the original villages on the Queen Charlotte Islands.

Where the Haidas really did come from is an unending puzzle, and in Alaska the origin and migration of races are subjects continually claiming one's attention. There is enough to be seen by superficial glances to suggest an Oriental origin, and those who believe in the emigration of the Indians from Asia by way of Behring Straits, or the natural causeway of the Aleutian Islands, in prehistoric times, find an array of strange suggestions and resemblances among the Haidas to encourage their theories. That the name of this tribe corresponds to the name of the great mountain range of Japan may be a mere coincidence, but a few scholars who have visited them say that there are many Japanese words and idioms in their language, and that the resemblance of the Haidas to the Ainos of northern Japan is striking enough to suggest some kinship. Opposed to this, however, is the testimony of Marchand, the French voyager, who visited the Haidas in 1791, and recognizing Aztec words and terminations in their speech, and resemblances to Aztec work in their monuments and picture-writings, first started the theory that they were from the south, and descendants of those who, driven out of Mexico by Cortez, vanished in boats to the north. To continue the puzzle, the Haidas have some Apache words in their vocabulary, and have the same grotesque dance-masks, and many of the same dances and ceremonies that Cushing describes in his sketches of life among the Zunis in New Mexico. Hon. James G. Swan, of Port Townsend, who has given thirty years to a study of the Indians of the northwest coast, has lately given much attention to the Haidas of the Queen Charlotte Islands, and has made large collections of their implements and art works for the Smithsonian Institute. He found the Haida tradition and representation of the great spirit,—the Thunder Bird,—to be the same as that of the Aztecs, and when he showed sketches of Aztec carvings to the Haidas they seemed to recognize and understand them at once. Copper images and relics found in their possession were identical with some silver images found in ruins in Guatemala by a British archæologist. Judge Swan has collected many strange legends and allegories during his canoe journeys to the isolated Haida villages, and his guide and attendant, Johnny Kit-Elswa, who conducts him to the great October feasts and dances, is a clever young Haida silversmith and a remarkable genius. Judge Swan has written a memoir on Haida tattoo masks, paintings, and heraldic columns, which was published as No. 267 of the *Smithsonian Contributions to Knowledge*, January, 1874. *In The West Shore* magazine of August, 1884, he published a long article with illustrations upon the same subjects, and his library and cabinet, his journals and sketch-books, contain many wonderful things relating to the history and life of these strange people.

CHAPTER V.

FORT WRANGELL AND THE STIKINE.

Those who believe that all Alaska is a place of perpetual rain, fog, snow, and ice would be quickly disabused could they spend some of the ideal summer days in that most lovely harbor of Fort Wrangell. Each time the sky was clearer and the air milder than before, and on the day of my third visit the fresh beams of the morning sun gave an infinite charm to the landscape, as we turned from Clarence Straits into the narrower pass between the islands, and sailed across waters that reflected in shimmering, pale blue and pearly lights the wonderful panorama of mountains. Though perfectly clear, the light was softened and subdued, and even on such a glorious sunny morning there was no glare nor harshness in the atmosphere. This pale, soft light gave a dreamy, poetic quality to the scenery, and the first ranges of mountains above the water shaded from the deep green and russet of the nearer pine forests to azure and purple, where their further summits were outlined against the sky or the snow-covered peaks that were mirrored so faithfully in the long stretches of the channel. The sea water lost its deep green tints at that point, and was discolored and tinged to a muddy tea green by the fresh current of the Stikine River, which there reaches the ocean.

The great circle of mountains and snow-peaks, and the stretch of calm waters lying in this vast landlocked harbor, give Fort Wrangell an enviable situation. The little town reached its half-century of existence last summer, but no celebrations stirred the placid, easy-going life of its people. It was founded in 1834 by order of Baron Wrangell, then Governor of Russian America and chief director of the fur company, who sent the Captain-Lieut. Dionysius Feodorovich Zarembo down from Sitka to erect a stockade post on the small tongue of land now occupied by the homes, graves, and *totem* poles of the Indian village. It was known at first as the trading post of St. Dionysius, and, later, it assumed the name of Wrangell, the prefix of Fort being added during the time that the United States garrisoned it with two companies of the 21st Infantry. The Government began building a new stockade fort there immediately after the transfer of the territory in 1867, and troops occupied it until 1870, when they were withdrawn, the post abandoned, and the property sold for $500. The discovery of the Cassiar gold mines on the head waters of the Stikine River in 1874 sent a tide of wild life into the deserted street of Fort Wrangell, and the military were ordered back in 1875 and remained until 1877, when General Howard drew off his forces, and the government finally recalled the troops from all the posts in Alaska.

During the second occupation of the barracks and quarters at Fort Wrangell, the War Department helped itself to the property, and, assigning a nominal sum for rent, held the fort against the protest of the owner. The Cassiar mines were booming then, and Fort Wrangell took on something of the excitement of a mining town itself, and being at the head of ocean navigation, where all merchandise had to be transferred to small steamers and canoes, rents for stores and warehouses were extravagantly high. Every shed could bring a fabulous price. The unhappy owner, who rejoices in the euphonious name of W. King Lear, could only gnash his teeth and violently protest against the monthly warrants and vouchers given him by the commandant of the post. Since the troops have gone, the Government has done other strange things with the property that it once sold in due form, and Mr. Lear has a just and plain claim against the War Department for damages. The barracks and hospital of the old fort are now occupied by the Presbyterian Mission. No alteration, repairs, or improvements having been made for many years, the stockade is gradually becoming more ruinous, weather-worn, and picturesque each year, and the overhanging block-house at one corner is already a most sketchable bit of bleached and lichen-covered logs.

The main street of Fort Wrangell, untouched by the hoof of horse or mule for these many years, is a wandering grass-grown lane that straggles along for a few hundred feet from the fort gate and ends in a foot-path along the beach. The "Miners' Palace Restaurant," and other high-sounding signs, remain as relics of the livelier days, and listless Indian women sit in rows and groups on the unpainted porches of the trading stores. They are a quiet, rather languid lot of *klootchmans*, slow and deliberate of speech, and not at all clamorous for customers, as they squat or lie face downward, like so many seals, before their baskets of wild berries. In the stores, the curio departments are well stocked with elaborately carved spoons made of the black horns of the mountain goat; with curiously-fashioned halibut hooks and halibut clubs; with carved wooden trays and bowls, in which oil, fish, berries, and food have been mixed for years; with stone pipes and implements handed down from that early age, and separate store-rooms are filled with the skins of bears, foxes, squirrels, mink, and marten that are staple articles of trade. Occasionally there can be found fine specimens of a gray mica slate set full of big garnet crystals, like plums in a pudding, or sprinkled through with finer garnets that show points of brilliancy and fine color. This stone is found on the banks of a small creek near the mouth of the Stikine River, and great slabs of it are blasted off and brought to Fort Wrangell by the boat-load to be broken up into small cabinet specimens in time for the tourist season each summer. None of the garnets are clear or perfect, and the blasting fills them with seams and flaws. The best silver bracelets at Fort Wrangell are made by a lame Indian, who as the chief artificer and silversmith of the tribe has quite a local reputation. His bracelets are beautifully chased and decorated, but unfortunately for the integrity of Stikine art traditions, he has given up carving the emblematic beasts of native heraldry on heavy barbaric wristlets, and now only makes the most slender bangles, adapted from the models in an illustrated jeweller's catalogue that some Philistine has sent him. Worse yet, he copies the civilized spread eagle from the half-dollar, and, one can only shake his head sadly to see Stikine art so corrupted and debased. For all this, the lame man cannot make bracelets fast enough to supply the market, and at three dollars a pair for the narrower ones he pockets great profits during the steamer days.

On the water side of the main street there is a queer old flat-bottomed river-boat, stranded high and dry, that in its day made $135,000 clear each season that it went up the Stikine. It enriched its owner while in the water, and after it went ashore was a profitable venture as a hotel. This Rudder Grange, built over from stem to stern, and green with moss, is so settled into the grass and earth that only the shape of the bow and the empty box of the stern wheel really declare its original purpose. There is a bakeshop in the old engine-room, and for the rest it is the Chinatown of Fort Wrangell. A small cinnamon-bear cub gambolled in the street before this boat-house, and it stood on its hind legs and sniffed the air curiously when it saw the captain of the ship coming down the street, bestowing sticks of candy on every child in the way. Bruin came in for his share, and formed the centre for a group that watched him chew up mint sticks and pick his teeth with his sharp little claws.

The houses of the Indian village string along the beach in a disconnected way, all of them low and square, built of rough hewn cedar and pine planks, and roofed over with large planks resting on heavy log beams. One door gives entrance to an interior, often twenty and forty feet square, and several families live in one of these houses, sharing the same fireplace in the centre, and keeping peacefully to their own sides and corners of the common habitation. Heraldic devices in outline sometimes ornament the gable front of the house, but no paint is wasted on the interior, where smoke darkens everything, the drying salmon drip grease from the frames overhead, and dogs and children tumble carelessly around the fire and over the pots and saucepans. The entrances have sometimes civilized doors on hinges, but the aborigine fashion is a *portière* of sealskin or walrus hide, or of woven grass mats. When one of the occupants of a house dies he is never taken out by the door where the others enter, but a plank is torn off at the back or side, or the body is hoisted out through the smoke hole in the roof, to keep the spirits away.

Before many of the houses are tall cedar posts and poles, carved with faces of men and beasts, representing events in their genealogy and mythology. These tall *totems* are the shrines and show places of Fort Wrangell, and on seeing them all the ship's company made the hopeless plunge into Thlinket mythology and there floundered aimlessly until the end of the trip. There is nothing more flexible or susceptible of interpretations than Indian traditions, and the Siwash himself enjoys nothing so much as misleading and fooling the curious white man in these matters. The truth about these *totems* and their carvings never will be quite known until their innate humor is civilized out of the natives, but meanwhile the white man vexes himself with ethnological theories and suppositions. These *totems* are for the most part picture writings that tell a plain story to every Siwash, and record the great events in the history of the man who erects them. They are only erected by the wealthy and powerful members of the tribe, and the cost of carving a cedar log fifty feet long, and the attendant feasts and ceremonies of the raising, bring their value, according to Indian estimates, up to one thousand and two thousand dollars. The subdivisions of each tribe into distinct families that take for their crest the crow, the bear, the eagle, the whale, the wolf, and the fox, give to each of these sculptured devices its great meaning. The *totems* show by their successive carvings the descent and alliances of the great families, and the great facts and incidents of their history. The representations of these heraldic beasts and birds are conventionalized after certain fixed rules of their art, and the grotesque heads of men and animals are highly colored according to other set laws and limitations. Descent is counted on the female side, and the first emblem at the top of the totem is that of the builder, and next that of the great family from which he is descended through his mother.

In some cases two *totem* poles are erected before a house, one to show the descent on the female side, and one to give the generations of the male side, and a pair of these poles was explained for us by one of the residents of Fort Wrangell, who has given some study to these matters. The genealogical column of the mother's side has at the top the eagle, the great *totem* or crest of the family to which she belonged. Below the eagle is the image of a child, and below that the beaver, the frog, the eagle, the frog, and the frog for a third time, show the generations and the sub-families of the female side. By some interpreters the frog is believed to indicate a pestilence or some great disaster, but others maintain that it is the recognized crest of one of the sub-families. The male *totem* pole has at the top the image of the chief, wearing his conical hat, below that his great *totem*, the crow. Succeeding the crow is the image of a child, then three frogs, and at the base of the column the eagle, the great *totem* of the builder's mother.

TOTEM POLES AT FORT WRANGELL.

In front of one chief's house a very natural-looking bear is crouched on the top of a pole, gazing down at his black foot-tracks, which are carved on the sides of the column. A crossbeam resting on posts near this same house used to show three frogs sitting in line, and other grotesque fantasies are scattered about the village. With the advance of civilization the Indians are losing their reverence for these heraldic monuments, and some have been destroyed and others sold; for the richest of these natives are so mercenary that they do not scruple to sell anything that belongs to them. The disappearance of the *totem* poles would rob these villages of their greatest interest for the tourists, and the ethnologist who would solve the mysteries and read the pictures finally aright, should hasten to this rich and neglected field.

In their mythology, which, as now known, is sadly involved through the medium of so many incorrect and perverted explanations, the crow or raven stands supreme as the creator and the first of all created things. He made everything, and all life comes from him. After he had made the world, he created woman and then man, making her supreme as representative of the crow family, while man, created last, is the head of the wolf or warrior's family. From them sprang the sub-families of the whale, the bear, the eagle, the beaver, and the frog. The Stikine Indians have a tradition of the deluge, in which the chosen pair were given the shape of crows until the water had subsided, when they again returned to the earth and peopled it with their descendants. No alliances are ever made within the great families, and a crow never marries a crow, but rather a member of the whale, bear, or wolf families. The man takes the *totem* of his wife's family, and fights with them when the great family feuds arise in the tribe.

GRAVE AT FORT WRANGELL.

On many of the *totem* poles the chiefs are represented as wearing tall, conical hats, similar to those worn by certain classes in China, and this fact has been assumed by many ardent ethnologists to give certain proof of the oriental origin of these people, and their emigration by way of Behring's Straits. Others explain the storied hats piled one on top of another, as indicating the number of *potlatches*, or great feasts, that the builder has given. Over the graves of the dead, which are square log boxes or houses, they put full-length representations of the dead man's totemic beast, or smooth poles finished at the top with the family crest. One old chief's tomb at Fort Wrangell has a very realistic whale on its moss-grown roof, another a bear, and another an otter. The Indians cremated their dead until the arrival of the missionaries, who have steadily opposed the practice. The Indian's idea of a hell of ice made him reason that he who was buried in the earth or the sea would be cold forever after, while he whose ashes were burned would be warm and comfortable throughout eternity.

These Thlinket Indians of the coast have broad heavy faces, small eyes, and anything but quickness or intelligence in their expression. They are slow and deliberate in speech, lingering on and emphasizing each aspirate and guttural, and any theories as to a fish diet promoting the activity of the brain are dispersed after watching these salmon-fed natives for a few weeks. Many of their customs are such a travesty and burlesque on our civilized ways as to show that the same principles and motives underlie all human action. When those expensive trophies of decorative art, the *totem* poles, are raised, the event is celebrated by the whole tribe. A common Indian can raise himself to distinction and nobility by giving many feasts and setting up a pole to commemorate them. After he owns a *totem* pole he can aspire to greater eminence. That man is considered the richest who gives most away, and at the great feasts or *potlatches* that accompany a house-warming or pole-raising, they nearly beggar themselves. All the delicacies of the Alaska market are provided by the canoe-full, and the guests sit around the canoes and dip their ancestral spoons into the various compounded dishes. Blankets, calico, and money are distributed as souvenirs on the same principle as costly favors are given for the German. His rank and riches increase in exact ratio as he tears up and gives away his blankets and belongings; and the Thlinket has satisfied pride to console himself with while he struggles through the hard times that follow a *potlatch*.

In the summer season Fort Wrangell is a peaceful, quiet place; the climate is a soothing one, and Prof. Muir extolled the "poultice-like atmosphere" which so calms the senses. The Indians begin to scatter on their annual fishing trips in June, and come back with their winter supplies of salmon in the early fall. Many of the houses were locked or boarded up, while the owners had gone away to spend the summer at some other watering-place. One absentee left this notice on his front door:—

**LET NO ONE OPEN OR SHUT THIS
HOUSE DURING MY ABSENCE.**

Over another locked door was this name and legend, which combines a well-witnessed and legal testament, together with the conventional door-plate of the white man:—

ANATLASH.

Let all that read know that I
Am a friend to the whites. Let no
One molest this house. In case of my
Death it belongs to my wife.

Thus wrote Anatlash, a man of tall *totems* and many blankets; and stanzas in blank verse after the same manner decorated the doorway of many Thlinket abodes.

The family groups within the houses were as interesting and picturesque as the *totem* poles without; and strangers were free to enter without formality, and study the ways of the best native society without hindrance. These people nearly all wear civilized garments, and in the baronial halls of Fort Wrangell there are imposing heaps of red-covered and brass-bound trunks that contain stores of blankets, festal garments, and family treasures. In all the houses the Indians went right on with their breakfasts and domestic duties regardless of our presence; and the white visitors made themselves at home, scrutinized and turned over everything they saw with an effrontery that would be resented, if indulged in in kind by the Indians. The women had the shrewdest eye to money-making, and tried to sell ancient and greasy baskets and broken spoons when they had nothing else in the curio line. In one house two giggling damsels were playing on an accordeon when we entered, but stopped and hid their heads in their blankets at sight of us. An old gentleman, in a single abbreviated garment, crouched by the fireside, frying a dark and suspicious-looking dough in seal oil; and the coolness and self-possession with which he rose and stepped about his habitation were admirable. He was a grizzled and surly-looking old fellow, but from the number of trunks and fur robes piled around the walls, he was evidently a man of wealth, and his airy costume rather a matter of taste than economy. Many of the men showed us buckskin pouches containing little six-inch sticks of polished cedar that they use in their great social games. These gambling sticks are distinguished by different markings in red and black lines, and the game consists in one man taking a handful, shuffling them around under his blanket, and making the others guess the marks of the first stick drawn out. These Indians are great gamblers, and they spend hours and days at their fascinating games. They shuffle the sticks to see who shall go out to cut and gather firewood in winter, and if a man is seen crawling out after an armful of logs, his neighbors shout with derision at him as a loser.

SILVER BRACELETS.

LABRETTES.

In addition to their silver bracelets, their silver earrings and finger rings, many of the women keep up the old custom of wearing nose rings and lip rings, that no amount of missionary and catechism, seemingly, can break them of. The lip rings used to be worn by all but slaves, and the three kinds worn by the women of all the island tribes are marks of age that take the place of family records. When a young girl reaches marriageable age, a long, flat-headed silver pin, an inch in length, is thrust through the lower lip. After the marriage festival the Thlinket dame assumes a bone or ivory button a quarter or half inch across. This matronly badge is a mere collar-button compared to the two-inch plugs of wood that they wear in their under lips when they reach the sere and yellow leaf of existence. This big labrette gives the last touch of hideousness to the wrinkled and blear-eyed old women that one finds wearing them, and it was from the Russian name for this trough in the lip—*kolosh*—that all the tribes of the archipelago were known as Koloshians, as distinguished from the Aleuts, the Innuits, and Esquimaux of the northwest.

Far less picturesque than the natives in their own houses were the little Indian girls at the mission-school in the old fort. Combed, cleaned, and marshalled in stiff rows to recite, sing, and go through calisthenic exercises, they were not nearly so striking for studies and sketches aboriginal, but more hopeful to contemplate as fellow-beings. Clah, a Christianized Indian from Fort Simpson, B. C., was the first to attempt mission work among the Indians at Fort Wrangell. In 1877 Mrs. McFarland was sent out by the Presbyterian Board of Missions, after years of mission work in Colorado and the west, and, taking Clah on her staff, she labored untiringly to establish the school and open the home for Indian girls. Others have joined her in the work at Fort Wrangell, and everyone on the coast testifies to good results already attained by her labors and example. She is known and reverenced among all the tribes, and the Indians trust in her implicitly, and go to her for advice and aid in every emergency. With the establishment of the new industrial mission-school at Sitka, Mrs. McFarland will be transferred to the girls' department of that institution. The Rev. Hall Young and his wife have devoted themselves to the good cause at Fort Wrangell, and will continue there in charge of the church and school. The Presbyterian missions have the strongest hold on the coast, and the Catholics, who built a church at Fort Wrangell, have given up the mission there, and the priest from Nanaimo makes only occasional visits to his dusky parishioners.

The steep hillside back of Fort Wrangell was cleared of timber during military occupancy, and on the lower slopes the companies had fine gardens, which remain as wild overgrown meadows now. In them the wild timothy grows six feet high, the blueberry bushes are loaded with fruit, salmon berries show their gorgeous clusters of gold and scarlet, and the white clover grows on long stems and reaches to a fulness and perfection one can never imagine. This Wrangell clover is the common clover of the East looked at through a magnifying glass, each blossom as large and wide-spread as a double carnation pink, and the fragrance has a strong spicy quality with its sweetness. The red clover is not common, but the occasional tops are of the deepest pink that these huge clover blossoms can wear. While the hillside looked cleared, there was a deep and tangled thicket under foot, the moss, vines, and runners forming a network that it took some skill to penetrate; but the view of the curved beach, the placid channel sleeping in the warm summer sunshine like a great mountain lake, and the ragged peaks of the snowy range showing through every notch and gap, well repaid the climb through it. It was a most perfect day when we climbed the ridge, the air as warm and mellow as Indian summer, with even its soft haze hung round the mountain walls in the afternoon, and from those superior heights we gazed in ecstasy on the scene and pitied all the people who know not Alaska.

When Professor Muir was at Fort Wrangell one autumn, he climbed to the summit of this first mountain on a stormy night to listen to the fierce music of the winds in the forest. Just over the ridge he found a little hollow, and gathering a few twigs and branches he started a fire that he gradually increased to quite a blaze. The wind howled and roared through the forest, and the scientist enjoyed himself to the utmost; but down in the village the Indians were terrified at the glow that illuminated the sky and the tree-tops. No one could explain the phenomenon, as they could not guess that it was Professor Muir warming himself during his nocturnal ramble in the forest, and it was with difficulty that the minister and the teachers at the mission could calm the frightened Indians.

On a second visit to Fort Wrangell on the *Idaho*, there was the same warm, lazy sunshine and soft still air, and as connoisseurs we could the better appreciate the fine carvings and ornamental work of these æsthetic people, who decorate every household utensil with their symbols of the beautiful. Mr. Lear, or "King Lear," welcomed us back to his comfortable porch, and as a special mark brought forth his great horn spoon, a work of the highest art, and a bit of bric-a-brac that cost its possessor some four hundred dollars. Mr. Lear is that famous man, who "swears by the great horn spoon," and this elaborately carved spoon, made from the clear, amber-tinted horn of the musk ox, is more than eighteen inches long, with a smooth, graceful bowl that holds at least a pint. This spoon constituted the sole assets of a bankrupt debtor, who failed, owing Mr. Lear a large sum; and the jocose trader first astonished us by saying that he had a carved spoon that cost him four hundred dollars. The amateur photographers on shipboard raved at sight of the beautiful amber spoon with its carved handle inlaid with abalone shell, and, rushing for their cameras, photographed it against a gay background of Chilkat blankets. Mr. Lear has refused all offers to buy his great horn spoon, routing one persistent collector by assuring him that he must keep it to take his medicines in.

The skies were as blue as fabled Italy when the *Idaho* "let go" from Fort Wrangell wharf that glorious afternoon, and we left with genuine regret. The Coast-Survey steamer *Hassler* came smoking around the point of an island just as we were leaving Fort Wrangell; and our captain, who would rather lose his dinner than miss a joke, fairly shook with laughter when he saw the frantic signals of the *Hassler*, and knew the tempestuous frame of mind its commander was working himself up to. After giving the *Hassler* sufficient scare and chase, the *Idaho* slowed up, and the mails that she had been carrying for three months were transferred to the Coast-Survey ship, while the skippers, who are close friends and inveterate jokers, exchanged stiff and conventional greetings, mild sarcasm, and dignified repartee from their respective bridges. The pranks that these nautical people play on one another in these out-of-the-way waters would astonish those who have seen them in dress uniforms and conventional surroundings, and such experiences rank among the unique side incidents of a trip.

A boat-race of another kind rounded off the day of my third and last visit to Fort Wrangell, and the Indians who had been waiting for a week made ready for a regatta when the *Ancon* was sighted. It took several whistles from our impatient captain to get the long war-canoes manned and at the stake-boat; and, in this particular, boat-races have some points in common the world round. Kadashaks, one of the Stikine chiefs, commanded one long canoe in which sixteen Indians sat on each side, and another chief rallied thirty-two followers for his war-canoe. It was a picturesque sight when the boatmen were all squatted in the long dug-outs, wearing white shirts, and colored handkerchiefs tied around their brows. While they waited, each canoe and its crew was reflected in the still waters that lay without a ripple around the starting-point near shore. When the cannon on the ship's deck gave the signal, the canoes shot forward like arrows, the broad paddles sending the water in great waves back of them, and dashing the spray high on either side. Kadashaks and the other chief sat in the sterns to steer, and encouraged and urged on their crews with hoarse grunts and words of command, and the Indians, paddling as if for life, kept time in their strokes to a savage chant that rose to yells and war whoops when the two canoes fouled just off the stake-boat. It was a most exciting boat-race, and bets and enthusiasm ran high on the steamer's deck during its progress. The money that had been subscribed by the traders in the town was divided between the two crews, and at night there was a grand *potlatch*, or feast, in honor of the regatta.

The trade with the Cassiar mines at the head of the Stikine River once made Fort Wrangell an important place, but the rival boats that used to race on the river have gone below, and the region is nearly abandoned. As early as 1862 the miners found gold dust in the bars near the mouth of the river; but it was twelve years later before Thibert and another trapper, crossing from Minnesota, found the gold fields and quartz veins at the head-waters of the stream, three hundred miles distant from Fort Wrangell, within the British Columbia lines. Immediately the army of gold-seekers turned there, leaving California and the Frazer River mines, and in 1874 there were two thousand miners on the ground, and the yield was known to have been over one million dollars. Light-draught, stern-wheel steamers were put on the river, and the goods and miners transferred from ocean steamers at Fort Wrangell were taken to Glenora at the head of navigation, one hundred and fifty miles from the mouth. From that point there was a steep mountain trail of another one hundred and fifty miles, and pack trains of mules carried freight on to the diggings. Freights from Fort Wrangell to the mines ranged at times from twenty to eighty and one hundred and sixty dollars per ton; and in consequence, when the placers were exhausted, and machinery was necessary to work the quartz veins, the region was abandoned.

The official returns as given by the British Columbia commissioners are not at hand for all of the years since the discovery of these mines, but for the seven years here given they show the great decrease in the bullion yield of the Cassiar fields:—

Years.	Number of miners.	Gold product.
1874	2,000	$1,000,000
1875	800	1,000,000
1876	1,500	556,474
1877	1,200	499,830
1879	1,800	....
1883	1,000	135,000

During this year of 1884 the steamers have been taken off the river, and Indian canoes are the only means of transportation. There are few besides Chinamen left to work the exhausted fields, and another year will probably find them in sole possession. While the mines were at their best, Fort Wrangell was the great point of outfitting and departure; and after the troops were withdrawn, the miners made it more and more a place of drunken and sociable hibernation, when the severe weather of the interior drove them down the river. They congregated in greatest numbers early in the spring, many going up on the ice in February or March, before the river opened; although no mining could be done until May, and the water froze in the sluices in September.

The Cassiar mines being in British Columbia, the rush of trade on the Stikine River caused many complications and infractions of the revenue laws of both countries, and great license was allowed. The exact position where the boundary line crosses the Stikine has not yet been determined by the two governments, and in times past it has wavered like the isothermal lines of the coast. The diggings at Shucks, seventy miles from Fort Wrangell, were at one time in Alaska and next time in British Columbia; and the Hudson Bay Company's post, and even the British custom house, were for a long time on United States soil before being removed beyond the debatable region. The boundary, as now accepted temporarily, crosses the river sixty-five miles from Fort Wrangell at a distance of ten marine leagues from the sea in a direct line, and, intersecting the grave of a British miner, leaves his bones divided between the two countries; his heart in the one, and the boots in which he died in the other.

Vancouver failed to discover the Stikine on his cruise up the continental shore, and, deceived by the shoal waters, passed by the mouth. It then remained for the American sloop *Degon*, Captain Cleveland, to visit the delta and learn of the great river from the natives in 1799. The scenery of the Stikine River is the most wonderful in this region, and Prof. John Muir, the great geologist of the Pacific coast, epitomized the valley of the Stikine as "a Yosemite one hundred miles long." The current of the river is so strong that while it takes a boat three days at full steam to get from Fort Wrangell up to Glenora, the trip back can be made in eight or twelve hours, with the paddle-wheel reversed most of the time, to hold the boat back in its wild flight down stream. It is a most dangerous piece of river navigation, and there have been innumerable accidents to steamboats and canoes.

Three hundred great glaciers are known to drain into the Stikine, and one hundred and one can be counted from the steamer's deck while going up to Glenora. The first great glacier comes down to the river at a place forty miles above Fort Wrangell, and fronting for seven miles on a low moraine along the river bank, is faced on the opposite side by a smaller glacier. There is an Indian tradition to the effect that these two glaciers were once united, and the river ran through in an arched tunnel. To find out whether it led out to the sea, the Indians determined to send two of their number through the tunnel, and with fine Indian logic they chose the oldest members of their tribe to make the perilous voyage into the ice mountain, arguing that they might die very soon anyhow. The venerable Indians shot the tunnel, and, returning with the great news of a clear passageway to the sea, were held in the highest esteem forever after. This great glacier is from five hundred to seven hundred feet high on the front, and extends back for many miles into the mountains, its surface broken and seamed with deep crevices. Two young Russian officers once went down from Sitka to explore this glacier to its source, but never returned from the ice kingdom into which they so rashly ventured. Further up, at a sharp bend of the river called the Devil's Elbow, there is the mud glacier, which has a width of three miles and a height of two hundred or three hundred feet where it faces the river from behind its moraine. Beyond this dirt-covered, boulder-strewn glacier, there is the Grand Cañon of the Stikine, a narrow gorge two hundred feet long and one hundred feet wide, into which the boiling current of the river is forced, and where the steamboats used to struggle at full steam for half an hour before they emerged from the perpendicular walls of that frightful defile. A smaller cañon near it is called the *Klootchman's*, or Woman's Cañon, the noble red man being always so exhausted by poling, paddling, and tracking his canoe through the Grand Cañon as to leave the navigation of the second one entirely to his wife. The Big Riffle, or the Stikine Rapids, is the last of these most dangerous places in the river; and at about this point, where the summit line of the mountain range crosses the river, the mythical boundary line is supposed to lie. The country opens out then into more level stretches, and at Glenora and Telegraph Creek, the steamboats leave their cargoes and start on the wild sweep down the river to Fort Wrangell again. As the boats are no longer running on the river, future voyagers who wish to see the stupendous scenery of this region will have to depend on the Indian canoes that take ten days for the journey up, or else feast and satisfy their imaginations with the thrilling tales of the old Stikine days that can be picked up on every hand, and study the topography of the region from the maps of Prof. Blake.

CHAPTER VI.

WRANGELL NARROWS AND TAKU GLACIERS.

If there were not so many more wonderful places in Alaska, Wrangell Narrows would give it a scenic fame, and make its fortune in the coming centuries when tourists and yachts will crowd these waters, and poets and seafaring novelists desert the Scotch coast for these northwestern isles. Instead of William Black's everlasting Oban, and Staffa, and Skye, and heroines with a burr in their speech, we will read of Kasa-an and Kaigan, Taku and Chilkat, and maidens who lisp in soft accents the deep, gurgling Chinook, or the older dialects of their races. Wrangell Narrows is a sinuous channel between mountainous islands, and for thirty miles it is hard to determine which one of the perpendicular walls at the end of the strait will finally stop us with its impassable front. There are dangerous ledges and rocks, and strong tides rushing through this pass, and the average depth of from four to twelve fathoms is very shallow water for Alaska. Although long known and used by the Indians and the Hudson Bay Company's traders, it was not considered a safe inside passage; and as Vancouver had not explored it, and there were not any complete charts, it was little traversed by regular commerce. After United States occupation, and the increased travel to Sitka, the perils of Cape Ommaney, off the south end of Baranoff Island, quite matched any dangers there might be in the unknown channel. Captain R. W. Meade, in command of the U. S. S. *Saginaw*, made a survey of the Narrows in 1869, and gradually the way through the ledges and flats and tide rips became better known. In 1884 Captain Coghlan, commander of the U. S. S. *Adams* carefully sounded and marked off the channel with stakes and buoys, and the navigators now only look for the favorable turn of the tide in going through the picturesque reaches.

Leaving Fort Wrangell in the afternoon, it was an enchanting trip up that narrow channel of deep waters, rippling between bold island shores and parallel mountain walls. Besides the clear, emerald tide, reflecting every tree and rock, there was the beauty of foaming cataracts leaping down the sides of snow-capped mountains, and the grandeur of great glaciers pushing down through sharp ravines, and dropping miniature icebergs into the water. Three glaciers are visible at once on the east side of the Narrows, the larger one extending back some forty miles, and measuring four miles across the front, that faces the water and the terminal moraine it has built up before it. The great glacier is known as Patterson Glacier, in honor of the late Carlisle Patterson, of the United States Coast Survey, and is the first in the great line of glaciers that one encounters along the Alaska coast. Under the shadow of a cloud the glacier was a dirty and uneven snow field, but touched by the last light of the sun it was a frozen lake of wonderland, shimmering with silvery lights, and showing a pale ethereal green, and deep, pure blue, in all the rifts and crevasses in its icy front.

With the appearance of this first glacier, and the presence of ice floating in the waters around us, the conversation of all on board took a scientific turn, and facts, fancies, and wild theories about glacial origin and action were advanced that would have struck panic to any body of geologists. Being all laymen, there was no one to expound the mysteries and speak with final authority on any of these frozen and well-established truths; and we floundered about in a sea of suppositions, and were lost in a labyrinth of lame conclusions.

A long chain of snow-capped mountains slowly unrolled as the ship emerged from Wrangell Narrows, more glaciers were brought to view, and that strange granite monument, the "Devil's Thumb," as named by Commander Meade, signalled us from a mountain top.

Farther up, in Stephens Passage, floating ice tells of the great glaciers in Holkam or Soundoun Bay, and beside the one great Soundoun glacier flowing into the sea, there are three other glaciers hidden in the high-walled fiords that open from the bay. One of the first and most adventurous visitors to the Soundoun glacier was Captain J. W. White, of the Revenue Marine, who anchored the cutter *Lincoln* in the bay in 1868. Seeing a great arch or tunnel in the front of the glacier, he had his men row the small boat into the deep blue grotto, and they went a hundred feet down a crystalline corridor whose roof was a thousand feet thick. The colors, he said, were marvellous, and, like the galleries cut in the Alpine glaciers, showed fresh wonders with each advance. At the furthest point the adventurous boatmen poured out libations and drank to the spirits of the ice kingdom. In 1876 gold was discovered, and the Soundoun placers were the first ones worked in Alaska. Professor Muir visited the glacier and mines of Soundoun Bay in 1879, and at Shough, a camp in a valley at the head of the inlet, found miners at work with their primitive rockers and sluices. In 1880 these mines yielded $10,000, and the miners believed the bed of gold-bearing gravel inexhaustible. The discovery of gold at Juneau drew the most of them away, and the Soundoun placers have hardly been heard of in later years.

Winding north, through a broad channel with noble mountain ranges on either side, we passed the old Hudson Bay Company's trading post of Taku, and at mention of this name those who believe in the Asiatic origin of the Alaska Indians cried out in delighted surprise: "There is a Chinese city of the same name and spelled in the same way as this—Taku."

Reaching the mouth of Taku Inlet, into which the Taku River empties, the floating ice gave evidence of the great glaciers that lie within; and, following up this fiord for about fifteen miles to a great basin, we came suddenly in sight of three glaciers. One sloped down a steep and rather narrow ravine, and its front was hidden by another turn in the overlapping hills. The second one pushed down between two high mountains, and, resting its tongue on the water, dropped off the icebergs and cakes that covered the surface of the dull, gray-green water. The front of this icy cliff stretched entirely across the half-mile gap between the mountains, and its face rose a hundred and two hundred feet from the water, every foot of it seamed, jagged, and rent with great fissures, in which the palest prismatic hues were flashing. As the tide fell, large pieces fell from this front, and avalanches of ice-fragments crashed down into the sea and raised waves that rocked our ship and set the ice-floes grinding together. On the other point of the crescent of this bay there lay the largest glacier, an ice-field that swept down from two mountain gorges, and, spreading out in fan shape, descended in a long slope to a moraine of sand, pebbles, and boulders. Across its rolling front this glacier measured at least three miles, and the low, level moraine was one mile in width. The moraine's slope was so gradual that when the small boats were lowered and we started for shore, they grounded one hundred feet from the water-mark and there stuck until the passengers were taken off one by one in the lightest boat, and then carried over the last twenty feet of water in the sailors' arms. It was a time for old clothes, to begin with, and everyone wore their worst when they started off; but at the finish, when the same set waded through a quarter of a mile of sand and mineral mud left exposed by the falling tide, and were dumped into the boats by the sailors, a near relative would not have owned one of us. The landing of the glacier pilgrims was a scene worthy of the nimblest caricaturist, and sympathy welled up for the poor officers and sailors who shouldered stout men and women and struggled ashore through sinking mud and water. The burly captain picked out the slightest young girl and carried her ashore like a doll; but the second officer, deceived by the hollow eyes of one tall woman, lifted her up gallantly, floundered for a while in the mud and the awful surprise of her weight, and then bearer and burden took a headlong plunge. The newly-married man carried his bride off on his back, and had that novel incident to put down in the voluminous journal of the honeymoon kept by the young couple.

We trailed along in files, like so many ants, across the sandy moraine, sinking in the soft "mountain meal," stumbling over acres of smooth rocks and pebbles, and jumping shallow streams that wandered down from the melting ice. Patches of epilobium crimsoned the ground with rank blossoms near the base of the glacier, and at last we began ascending the dull, dirty, gray ice hills.

There was a wonderful stillness in the air, and the clear, sunny, blue sky brooded peacefully over the wonderful scene. The crunching of the footsteps on the rough ice could be heard a long way, and from every crevice came the rumble and roar of the streams under the ice. Rising five hundred feet or more by a gradual incline of half a mile, we were as far from seeing the source of the glacier as ever; and the vast snow-fields from which the streams of ice emerge were still hidden by the spurs of the mountain round which they poured. At that point there were some deep crevasses in the ice, and leaning over we looked down into the bottomless rifts. The young Catholic priest, forgetting everything in the ardor of the moment and the ice-fever, labored like a giant, hurling vast boulders into the depths, that we might hear the repeated crashes as they struck from side to side, before the splash told that they had reached the subterranean river that roared so fiercely. In the outer sunshine the ice sparkled like broken bits of silver, but in the crevasses the colors were intensified from the palest ice-green to a deeper and deeper blue that was lost in shadowy purple at the last point. The travellers who had learned their glaciers in Switzerland sat amazed at the view before them, and owned that the glacier on which they were sitting was much larger and more broken than the *Mer de Glace*, while nothing in the Alps could equal the smaller glacier beyond, that lay glittering like a great jewel-house and dropping bergs of beryl and sapphire into the sea.

Where the two arms of the glacier united, the lines of converging ice-streams were marked by great trains of boulders and patches of dirt; and fragments of quartz and granite, and iron-stained rocks were souvenirs that the pilgrims carried off by the pocketful. We sat on rough boulders and looked down into the ice-ravines on every side, and sighed breathlessly in the ecstasy of joy. An earthly and material soul roused the scorn of the young Catholic divine by sitting down in that exalted spot to eat—to munch soda crackers from a brown-paper bundle—while the wreck of glaciers, the crash of icebergs, the grinding of ice-floes, and world-building were going on about him.

We ran down the glacier slopes hand in hand, in long lines that "snapped the whip" and went all-hands-round on the more level places, or crept in cautious file along the narrow ridges between crevasses. We drank from icy rills that ran in channels of clear green ice, and crossing the moraine, we waded through mud ankle deep and were carried to the boats. The receding tide had obliged the sailors to push the boats further and further off, and when one frail bark was about full there was a crash, an avalanche of ice went splashing into the sea from the smaller glacier up the bay, and a great wave curling from it washed the boat back and left it grounded. Men without rubber boots were then so well soaked and so plastered with glacier mud that they just stepped over the boat's side and helped the rubber-clad sailors float it off. The lower deck and the engine-room were hanging full and strewn with muddy boots and drying clothes all day, and the stewards were heard to wonder "what great fun there was in getting all their clothes spoiled, that the passengers need take on so over a glacier."

When Vancouver went to the head of Taku Inlet in 1794 he found "frozen mountains" surrounding it on every side, and his boats were so endangered by the floating ice, that his men gladly hurried away from it. Prospectors have had their camps at the mouth of the river at the head of the basin, and have searched the bars and shores of Taku River for miles across the mountain wall. Their evidence and that of the fur traders, who give scant notice to such things, prove the Indian traditions, that the ice is receding rapidly, and that the ice mountain that now sets back with a great moraine before it, came down to the water's edge in their fathers' days.

That day on the Taku glacier will live forever as one of the rarest and most perfect enjoyment. The grandest objects in nature were before us, the primeval forces that mould the face of the earth were at work, and it was all so far away and out of the everyday world that we might have been walking a new planet, fresh fallen from the Creator's hand. The lights and shadows on the hills, and the range of colors, were superb,—every tiny ice-cake in the water showing colors as rare and fleeting as the shades of an opal, while the gleaming ice-cliff, from which these jewels dropped, was aglow with all the prismatic lights and tinted in lines of deepest indigo in the great caverns and rifts of its front. The sunny, sparkling air was most exhilarating, and we sat on the after-deck basking in the golden rays of the afternoon sun, and looked back regretfully as the glaciers receded and were lost to sight by a turn in the fiord.

CHAPTER VII.

JUNEAU, SILVER BOW BASIN, AND DOUGLASS IS-LAND MINES.

Turning north from the mouth of Taku Inlet, and running up Gastineaux Channel, we were between the steepest mountain walls that vegetation could cling to, and down all those verdant precipices poured foaming cascades from the snow-banks on the summits. This channel between the mainland shore and Douglass Island is less than a mile in width, and the mountains on the eastern shore rise to two thousand feet and more in their first uplift from the water's edge. The snowy summits of the ranges back of it reach twice that altitude, and are the same mountains that shelter the glaciers of the north shore of Taku Inlet.

All of this Taku region is rich in the indications of precious minerals, and prospectors have explored miles of the most rugged mountain country in their search for float and gravel. The presence of gold along the shores of Taku River was long known, but the Taku Indians, who guarded the mouth of the river and kept the monopoly of the fur trade with the interior Indians, were known to be hostile and kept prospectors aloof. Prof. Muir found signs of gold in every stream in the territory, ground by and swept down from the higher ranges by the vast ice-sheet that once covered this region, and by the glaciers that are still at work in all the fiords and ravines. He believed that the great mineral vein extending up the coast from Mexico to British Columbia continued through Alaska and into Siberia. With British Columbian miners producing $1,000,000 and $2,000,000 each year, and Siberia yielding its annual $22,000,000, Professor Muir was certain that Alaska would prove to be one of the rich gold fields of North America. In one of his letters to the San Francisco *Bulletin* in 1879, he gave it as his belief that the richest quartz leads would be found on the mainland shores east of Sitka, and that the true mineral belt followed the trend of the continental shores. A year later his prophecy was verified, and the present mining town of Juneau, a hundred miles north and east of Sitka in a direct line, promises soon to distance the capital and become the most important town in the territory.

The town of Juneau straggles along the beach and scatters itself after a broken, rectangular plan, up a ravine that opens to the water front. Lying at the foot of a vertical mountain-wall, with slender cascades rolling like silver ribbons from the clouds and snow-banks overhead, and sheltered in a curve of the still channel, Juneau has the most picturesque situation of any town on the coast. There were about fifty houses in 1884, and the place claimed between three hundred and four hundred white inhabitants, with a village of Taku Indians on one side of the town, and Auk Indians on the other. The Northwest Trading Company has a large store at Juneau, and a barber's shop and the sign of "Russian Baths, every Saturday, fifty cents," shows that the luxuries of civilization are creeping in.

As a mining camp, this settlement dates back but a few years. In 1879 the Indians gave fine quartz specimens to the officers of the U. S. S. *Jamestown*, claiming to have found them on the shores of Gastineaux Channel. In the following summer a prospecting party was formed at Sitka, and left there headed by Joseph Juneau and Richard Harris. They camped on the present site of Juneau on Oct. 1, 1880, and followed up the largest of three creeks emptying into the channel near that point. Three miles back on this Gold Creek in the Silver Bow Basin, they found rich placers and outcropping quartz ledges. When they returned to Sitka with their sacks of specimens, there was a stampede and a rush for the new El Dorado, and the camp, established in midwinter, has since grown into a town. Harris took up a town site of one hundred and sixty acres, and in the spring of 1881 miners from British Columbia and from Arizona flocked to the new gold-fields.

The place was first called Pilsbury, for one prospector; then Fliptown, as a miner's joke; next Rockwell, for the officer of the U. S. S. *Jamestown*, who came down with a detachment of marines to keep the camp in order; fourthly it was named Harrisburg, and fifthly Juneau. This last name was formally adopted by the miners at a meeting held in May, 1882, and in the same conclave resolutions were passed ordering all Chinamen out of the district, and warning the race to stay away; which they have done. At the same time the miners perfected an organization, elected a recorder, and adopted a code of laws which should be enforced until the United States should establish civil government and declare it a land district. Even with this volunteer attempt at law and order, the ownership of mining claims was uncertain, as they belonged to the first and the strongest ones who began work in the spring. For want of a civil tribunal, miners' quarrels were settled by fists, shotguns, or an appeal to the man-of-war at Sitka. The whole town site and the Basin are staked off and claimed by three and four first owners, and lawsuits are impending over every piece of mining property. Without surveys, titles, or protection, the Juneau miners have done little more than the necessary assessment work each year, although some of the placers have paid richly. With things in such an insecure state, capitalists were not willing to venture anything in the development of these mines, and owners did little boasting of the richness of their lodes, lest more miscreants should be invited to jump their claims. The newly established district court, whose clerk is *ex officio* recorder of deeds, mortgages, and certificates of location of mining claims, will be overwhelmed with mining suits at its first sessions, and every claim will supply one or more cases for trial.

It is very difficult to ascertain the exact amounts produced by these mines, although from ten to fifty thousand dollars in gold is sent down by each steamer during the summer months. To avoid the heavy express charges, many of the provident miners carry down their own hard earnings in the fall, and buckskin bags, tin cans, and bottles of gold dust are among the curios put in the purser's safe. As far as known, $135,000 was washed from the placers in 1881, $250,000 in

1882, and about $400,000 in 1883.

After the first season's stir Juneau experienced a slow and steady growth, and has not yet set up its pretensions to a "boom." There is a calm and quiet to the town that disappoints one who looks for the wild and untrammelled scenes of an incipient Leadville. The roving prospectors and the improvident miners gather at Juneau when the frosts and snows of winter drive them from the basins and valleys of the mainland, and in that season Juneau comes nearest to wearing the air of a mining town with the fever and delirium of a boom about to come on. Tales of fabulous riches are then current, and around the contraband whiskey-bottle prospectors tell of finds that put Ormus and the Ind, Sierra Nevada and Little Pittsburg far behind.

The first time that I visited Juneau it was getting a large instalment of its annual rainfall of nine feet, and it was only by glimpses through the tattered edges of the clouds that one could see the slopes of the steep, green mountains, with the roaring cascades waving like snowy pennants against the forest screen. The ground was soaked and miry, and the least step from the gravelly beach or the plank walks plunged one ankle-deep in the black mud. Of the two beasts of burden in the town, the horse was busy hauling freight from the wharf, and the mule struck a melancholy pose beside an ancient schooner on the beach and refused to move. Depending upon such transportation, travel to the Basin mines was rather limited, and a few miners and Indians descending the steep trail from the forest, like Fra Diavolo in the first act, quite excited the fancy. After a contest with the best two hundred feet of the three miles of the steep yet miry trail, we were convinced that the mines would not pay on that drizzly afternoon. With the trees dripping around us and little rills running down on every side, it was rather paradoxical to have a wayfarer tell us that the miners were doing very little just then, for want of water. It was strange enough in a country of perpetual rain, with streams dropping down from eternal snows, that the system of reservoirs, ditches, and flumes should be incomplete. A sociable miner, with his hands in his pockets as far as his elbows, engaged us in conversation on a street corner, and we surrounded him with a cordon of dripping umbrellas and listened to his apologies for the state of the weather, couched in many strange idioms.

"We haven't any Indian agents, or constables, so there's never any trouble between us peaceable white men and the natives," said the miner. "There's no caboose and no tax-collector; and as fish is plenty, it's as good a place as any for a poor miner. Want of whiskey is the greatest drawback to the development of this country, and something will have to be done about it. Congress and them folks in Washington don't pay much attention to us, but we had an earthquake a while ago, so the Lord ain't forgotten us, if the government has," said the friendly miner, with a solemn smile. He promised to bring some quartz specimens to the ship for the ladies; but we never saw that friend again.

The miners thus failing us in picturesqueness and thrilling incidents, the Indians came in for a full share of attention. One village wanders along the beach below the wharf, and the other settlement is hidden behind a knoll at the other side of the town. In the latter, Sitka Jack has a summer-house as well as at Fort

Wrangell, but, instead of finding this potentate at home, his door was locked, and the neighbors said that he had gone up to Chilkat for the salmon fishing. On one of the largest houses in the village was the sign: "Klow-kek, Auke Chief." Over another doorway was written:

> "Jake is a good boy, a working man,
> Friend of the whites, and demands protection."

The Indians came from both villages and huddled in groups on the wharf. Nearly all of them were barefooted, for those rich enough to afford shoes take them off and put them away when the ground is wet or muddy. They seemed quite unconscious of the weather, and, though unshod, were wrapped in blankets and in many cases carried umbrellas. The women and children tripped down in their bare feet, and sat around on the dripping wharf with a recklessness that suggested pneumonia, consumption, rheumatism, and all those kindred ills from which they suffer so severely. Nearly all the women had their faces blacked, and no one can imagine anything more frightful and sinister on a melancholy day than to be confronted by one of these silent, stealthy figures, with the great circles of the whites of the eyes alone visible in the shadow of the blanket. A dozen fictitious reasons are given for this face-blacking. One Indian says that the widows and those who have suffered great sorrow wear the black in token thereof. Another native authority makes it a sign of happiness, while occasionally a giggling dame confesses that it is done to preserve the complexion. Ludicrous as this may seem to the bleached Caucasian and the ladies of rice-powdered and enamelled countenances, the matrons of high fashion and the swell damsels of the Thlinket tribes never make a canoe voyage without smearing themselves well with the black dye, that they get from a certain wild root of the woods, or with a paste of soot and seal oil. On sunny and windy days on shore they protect themselves from tan and sunburn by this same inky coating. On feast days and the great occasions, when they wash off the black, their complexions come out as fair and creamy white as the palest of their Japanese cousins across the water, and the women are then seen to be some six shades lighter than the tan-colored and coffee-colored lords of their tribe. The specimen women at Juneau wore a thin calico dress and a thick blue blanket. Her feet were bare, but she was compensated for that loss of gear by the turkey-red parasol that she poised over her head with all the complacency of a Mount Desert belle. She had blacked her face to the edge of her eyelids and the roots of her hair; she wore the full parure of silver nose-ring, lip-ring, and ear-rings, with five silver bracelets on each wrist, and fifteen rings ornamenting her bronze fingers; and a more thoroughly proud and self-satisfied creature never arrayed herself according to the behests of high fashion. The children pattered around barefooted and wearing but a single short garment, although the day was as cold and drear as in our November. Not one of these poor youngsters even ventured on the croopy cough, that belongs to the civilized child that has only put his head out of doors in such weather. One can easily believe the records and the statements as to the terrible death rate among these people, and marvel that any ever live beyond their infancy. So few old people are seen among them as to continually cause remark, but by their Spartan system only the strongest can possibly survive the exposure and hardships of such a life. Consumption is the common ailment and carries them away in numbers, yet they have no medicines or remedies of their own, trust only to the incantations and hocus-pocus of their medicine-men, and take not the slightest care to protect themselves from exposure. Great epidemics have swept these islands at times, and forty years ago the scourge of smallpox carried off half the natives of Alaska. The tribes never regained their numbers after that terrible devastation, and since then black measles and other diseases have so reduced their people that another fifty years may see these tribes extinct. The smoke of their dwellings and the glare from the snow in winter increases diseases of the eye, and most interesting cases for an oculist are presented in every group.

Indian women crouched on the wharf with their wares spread before them, or wandered like shadows about the ship's deck, offering baskets and mats woven of the fine threads of the inner bark and roots of the cedar, and extending arms covered with silver bracelets to the envious gaze of their white sisters. There was no savage modesty or simplicity about the prices asked, and their first demands were generally twice what the articles were worth. They are keen traders and sharp at bargaining, and no white man outwits these natives. Conversation was carried on with them in the Chinook jargon, the language compounded by Hudson Bay Company traders from French, English, Russian, and the dialect of the Chinook tribe once living at the mouth of the Columbia River. The Indians from California to the Arctic Ocean understand more or less of this jargon, and in Oregon and Washington Territory Chinook is a most necessary accomplishment.

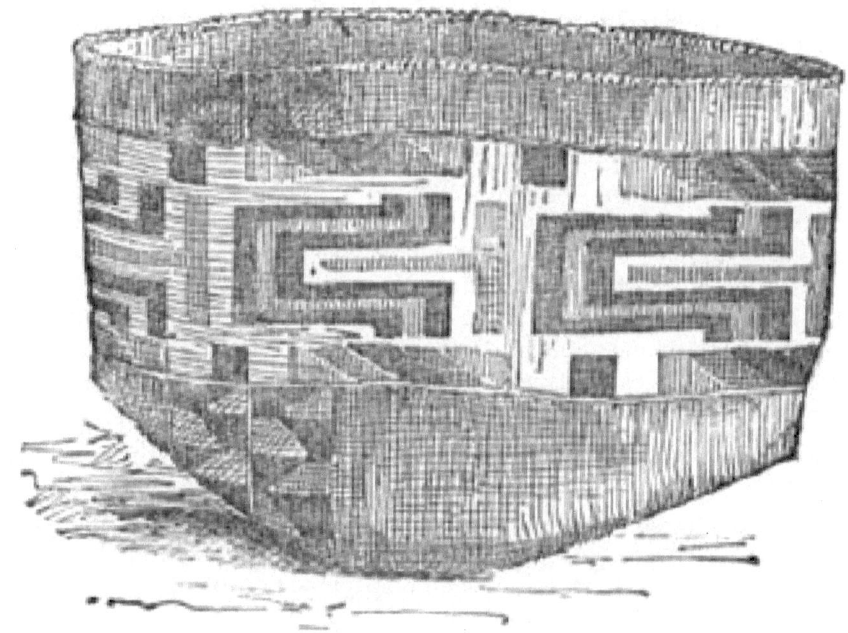

A THLINKET BASKET.

At the traders' stores in town we found whole museums of Indian curios, and revelled in the oddities and strange art-works of the people. The round baskets of split cedar, woven so tightly as to be waterproof, and ornamented in rude geometrical designs in bright colors, are the first choice for souvenirs among tourists. After that the carvings, the miniature totems and canoes, the grotesque masks and dance rattles, take the eye. There were, too, the fine ancestral spoons made from the horns of mountain goat and musk ox, and finished with handles carved in full and high relief, and inlaid with bits of abalone-shell, bears' teeth, and lucky stones from the head of the codfish. Of furs and skins every store held a great supply, and when bearskins and squirrel robes had no effect the traders would bring out their treasures of otter, fox, and seal, and show the bales of furs that awaited transportation to the south. A robe of gray squirrel two yards square was bought for one dollar and fifty cents, and sealskins at eight dollars, silver-fox skins for twenty-five dollars, and sea-otter skins for one hundred dollars, continued the ascending scale of prices. The real entertainment of the day came after we had bought our baskets and spoons and carvings at the traders' stores, and were enjoying a few dry hours in the cabin. Then the Indian women came tapping at the windows with their bracelets, and the keen spirit of the trade having possessed us, we made wonderful bargains with the relenting savages. A tap on the window, and the one word "Bracelet!" or the Chinook *Klickwilly*," would bring all the ladies to their feet, and the mechanical "how much" that followed became so automatic during the day, that when the porter rapped at night for lights to be put out, he was greeted with a "how much" in response. For each bracelet the Indians wailed out a demand for *"mox tolla,"* two dollars in our tongue. They finally came down to *"ict tolla sitcum,"* or one dollar and fifty cents, and rapidly disposed of their treasures. Some lucky purchasers happened upon the unredeemed pledges in the pawn branch of a jolly old trader's store, and for *"sitcum tolla,"* or fifty cents, walked off with flat silver bracelets a quarter of an inch wide, carved in rude designs of leaves and scrolls.

Even Indian society is dull in the summer time, as they all go off in great parties to catch their winter supplies of fish. While the salmon are running no Indian wants to stay at home in the village, but no angler can imagine that they need go far to drop the line, when one copper-colored Izaak dropped his halibut hook off the Juneau wharf and pulled up a fish weighing nine hundred pounds. Being clubbed on the head and hauled up with much help, the monster halibut was sold for two dollars and fifty cents, which statement completes about as remarkable a fish story as one dares to tell, even at this distance.

Halibut of ninety and one hundred pounds have been caught over the ship's side in these channels, and Captain Cook tells of one weighing five hundred pounds, and other navigators of those weighing nine hundred pounds. Halibut is a staff of life to the Indians, and their *menu* always comprises it. They catch the halibut with elaborately-carved wooden hooks made of red cedar or the heart of spruce roots, fastened to lines of twisted cedar bark, or braided seaweed. Clubs carved with the fisherman's *totem* and other designs are used to kill them with when drawn up to the side of the canoe. At many of the fisheries a great deal of halibut is salted and packed before the salmon season begins, and halibut fins are choice morsels that command a higher price by the barrel than salmon bellies.

The second time that I saw Juneau it was like another place in the last golden glow of the afternoon sun. They had been having clear weather for weeks, and under a radiant blue sky Juneau was the most charming little mountain nook and seashore village one could look for. The whole summit ranges of the mountains on the Juneau shore and on the island were visible, and at a distance the little white houses of the town looked like bits of the snowbanks, that had slid three thousand feet down the track of the cascades to the beach. We determined on an early start for the mines the next morning, anxious to see the places that baffled the pilgrims the first time.

The site of the mining camp in the Silver Bow Basin is even more picturesque, and the trail from Juneau leads straight up the mountain side, then down to a second valley, and along the wild cañon of Gold Creek and into the basin of the Silver Bow. All the way it leads through dense forests and luxuriant bottom land, where the immense pine-trees, the thickets of ferns and devil's club, and the rank undergrowth of bushes and grasses, continually excite one's wonder. We rose at half past five in order to go out to the basin and get back before the ship sailed at ten o'clock, and in the fresh, dewy air and the pure light of the early morning it was a walk through an enchanted forest and a happy valley. The trail wound up to fifteen hundred feet, dropped by long jumps and slides to the first level of the cañon and reached fifteen hundred feet above the sea again in the Basin. The devil's club, a tall, thorny plant with leaves twelve and more inches across, grew in impassable clumps in the woods, and the sunlight falling on these large leaves gave a tropical look to the forest. The devil's club is the prospectors' dread, and the thorny sticks used to do to switch witches with in the Indians' old uncivilized days. *Echinopanax horrida* is the botanist's awful name for it, and that alone is caution enough for one to avoid it. There were thickets of thimbleberry bushes covered with large, creamy-white blossoms; and clusters of white ranunculus, white columbine, blue geranium, and yellow monkey flowers grew in patches and dyed the ground with their massed colors. The ferns were everywhere, and under bushes and beside fallen logs, delicate maidenhair ferns, with fine ebony stems, were gathered by the handful. We met a few well-dressed Indians hurrying to town, and an occasional miner, who gave us a cheery greeting.

Blue jays flitted down the path before us, flashing their beautiful wings in the sunshine; and where the cañon grew steeper and narrower, Gold Creek roared like a muddy Niagara. High up in a ravine a melting snowbank disclosed a great cave underneath, and its edges were fringed with waving grasses and flowers. Even hydraulic mining cannot scar and disfigure this country, where a mantle of green clothes every bare patch in a second season, and mosses and lichens cover the stones and boulders. The moss or sphagnum, that covers the ground, is as great an obstacle to the prospectors' search as the thickets of "devil's club." A campfire built on this moss gradually burns and sinks through, and the miner, returning to his open fire, often finds it lying deep in a well-hole that it has made for itself. In view of the obstacles encountered, the discovery of these mining regions is most remarkable, and is the greatest monument to the prospectors' zeal.

We passed picturesque little log cabins and crossed the débris of hydraulic mines, watched the men in a narrow gulch cleaning up their sluices, and going around the corner of Snowslide Gulch, just this side of Specimen Gulch, we met Mr. B. and his dog. Down we all sat, dog included, and indulged in the light and dry repast that we carried in our pockets. Mr. B. was a typical and ideal miner, and in his high boots, canvas trousers, flannel shirt, big felt hat, and heavy gold watch chain, made exactly the figure for the landscape, as he rested on a big boulder beside the roaring creek. We started to tell him the great news that Alaska at last had a governor and a government, and, bethinking ourselves of the little side incident of Presidential nominations, began to tell him about them. He manifested so little excitement over Blaine and Logan that we asked if his seven years without seeing the polls had made him so indifferent.

"Oh! Lord no; I'm a Democrat though, I guess, ma'am," said Mr. B., apologetically.

"Then we'll never tell you who they have nominated, if you are on that side," said a Republican, firmly, and Mr. B.'s Homeric laugh made that mountain glen ring before he was enlightened as to Cleveland and Hendricks.

Our miner told us of a piece of quartz that he had found the day before, that looked "as if the gold had been poured on hot and had spattered all over it," and then we had to part with him and hurry on in different ways.

Silver Bow Basin is a place to delight an æsthetic miner with in the way of landscape, and any one with a soul in him would surely appreciate that little round valley sunk deep in the heart of great mountains, with snow-caps on every horizon line, a glacier slipping from a great ravine, and waterfalls tumbling noisily down the slopes. A little cluster of cabins is set in the middle of this Basin, and tiny cabins, dump piles, and lines of flumes can be seen on the sides of the steep mountains. The camp had fallen away in numbers since the preceding year, and the mining community dwindled from two hundred to less than one hundred workers. As the placers showed signs of exhaustion, the roving adventurers had left, and the most of those living in the basin were chiefly occupied in holding down their quartz claims until the reign of law and the rush of capitalists should begin. Placer claims that had yielded thirty dollars and fifty dollars a day to the man were abandoned, as the débris from the old glaciers and land-slides came to an end. Across the range in Dix Bow Basin the same conditions existed. Returning on the trail, we met a few miners going back to their cabins and claims, and one sociable fellow stopped for a time to talk to us. He complimented the small party on our energy in taking that early stroll, and in the most regretful way apologized for the roughness and wildness of the very surroundings with which we were so enraptured. A jolly old fellow with a shrewd twinkle in his eye came up the trail swinging his coat gayly, and, planting himself in the pathway, took off his hat with a fine flourish and said to me, "Madam, I was told to watch out for you on this road, and to look you squarely in the eye and tell you to hurry back to the ship or you would be left." There was a shout all round at this unmistakable message of the skipper, and the gay miner enjoyed it most of all. Timing ourselves by our watches, we lingered long on the last mile, sitting on a log in the cool shade of the forest, where the trail almost overhung the little town. We could watch the people walking in the streets beneath, and in the still, slumbering sunshine almost catch the hum of their voices. Pistol-shots raised crashing echoes between the high mountain walls, and set all the big ravens to croaking in hoarse concert.

On the east shore of Douglass Island, opposite Juneau, the group of Indian huts and canoes on the beach, and the skeleton of a flume stalking across a gorge and down to the water, tell of the mining camp there. Running across the narrow channel, the ship anchored off the Treadwell mine, on Douglass Island, and while the miners' supplies were being put in the lighter, we all went ashore and climbed the steep and picturesque trail to the mill. The superintendent took his lantern and marshalled the file into the tunnel to see the air-drill at work, and then we all filed out again. The Treadwell is one of the remarkable mines on the Pacific coast, and said to be one of the largest quartz ledges in the world. The vein is over four hundred feet wide, cropping out on the surface and crossed by three tunnels. The ore is not high grade, but is easily mined and milled, and the supply is inexhaustible. The owners are Messrs. Treadwell, Frye, Freeborn, and Hill, of San Francisco, and Senator J. P. Jones of Nevada. So far only a small 15-stamp mill has been at work on the ore, but the owners have decided to erect a 120-stamp mill this year and develop the property systematically. The progress of the Treadwell mine has been carefully watched by miners and capitalists, and its success has done much to encourage others to hold on to their properties in the face of all the discouragements they have had to undergo through government neglect.

The Bear Ledge, owned by Captain Carroll and his partners, adjoins the Treadwell or Paris claim, and is a continuation of the same rich vein; and from the richness and extent of these and other mines, it is believed that a large town will eventually spring up on the island. A town-site was located and called Cooperstown, in 1881, soon after the discovery of gold on the island, but so far only the tents of placer miners have marked it. For two seasons lawless bodies of men worked the placers on the surface of the Treadwell lode, and, as there was no power to appeal to, the Treadwell company were forced to endure it. During the summer of 1883, over twenty-five thousand dollars was taken from the surface of the ledge in this way. The miners pounded up the rich, decomposed quartz in hand-mortars, and as it was impossible to extract all the gold by the rude process employed, they dumped over into the channel richer quartz, in many instances, than had been worked in the Treadwell mill. The deposit of decomposed quartz on the top of the ledge was in some places ten feet deep, and in working it the squatters took the water of the Paris, or Hayes Creek, and shut off the mill supply entirely. There was a sharp contest between the mill-owners and the hydraulic miners, and the man-of-war at Sitka had to be sent for before the matter was adjusted. They pledged themselves, "until such time as they should have civil law," to let the mill have the use of the water for twelve hours and the miners for the other twelve hours of each twenty-four, and the squatters were not to blast the lode, but only wash the surface ground.

An island gold field is a rarity in mining annals, but all Douglass Island is said to be seamed with quartz lodes, and it is ridged with high mountains from end to end of its twenty-mile boundaries. It was eighty-seven years after Vancouver's surveys before the prospectors found the gold on its shores, but the miners have retained the old nomenclature, and the island is still Douglass Island, as Vancouver named it in honor of his friend, the Bishop of Salisbury.

CHAPTER VIII.

THE CHILKAT COUNTRY.

Juneau is far enough north to satisfy any reasonable summer ambition, and with its latitude of 58° 16′ N., the young mining town and future metropolis is but little above the line of Glasgow, Edinburgh, Copenhagen, and Moscow. The deep waters of Gastineaux Channel are obstructed by ledges just north of Juneau, and the eighteen feet fall of the regular tides leaves islands and reefs visible in mid-channel. For this reason the ship had to return on its course, and round Douglass Island, before it could continue further north, and when that island of solid gold quartz was left behind, the vessel entered a maze of smaller islands and threaded its way into the grand reaches of Lynn Canal. Vancouver named this arm of the sea for the town of Lynn, in Norfolk, England, the place of his nativity, and his explorers began the song of praise that is chanted by every summer traveller who follows their course up the high-walled, glacier-bound fiord. The White Mountains present bold barriers on the west, and along the eastern shores the great continental range fronts abruptly on the water. Each point or peak passed brought another glacier into view, nineteen glaciers in all being visible on the way up the canal. The great Auk glacier was first seen, and then the Eagle glacier, toppling over a precipice three thousand feet in air, their frozen crests and fronts turning pinnacles of silver and azure to the radiant sun.

Not even "the blue Canary Isles" could have offered a more "glorious summer day" than the one that we enjoyed while the *Idaho* steamed straight up Lynn Canal, headed for the north pole. The sun shone so warmly on deck that we laid aside wraps, and sat under the grateful shade of an umbrella. There was a sparkle and freshness to the air, and under an ecstatic blue sky fleecy white clouds drifted about the mountain summits and mingled their vapory outlines with the fields of snow. We revelled in the beauties of the scenes, and appreciated at the moment that this passage leading to the Chilkat country is perhaps the finest fiord of the coast. Lynn Canal slumbered as a sapphire sea between its high mountain walls, with scarcely a ripple on its surface. The blue expanse was streaked with a greenish gray where the turbid streams poured in from the melting glaciers, and was marked with a distinct line where the azure water changed to green, and then it faded away into gray again, where the fresh waters of the Chilkat River flowed in.

At the head of Lynn Canal a long point juts out into the current, with the Chilkat Inlet opening at the left, and the Chilkoot Inlet at the right. Opposite this tongue of land on the Chilkat side is the great Davidson glacier, sweeping down a gorge between two mountains, and spreading out like an opened fan. The glacier is three miles across its front and twelve hundred feet high, where it slopes to reach the level ground, and it is separated from the waters of the inlet by a terminal moraine covered with a thick forest of pines. The symmetry of its outlines and the grand slope of its broken surface are most impressive, and this mighty torrent, arrested in its sweep, shows in every pinnacle and crevice all the blues of heaven, the palest tints of beryl and glacier ice, and the sheen of snow and silver in the sunshine. It is worthily named for Professor George Davidson, the astronomer, and its lower slopes were explored by him during his visits to the Chilkat country on government and scientific missions.

Rounding a sharp point beyond the glacier, the *Idaho* swept into a circling, half-moon cove, where a picturesque Indian camp nestled at the foot of the precipitous Mount Labouchere, not named for the witty editor of the London *Truth*, but for one of the Hudson Bay Company's steamers that first penetrated these waters and anchored regularly in this Pyramid Harbor. The cannon-shot, which was such an important feature in the progress of the *Idaho*, gave a tremendous echo from mountain to mountain, and glacier to glacier, and thundered and rolled down the inlet for uncounted seconds, as the anchor dropped. The tents and bark huts, and the trader's store of the little settlement, showed finely against the deep green mat at the foot of the vertical mountain, and in the early afternoon all lay in clear shadow, and the mountain seemed to almost overhang the ship as she swung round from her anchor chain. There was an excited rushing to and fro on shore; dogs and Indians gathered at the beach, and canoes put off before the ship's boats were lowered to take us ashore.

THE DAVIDSON GLACIER.

The Northwest Trading Company's large store and salmon cannery were quite overlooked in the travellers' hasty rush for the Indian tents, that were scattered in groups along the narrow clearing between tide-water and mountain wall. Before each tent and cabin were frames, hung with what looked to be bits of red flannel at a distance, but proved to be drying salmon when we reached them. It was a gaudy and effective decoration, and a Chilkat salmon is as bright a color, when caught, as a lobster after it has been boiled. Though a warlike and aggressive people, the Chilkats practise many of the arts of peace, and the wood-carvings and curios that they had for sale were eagerly bought. Miniature totem poles and canoes, pipes, masks, forks, and spoons changed ownership rapidly, and Indians and passengers regretted that there were no more. Bone sticks, used for marten-traps by the Tinneh tribes of the interior, were to be had, with every stick topped with some totemic beast, and there were queer little fish and toys of soapstone, made by the same peaceful natives. Copper bracelets, covered with Chilkat designs, were offered by a lame rascal, who said, "Gold! gold!" to the eager curio-seekers who snatched at his shining wares. Copper knives and arrow-tips were also displayed, and articles of this metal are distinctly Chilkat work, as the art of forging copper was long a secret of theirs. Relics of the stone age were brought forth, and granite mortars and axes, and leather dressers of slate, offered for sale. Stone-age implements are being rapidly gathered up in this country, and a trader, who has received and filled large orders for eastern museums and societies, threatens to bring up a skilled stone-cutter to supply the increasing demands of scientists, now that the Indians have parted with most of their heirloom specimens.

CHILKAT BLANKET.

In one tent two women were at work weaving a large Chilkat blanket on a primitive loom. These blankets, woven from the long fleece of the mountain goat, have been a specialty of the Chilkats as long as white men have known them. The chiefs who met Vancouver were wrapped in these gorgeous totemic blankets or cloaks, and in early days they were commonly worn by the chiefs and rich men. Since the traders have introduced the woollen blankets of commerce, the native manufactures have been neglected, and now that the art is dying out, the few that remain in the possession of the natives are highly valued and only taken from their cedar boxes on the occasion of great feasts and ceremonies. These blankets are found among all the Thlinket tribes, and the Haidas at Kasa-an Bay had many Chilkat cloaks and garments stored away in their cabins. The blankets average two yards in width and about one yard in depth, and are bordered at the ends and across the bottom with a deep fringe. The colors are black, white, and yellow, with occasional touches of a soft, dull blue. Soot, or bituminous coal, gives the base for the black dye, and they get the pure, brilliant yellow from a moss that grows on the rocks. The blue is made by boiling copper and seaweeds together. They make fine trophies for wall decorations, or, as rugs or lambrequins, are superior to the Navajo and Zuni blankets of the New Mexico Indians. The totemic figures woven in these cloaks tell allegories and legends to the natives, and the conventionalized whales, eagles, and ravens are full of meaning, recording the great battles between the clans, the incidents of family history, and deeds at arms. The price of a blanket ranges from twenty to forty dollars; the fineness of the work, the beauty of the design, and the anxiety of the purchaser all helping to increase the price.

As in all Indian villages, the fierce, wolfish-looking dogs showed an inclination to growl and snap at the white people, but the hard-featured, strong-minded women of the Chilkat tribe silenced them with a word, or a skilfully thrown brand snatched from the family camp fire. The children and the dogs were always getting under foot and crowding into each group, and in the Alpine valley, where the afternoon shadows brought a pleasant sharpness to the air, the youngsters were as scantily clad as in the tropics. They sat on the damp ground and stole handfuls of rice from the pots boiling on the fires, or furtively dipped the spoons into the mess one minute and hit the dogs with the table utensil the next. One boy, who had sold a great many little carved toys to the visitors, dashed off into a thicket of wild roses, and gallantly brought back fragrant pink blossoms for his customers. Sitka Jack's carved canoe was drawn up on shore, and that grandee at last appeared to us, and after selling his own pipe and carved possessions, he wandered about and interfered in every one's bargains by urging the natives to ask more for their curios.

Of the white celebrities residing at Pyramid Harbor, there was one with the enviable fame of being "the handsomest man in Alaska," and when he went gliding out to the ship in a swift native canoe, and appeared on deck as if just stepped aside from a Broadway stroll, there was a perceptible flutter in the ladies' cabin. Another fine-looking man of distinguished manner, found wandering on shore, proved to be a French count, who, having dissipated three fortunes in the gayeties of a Parisian life, has hidden himself in this remote corner of the world to ponder on the philosophy of life, and wait for the favorable stroke that shall enable him to return and shine once more among his gay comrades of the boulevard, the Bois and the opera foyer.

At Pyramid Harbor the ship reached the most northern point on her course and the end of the inside passage. At 59° 11′ N. we were many degrees distant from the Arctic Circle, but, although it was mid-July, the sun did not set until half past nine o'clock by ship's time, and the clear twilight lasted until the royal flush of sunrise was bathing the summits of the higher mountains. At midnight fine print could be read on deck, and at the hour when churchyards yawn the amateur photographers turned their cameras upon the matchless panorama before them, and the full witchery of that serene northern night was felt when the crescent of the young moon showed itself faint and ethereal in the eastern sky.

We had been watching a rocky platform up on the mountain side, in the hopes of seeing the bear with her cubs, who, living in some crevice near there, was said to promenade on her airy perch at all hours of the day and look down defiantly on the settlement. We were tiring of that cuckoo-clock amusement, when a shaggy man came on the scene and said to the photographers, —

"You ought to have been here in June, if you wanted to see long days. You never would know when it was time to go to bed then."

"Doesn't it ever get dark here?" we yawned at him in chorus.

"Sometimes," he answered. "'Bout long enough to get your overcoat off, I reckon."

A year later there was the same beautiful trip up Lynn Canal, and as a mark of growth and progress the *Ancon* found a large wharf to tie up to at Pyramid Harbor. The cannery building had been enlarged, and the Indian tents replaced with log and bark houses. The cannery, that had been a losing venture in the first year, gave promise of better returns, and Pyramid Harbor wore quite a prosperous air. The Indians and their curios were again the sole distracting interest of the passengers, and the Chilkats, as before, sold everything desirable that they owned.

A strapping young Indian seized upon us as we were wandering on shore, rattled off the few words, "My papa, Sitka Jack, my papa heap sick," and soon we were chasing over grass and gravel, at the heels of this young Hercules, to his neat log house. The son of Sitka Jack showed first the curios he had for sale, and then his pretty wife, who wore a yellow dress and a bright blue blanket, and had a clean face illuminated by soft black eyes and rosy cheeks. Lastly he led us at a quickstep to the place where his venerable papa sat crouched in a blanket. The son spoke English well, but so rapidly, that he brought himself up breathless every few minutes, and the docile, infantile way in which this six-footed fellow spoke of his "papa" more than amused us.

The "papa" is one of the head chiefs of the Sitka tribe, but goes to Chilkat Inlet every summer to visit his wife's relations during the salmon season. He is an arrant old rascal, and has made a great deal of trouble at times; but in his feeble old age he has a kindly and pleasant smile, and a quiet dignity that is in great contrast to his vehement, impetuous young son. Mrs. Sitka Jack is the sister of Doniwak, the one-eyed tyrant who rules the lower Chilkat village, and now that her liege is becoming helpless, her influence is more supreme than ever. She sat like a queen, kindly relaxing some of the grimness of her expression when she saw that we had been buying from her son, but everything indicated that she had the most eloquent and obstreperous chief of the Sitkans completely disciplined. One of her Chilkat nephews was introduced to us by her glib son, and the hulking young savage fairly crushed our civilized hands in his friendly grasp, and critically examined our purchases.

A wild-looking old medicine-man, with long red hair, hovered on the outskirts of the group, and finally showed us, with innocent pride, a naval officer's letter of credentials, which testified to his having a good ear for music, since he neither flinched nor winked, when a large cannon was slyly touched off at his elbow, during one of his visits on board a man-of-war.

Three-Fingered Jack, a celebrity of another order, wandered about the camp arrayed in the cast-off uniform of a naval officer, with his breast pinned full of tin and silver stars, like a German diplomat. Sitka Jack's son looked quite unconscious while the three-fingered lion passed by; but when we directed his attention to him, the son of his papa gave a pitying, contemptuous look and declared that he did not know who it was. As well might we have asked one of the Capulets who Romeo was.

Kloh-Kutz, or Hole-in-the-Cheek, the head chief of the Chilkats, appeared to us only in flying glimpses, as he ran up and down the steps of the trader's store. He is a wrinkled old fellow now, and the hole left in his cheek by a wound is decorated by a large bone button similar to those that the women wear in their cheeks. When Professor Davidson, of the Coast Survey, went to the Chilkat country in 1867, on the revenue cutter *Lincoln*, Capt. J. W. White commanding, to gather material for a report upon the topography, climate, and the resources of Alaska, called for by the Congressional committees having the matter of the purchase of the territory in charge, he first made the acquaintance of Kloh-Kutz, then in his prime.

In 1869 Professor Davidson revisited the Chilkat country to observe the total eclipse of the sun, and, by invitation of Kloh-Kutz, established his observatory at the village of Klu-Kwan, twenty miles up the Chilkat River. The station was called Kloh-Kutz in honor of the distinguished patron and protector of the scientists, who gave them the great council-house for a residence. In the ardor of his hospitality Kloh-Kutz was going to have the name "DAVIDSON" tattooed on his arm, but at the suggestion of the astronomer gave up that elaborate design, and had "SEWARD" traced across his biceps with a needle and thread dipped in soot and seal oil and drawn through the flesh. He was quite willing to wear his name when he learned that Seward was the great *Tyee*, or chief, who bought the country of the Russians and thereby raised the price of furs so greatly.

In advance of the eclipse, Professor Davidson told his host what would happen; that the sun would be hidden at midday, and darkness fall upon the land on the 7th of August, and that it would come as a great shadow sweeping down the valley of the Chilkat. The Indians had always gathered and silently watched the white men when they pointed their strange instruments at the sun each day, but they fled in terror when the great darkness began to come, and did not return until the eclipse was over. They regarded Professor Davidson with the greatest awe, as a wonderful medicine-man who could perform such great miracles at will; and Kloh-Kutz, delighted with the great trick of his friend, made a serious offer of all his canoes, blankets, and wives, if the astronomer would tell him "how he did it," and divulge the secret confidentially to a brother conjurer.

The evening before the eclipse, word reached Professor Davidson that Secretary Seward and his party were at the mouth of the Chilkat River, to convey him back to Portland on their steamer, as soon as his observations were completed. Kloh-Kutz was invited to come down and meet the great *Tyee*, and hold a council with Gen. Jeff. C. Davis, the military commandant, who had gone up from Sitka with the Seward party. Kloh-Kutz chose the flower of Chilkat chivalry to go below with his great war canoe and carry a letter from Professor Davidson to Mr. Seward, urging him to "come up hither" and see the territory he had bought; and luring on the ex-premier by saying that he had discovered an iron mountain, the ore of which was seventy per cent iron. Referring to this fact in a speech made at a public meeting in Sitka afterwards, Mr. Seward said:

"When I came there I found very properly he had been studying the heavens so busily that he had but cursorily examined the earth under his feet; that it was not a single iron mountain he had discovered, but a range of hills, the very dust of which adheres to the magnet, while the range itself, 2,000 feet high, extends along the east bank of the river thirty miles."

Mr. Seward and his son, and General Davis, with two staff officers, and others of the party, left the ship in three canoes early on the morning of the day of the eclipse. They were half way up to Klu-Kwan village,when the shadow began to cross the sun, and the weird, unearthly light fell upon the land. The Indians in the canoe said the sun "was very sick and wanted to go to sleep," and they refused to paddle any further. The canoes were beached quickly, and the visitors made a sociable camp-fire for themselves, and cooked their dinner by its blaze. Late in the afternoon they reached the village, and that evening Kloh-Kutz made a call of ceremony upon the guests in the council-house. There was an array of Chilkat chiefs and Chilkat women to witness the meeting of the Tyees, and after a speech of welcome, Kloh-Kutz drew up his sleeve dramatically and showed the "Seward" tattoed with his *totems* on his arm. The great diplomat was quite astonished and bewildered, and the handwriting on the wall hardly made a greater sensation in Belshazzar's court.

The next morning the *wa-wa*, or official council, was held with the aid of two interpreters, one to translate English into Russian, and the other to translate Russian into Chilkat. Believing that if Mr. Seward bought Alaska, he must still own it in person, Kloh-Kutz ignored Gen. Davis, as being only the great Tyee's servant, and addressed himself directly to the supposed ruler of the whole country. His grievance was that, ten years before, three Chilkats had been killed at Sitka, and now, "What is the great Tyee going to do about it?" Kloh-Kutz was not to be put off by the diplomatic answer that the murder had happened during Russian days. He said that "the Tyee of the Russians was so poor that he could not keep his land

and had to sell it," but for all that he must have reparation for the loss of his three Chilkats. To his mind one Chilkat was worth three Sitkans, and if the Tyee would let him kill nine Sitkans, the account would be squared. With a finesse worthy of a diplomat who had dealt with all the great nations of the earth, Mr. Seward finally brought Kloh-Kutz down to accepting forty blankets as an indemnity, and he and his sub-chief Colchica and their wives led the guard of honor that escorted the great Tyee back to his ship. Captain C. C. Dall, who commanded the steamer *Active* during that memorable cruise, gave a great entertainment to the chiefs on board, and fireworks rounded off that memorable evening. Mr. Seward presented a flag to the Chilkat chief, and at the banquet in the cabin, he and Professor Davidson gave astronomy by easy lessons to their Chilkat visitors, and disclaimed any agency in the eclipse as an accompaniment of the Tyee's visit.

Kloh-Kutz is delighted yet to show his Seward tattoo mark to any one, and to tell of the visit of the great Tyee. He is a chief of advanced and liberal notions, a high-strung, imperious old fellow, and has a fine countenance, marred only by the wound in his cheek, which was received at the hands of one of his own tribe during some internecine troubles. His assailant held a revolver close to Kloh-Kutz's head, and when the chief looked scornfully at it, the trigger was snapped. Weak powder prevented the ball from inflicting any more serious injuries than to enter his cheek and tear away a few teeth. Kloh-Kutz swallowed his teeth and handed the bullet back to his assailant with a fine gesture, saying: "You cannot hurt me. See!"

A few years since a young German was sent up to establish the trading post at Pyramid Harbor, and was introduced to Kloh-Kutz as a great Tyee. When the agent failed to recognize, or understand the meaning of the "Seward" on his arm, Kloh-Kutz was disgusted, and refused to treat with him as anything but a mere trader.

"How can he be a Tyee, if he does not know the chief of all the Tyees?" scornfully said Kloh-Kutz.

On the east shore of Chilkat Inlet, opposite Pyramid Harbor, is the rival trading station of Chilkat, where Kinney, the Astoria salmon packer, has another cannery. In the rivalry and competition of the first year (1883) between the Pyramid Harbor and Chilkat canneries, the price of salmon rose from two to fifteen cents for a single fish, and the Indians, once demoralized by opposition prices, refused to listen to reason when the canneries had to, and Chinese cheap labor was imported. There has been wrath in the Chilkat heart ever since the Chinese cousins went there, and old Kloh-Kutz indignantly said: "If Indian know how to make *hoochinoo* (whiskey) out of an oil can and a piece of seaweed, he knows enough to can salmon."

During its first year the Kinney cannery shipped sixty barrels of salt salmon and 2,890 cases of canned salmon, working at a great disadvantage for want of proper nets. In 1884 the amount of salmon shipped was doubled.

Chilkat and Pyramid Harbor are rivals also in the fur trade, and at Chilkat especially, the skins and furs shown were finer than had been seen at any of the other trading places. The shrewd Chilkats are as hard bargainers as the old Hudson Bay Company people ever were, and they get the furs from the interior tribes for a mere trifle in comparison to what they demand for the same pelts from the traders. In Hudson Bay Company trades, the cheap flint-lock muskets used to be sold to the Indians, by standing the gun on the ground and piling up marten skins beside it, until they were even with the top of the gun-barrel. That hoax is equalled now by the tricks of the Chilkats, who sell gunpowder to the unsophisticated men of the interior tribes at an average rate of twenty-five dollars a pound, and boast of their smartness at this kind of bargaining which brings a profit of one hundred and even two thousand per cent. Only one tourist was ever known to get the better of a Chilkat at a bargain, and that was when a common red felt tennis hat, bought for half a dollar at Victoria, was exchanged for a silver bracelet by a Chicago man, who regretted for the rest of his trip that he had not bought a box of hats to trade for curios.

Back of the Chilkat cannery a few miles, and facing on Chilkoot Inlet, is the mission station of Haines, named for a benevolent lady of Brooklyn, N. Y., who supports the establishment, presided over by the Rev. E. S. Willard and his wife.

Either the Chilkat, or the Chilkoot Inlet gives entrance to a chain of rivers and lakes, that, leading through gorges and mountain passes, conducts the prospector by a final portage to Lewis River, one of the head tributaries of the Yukon. The Chilkat Indians, with a fine sense of the importance of their position, have always closely guarded these approaches to the interior, and prevented the Indians of the back country from ever coming down to the coast and the white traders. They have thus held the monopoly of the fur trade of the region, and, while keeping the interior Indians back, have been quite as careful not to let any white men across.

On account of this guard, Vancouver's men experienced some of the hospitable attentions of the Chilkats when they were exploring the channel in 1794. A canoe-load of natives bore down upon Whidby's boat, and urged the Englishmen to accompany them on up the Chilkat River to the great villages, where eight chiefs of consequence resided. Vancouver's men declined the invitation, and the chief, commanding the first canoe, made hostile flourishes with the brass speaking-trumpet and other nautical insignia that he carried. They followed the boats out to the mouth of the channel, and alarmed the Englishmen greatly, as they feared an attack by the whole tribe at any moment.

The Russian and Hudson Bay Company's ships traded with the Chilkats for a half century without ever dealing directly with one of the natives of the interior, from whom came the vast stores of furs that were exchanged each year. The Chilkats met the men of the Tinneh (interior) tribes at an established place many miles from the mouth of the river, and occasionally, as a matter of diplomacy, they would bring a great Tinneh chief down under escort, and allow him to look at the "fire ship" of the traders.

The first man to run the gauntlet of the Chilkoot Pass was a red-headed Scotchman in the employ of the Hudson Bay Company, who left Fort Selkirk in 1864 and forced his way alone through the unknown country to Chilkoot Inlet. The Indians seized the adventurer and held him prisoner until Captain Swanson, with the Hudson Bay Company steamer *Labouchere*, came up and took him away. In 1872 one George Holt dodged through the Chilkoot Pass, and went down the Lewis River to the Yukon. In 1874 Holt again crossed the Chilkoot Pass, followed the Lewis River to the Yukon, and then down that mighty stream to a place near its mouth, where he crossed by a portage to the Kuskokquin River, and thence to the sea.

In 1877 a party of miners set out from Sitka under the leadership of Edmund Bean, and attempted to cross by the Chilkoot Pass, but the Indians obliged them to turn back.

In 1878 and in 1880, prospecting parties left Sitka for the head waters of the Yukon, and the latter company, through the clever diplomacy and active interest of Captain Beardslee, commanding the U. S. S. *Jamestown*, were hospitably received by the Chilkats and guided through their country, when convinced that they would not interfere with their fur trade. They found indications of gold all the way, and large gravel deposits. This party descended the Lewis River to Fort Selkirk and there divided, one set of prospectors going down to Fort Yukon, and the others up the Pelly River and thence to the head waters of the Stikine River and the Cassiar region of British Columbia.

In the spring of 1882 a party of forty-five miners, all old Arizona prospectors, left Juneau for the head waters of the Yukon. They returned in the fall, and reported discoveries of gold, silver, copper, nickel, and bituminous coal in the region between the Copper and Lewis Rivers.

In the spring of 1883 one Dugan led a party from Juneau over the divide. In September they sent back by Indians for an additional supply of provisions, intending to remain in the interior all winter. They reported placer mines yielding one hundred and fifty dollars a day to the man, but another party, that left Juneau soon after Dugan, returned in September without having found any placers that yielded more than twenty-five dollars a day.

Altogether more than two hundred prospectors crossed from Lynn Canal to the Yukon country during the first three years after the Chilkats raised their blockade. The Chilkats kept control of the travel, and charged six and ten dollars for each hundred pounds of goods that they packed across the twenty-four-mile portage intervening between the river and the chain of lakes.

In May, 1883, Lieut. Schwatka and party crossed this same divide, and made a quick journey of more than two thousand miles by raft down the Lewis River to the Yukon, and down the Yukon to St. Michael's Island in Behring Sea, and thence to San Francisco by the revenue cutter *Corwin*.

In April, 1884, Dr. Everette, U. S. A., and two companions went over the Chilkat Pass to work their way westward to Copper River and descend it to its mouth. In June, Lieut. Abercrombie, U. S. A., and three companions were landed at the mouth of Copper River, with orders to ascend that stream and descend the Chilkat to Lynn Canal. These expeditions were sent out by order of General Miles, commanding the Department of the Columbia, who visited Alaska in 1882, and has since manifested a great interest in the Territory.

The present maps of this upper region of the Yukon give only the general courses of the rivers, and have not changed in any important details the Russian charts. A unique map of the country is one drawn by Kloh-Kutz and his wife for Professor Davidson, and which was made the basis and authority for one official chart, the original remaining in Professor Davidson's possession at San Francisco. Kloh-Kutz has known the Yukon route from childhood, and, lying face downward, he and his wife drew on the back of an old chart all the rivers, with the profile of the mountains as they appear on either side of the watercourses. The one great glacier in which the Chilkat and the Lewis branch of the Yukon River head, is indicated by snow-shoe tracks to show the mode of progress, and the limit of each of the fourteen days' journey across to Fort Selkirk is marked by cross lines on this original Chilkat map. The father of Kloh-Kutz was a great chief and fur-trader before him, and was one of the party of Chilkats that went across and burned Fort Selkirk in 1851, in retaliation for the Hudson Bay Company's interference with their fur trade with the Tinnehs.

The Doctors Krause, of the Geographical Society of Bremen, who spent a year at the mouth of the Chilkat lately, made some explorations of the region about the portages of the Yukon, and their maps and publications have been of great value to the Coast Survey. There are dangerous rapids and cañons on the watercourses leading to the Yukon, and none but miners and the most adventurous traders will probably ever avail themselves of this route; although by going some six hundred miles up to Fort Yukon, which is just within the Arctic Circle, the land of the midnight sun is reached. Professor Dall, who spent two years on the Yukon, has fully described the country below Fort Yukon in his "Resources of Alaska;" and the Schiefflin Brothers, of Tombstone, Arizona, who followed his path on an elaborately planned prospecting expedition in 1882, added little and almost nothing more to the general knowledge of the region. The Schiefflins found gold, but considered the remoteness from the sources of supplies, and the long winters, too great obstacles for any mines to be ever successfully worked there. There are fur-traders' stations all along the two thousand miles of the great stream, and within the United States boundaries, the Alaska Commercial Company, and the Western Fur Company of San Francisco, buy the pelts from the Indians, and divide the great fur trade of this interior region.

CHAPTER IX.

BARTLETT BAY AND THE HOONIAHS.

From Pyramid Harbor the ship went south to Icy Straits and up the other side of the long peninsula to Glacier Bay, so named by Captain Beardslee in 1880. At the mouth of it, in unknown and unsurveyed waters, began the search for a new trading station in a cove, since known as Bartlett Bay, in honor of the owner of the fishery, a merchant of Port Townsend.

Vancouver's boats passed by Glacier Bay during his third cruise on this coast, and his men saw only frozen mountains and an expanse of ice as far as the eye could reach. It is only within a decade that anything has been known of the extent of the great bay at the foot of the Fairweather Alps, and no surveys have been made of its shores to correct the imperfect charts now in use. Revenue cutters, men-of-war, and traders' ships had gone as far as the entrance, but were prevented from advancing by adverse winds and currents, floating ice, and shoaling waters. The old moraine left by the ice-sheet that once covered the whole bay forms a bar and barrier at its mouth, and the channel has to be sought cautiously.

Skirting the wooded shores and sailing through ice floes, every glass was brought into requisition for signs of life on land. Towards noon a white man and two Indians were sighted signalling from a canoe, and the steamer waited while they paddled towards it. They had been off on an unsuccessful hunt for the sea otter, and gladly consented to have their canoe hauled up on deck and to impart all their knowledge of Bartlett Cove. At three o'clock a resounding bang from the cannon announced to the Hooniah natives on shore, that the first ship that had ever entered that harbor was at hand. A canoe came rapidly paddling towards us, and a wild figure rose in the stern and shouted to the captain to "go close up to the new house and anchor in thirteen fathoms of water." This was Dick Willoughby, the first American pioneer in Alaska, a local genius, and a far-away, polar variety of "Colonel Sellers," most interesting to encounter in this last region of No-Man's Land. Dick Willoughby came to this northwest coast in 1858, emigrating from Virginia by way of Missouri. Since that time he has ranged the Alaskan shores from the boundary line to Behring's Straits, trading with the Indians, and prospecting for all the known minerals. Willoughby's mines and possessions are scattered all up and down the coast, and there is not a new scheme or enterprise in the territory in which he has not a share. His mines, if once developed to the extent he claims possible, would make him greater than all the bonanza men, and in crude and well-stored gold, silver, iron, coal, copper, lead, and marble he is fabulously rich. In all the twenty-five years he has spent here, Dick Willoughby has gone down to San Francisco but once, and then was in haste to get back to his cool northern home.

A little Indian camp edged the beach below Willoughby's log house and store, and the natives came out to look at us, with quite as much interest as we went on shore to see them. A small iceberg, drifted near shore, was the point of attack for the amateur photographers, and the Indian children marvelled with open eyes at the "long-legged gun" that was pointed at the young men, who posed on the perilous and picturesque points of the berg. Icebergs drifting down the bay, and small cakes of ice washing in shore with the rising tide, secured that luxury of the summer larder to the Indians, and in every tent and bark house on shore there was to be found a pail or basket of ice-water. In Willoughby's store there were curios and baskets galore, and after his long and quiet life in the wilderness the poor man was nearly distracted, when seven ladies began talking to him at once, and mixed up the new style nickel pieces with the money they offered him.

The packing-house had just been built, and the ship unloaded more lumber, nets, salt, barrel-staves and hoops, and general merchandise and provisions for the new station. The small lighters and canoes in which the freight was taken ashore made unloading a slow process, although the whole native population assisted. The small boys joined in the carnival, and little Indians of not more than six years trooped over the rocky beach barefooted, and carried bundles of barrel-staves and shingles on their heads.

We roamed the beach, hunting for the round, cuplike barnacles that the whales rub off their tormented sides, and the children, quick to see what we were looking for, trooped up the beach ahead of us, and soon returned with dozens of them that they sold for a good price. Back in the little valley and natural clearing, the ground was covered with wild flowers and running strawberry vines, and the botanist was up to his shoulders in strange bushes, up to his ankles in mire, and in wild ecstacy at his finds. When we complimented Dick Willoughby upon the promising appearance of his little vegetable garden, and the great crop of strawberries coming on, he assured us that in a few weeks the ground would be red with fruit, and that he did not know but that he would be canning the wild strawberries by another year.

In one tent the best Indian hunter lay dying from the wounds received in an encounter with a bear, his face being stripped of flesh by the clawing of the fierce animal, and his body frightfully mangled. The Indians, to whom remnants of their superstition cling, viewed him sadly as one punished by the spirits. Their old shamans taught them that the spirit of a man resided in the black bear, and it was sacrilege to slay this animal, representing their great totem. The old men mutter prayers whenever they find the tracks of a bear, and cannot be induced to bring in the skin entire. It is rare to find an Alaska bear skin with the nose on, the Indians believing that they have appeased the spirit if they leave that sacred particle untouched. The black, the grizzly, and the rare St. Elias silver bear are found in this Hooniah country, and their skins at the trader's store ranged in price from eight to twenty dollars.

The mountain goat—*Aplocerus Montana* by his full name—disports himself on all the crags around Glacier Bay, and leaps through the glacial regions of the Fairweather Alps. He has a long, silvery white hair, that is not particularly fine, but his sharp, little black horns are great trophies for the hunter, and are carved into spoon handles by the expert craftsmen of all the Thlinket tribes.

THLINKET BIRD-PIPE (SIDE AND BOTTOM).

The cool waters of Glacier Bay, filled with floating ice, are the great summer resort for the wary sea otter and the hair seal. The fur seal is occasionally found, but not in such numbers as to make it a feature of the hunting season; and as the pelts are stretched and dried before being brought in by the Indians, they are valueless to the furrier. The Hooniahs inhabiting this bay and the shores of Cross Sound and Icy Straits claim the monopoly of the seal and otter fisheries, and have had great wars with the other tribes who ventured into their hunting grounds. Indians even came up from British Columbia, and a few years ago the Hooniahs invoked the aid of the man-of-war to drive away the trespassing "King George men."

The seal is food, fuel, and raiment to them, and square wooden boxes of seal oil stand in every Hooniah tent. Age increases its qualities for them, and rancid seal oil and dried salmon, salmon eggs, or herring roe, mixed with oil, and a salad of seaweed dressed with oil, are the national dishes of all the Thlinket tribes. Boiled seal flippers are a great dainty, and in one Hooniah tent we peered into the family kettle, and saw the black flippers waving in the simmering waters like human hands. It looked like cannibalism, but the old man who was superintending the stew said: "Seal! Seal all same as hog." The Chinook term for seal is *cocho Siwash*, or, literally, "Indian hog," and it quite corresponds to American pork in its universal use.

In one smoky tent, a native silversmith was hard at work, pounding from half dollar pieces the silver bracelets which are the chief and valued ornaments of the Thlinket women. This Tiffany of the Hooniah tribe nodded to us amiably, carefully examined the workmanship of the bracelets we wore, and then went on to show us how they were made. We sat fascinated for nearly an hour in the thick smoke that blew in every direction from the fire, to watch this artist make bracelets with only the rudest implements. He first put the coin in an iron spoon and set it on the coals for some minutes, and when he drew out the spoon, and took the silver disk between a pair of old pincers, he nodded his head to us and muttered *Klimmin* — the Chinook word for soft. Holding it with the pincers, he hammered it on an old piece of iron, and heating it, turning it, and pounding away vigorously, he soon laid a long slender strip of silver before us. Another heating, a deft hammering and polishing, and the bracelet was ready to be engraved with a clumsy steel point in simple geometrical designs, or with the conventionalized dog-fish, salmon, seals, and whales of Hooniah art. After that it was heated and bent into shape to fit the wrist.

For these *Klickwillies*, or bracelets, the white visitors were asked three dollars a pair, while the native rule is to pay the silversmith just twice the value of the coins used. He was an amiable old fellow, this Hooniah silversmith, and he kept no secrets of his art from us, bringing out finger rings, nose rings, long silver lip pins, and earrings to show us. The Indian women in his tent were well bedecked with silver ornaments, and if all three of them were his wives, the silversmith's trade must be a profitable one. Each woman had her wrists covered with rows of closely fitting bracelets, always in odd numbers, and double rows of rings were on their fingers. The men of these tribes sport the nose ring as well as the women, and are not satisfied with wearing one pair of earrings at a time, but pierce the rim of the ear with a succession of holes, and wear in each one a silver hoop, a bead, or a charm, in memory of some particular deed.

The Hooniahs are next to the Haidas in skill and intelligence, and in the graves of their medicine men are found carvings on bone, and fossil ivory, mountain goat horns, and shells, that prove that they once possessed even greater skill in these things. On the grave cloth of one shaman buried near a village on Cross Sound, were lately found some flat pieces of ivory and bone, four and six inches long, carved with faces and totemic symbols. Age had turned them to a deep rich yellow and brown, and a slight rubbing restored the brilliant polish, that enhanced them when they were first sewed to the blankets and wrappings of the dead shaman. His rattles, masks, drums, and implements of his profession, buried with him, were of the finest workmanship, and proved the superiority of the ancient carvers.

The Hooniah women weave baskets from the fine bark of the cedar and from split spruce roots, and ornament them with geometrical patterns in brilliant colors, but the weaving that we saw was not as fine as that of some of the more southern tribes.

CHAPTER X.

MUIR GLACIER AND IDAHO INLET.

When Dick Willoughby told of the great glacier thirty miles up the bay, the thud of whose falling ice could be heard and felt at his house, and declared that it once rattled the tea-cups on his table, and sent a wave washing high up on his shore, the captain of the *Idaho* said he would go there, and took this Dick Willoughby along to find the place and prove the tale. Away we went coursing up Glacier Bay, a fleet of one hundred and twelve little icebergs gayly sailing out to meet us, as we left our anchorage the next morning. Entering into these unknown and unsurveyed waters, the lead was cast through miles of bottomless channels, and when the ship neared a green and mountainous island at the mouth of the bay, the captain and the pilot made me an unconditional present of the domain, and duly entered it on the ship's log by name. It is just off Garden Point, and for a summer resort Scidmore Island possesses unusual advantages. Heated and suffering humanity is invited to visit that emerald spot in latitude 58° 29′ north, and longitude 135° 52′ west from Greenwich, and enjoy the July temperature of 45°, the seal and salmon fishing, the fine hunting, and the sight of one of the grandest of the many great glaciers that break directly into the sea along the Alaska coast.

The gray-green water, filled with sediment, told that glaciers were near, and icebergs, from the size of a house down to the merest lumps, circled around us, showing the ineffable shades of pale greens and blues, and clinking together musically as the steamer passed by. The tides rush fiercely in and out of Glacier Bay, and heavy fogs add to the dangers of navigation, and Captain Beardslee and Major Morris, who entered it in the little steamer Favorite in 1880, were obliged to put back without making any explorations. The charts as they now appear are very faulty, the sketches having been made from information given by Mr. Willoughby and Indian seal hunters, and from brief notes furnished by Professor Muir. At the head of every inlet around the great bay there are glaciers, and Mr. Willoughby said that in five of these fiords there are glaciers a mile and a half wide, with vertical fronts of seamed ice rising two hundred and four hundred feet from the water. In one of them a small island divides the ice cataract, and Niagara itself is repeated in this glacial corner of the north. At low tide, bergs and great sections of the fronts fall off into the water, and Glacier Bay is filled with this debris of the glaciers, that floats out from every inlet and is swept to and fro with the tides.

Dick Willoughby stood on the bridge with the navigators, and gave them the benefit of his experience. After a while he came back to the group of ladies on deck, and, sitting down, shook his head seriously and said:—

"You ladies are very brave to venture up in such a place. If you only knew the risks you are running—the dangers you are in!" And the pioneer's voice had a tone of the deepest concern as he said it.

We received this with some laughter, and expressed entire confidence in the captain and pilot, who had penetrated glacial fastnesses and unknown waters before. A naval officer on board echoed the Willoughby strain, and declared that a commander would never attempt to take a man-of-war into such a dangerous place, and deprecated Captain Carroll's daring and rashness. The merchant marine was able to retaliate when this naval comment was repeated, and Glacier Bay was suggested as the safest place for a government vessel's cruise, on account of the entire absence of schooners.

DIAGRAM OF THE MUIR GLACIER.

The lead was cast constantly, and the *Idaho* veered gracefully from right to left, went slowly, and stopped at times, to avoid the ice floes that bore down upon it with the outgoing tide. Feeling the way along carefully, the anchor was cast beside a grounded iceberg, and the photographers were rowed off to a small island to take the view of the ship in the midst of that Arctic scenery. Mount Crillon showed his hoary head to us in glimpses between the clouds, and then, rounding Willoughby Island, which the owner declares is solid marble of a quality to rival that of Pentelicus and Carrara, we saw the full front of the great Muir Glacier, where it dips down and breaks into the sea, at the end of an inlet five miles long.

The inlet and the glacier were named for Professor John Muir, the Pacific coast geologist, who, as far as known, was the first white man to visit and explore the glaciers of the bay. Professor Muir went up Glacier Bay, with the Rev. S. Hall Young, of Fort Wrangell, as a companion, in 1879. They travelled by canoe, and Professor Muir, strapping a blanket on his back, and filling his pockets with hard tack, started off unarmed, and spent days of glacial delight in the region. These were the only white men who had preceded us, when Captain Carroll took the *Idaho* up the bay in 1883, on what was quite as good as a real voyage of exploration.

Of all scenes and natural objects, nothing could be grander and more impressive than the first view up the inlet, with the front of the great glacier, the slope of the glacial field, and the background of lofty mountains united in one picture. Mount Crillon and Mount Fairweather stood as sentries across the bay, showing their summits fifteen thousand feet in air, clear cut as silhouettes against the sky, and the stillness of the air was broken only by faint, metallic, tinkling sounds, as the ice floes ground together, and the waters washed up under the honeycombed edges of the floating bergs. Steaming slowly up the inlet, the bold, cliff-like front of the glacier grew in height as we approached it, and there was a sense of awe as the ship drew near enough for us to hear the strange, continual rumbling of the subterranean or subglacial waters, and see the avalanches of ice that, breaking from the front, rushed down into the sea with tremendous crashes and roars. Estimates of the height of the ice cliff increased with nearness, and from a first guess of fifty feet, there succeeded those of two hundred and four hundred feet, which the authority of angles has since proven as correct.

The *Idaho* was but an eighth of a mile from the front of the glacier, when the anchor was cast in eighty-four fathoms of water at low tide, and near us, in the midst of these deep soundings, icebergs loaded with boulders lay grounded, with forty feet of their summits above water. Words and dry figures can give one little idea of the grandeur of this glacial torrent flowing steadily and solidly into the sea, and the beauty of the fantastic ice front, shimmering with all the prismatic hues, is beyond imagery or description.

According to Professor Muir, the glacier measures three miles across the snout, or front, where it breaks off into the sea. Ten miles back it is ten miles wide, and sixteen tributary glaciers unite to form this one great ice-river. Professor Muir ascended to the glacier field from the north side, and, following its edges for six miles, climbed the high mountain around which the first tributary debouches from that side. He gives the distance from the snout of the glacier to its furthest source in the great nève, or snow-fields, as forty miles. Detailed accounts of Professor Muir's canoe journeys in glacier land were given in his letters to the San Francisco *Bulletin*, and they abound in the most beautiful and poetic descriptions of the scenery. His paper on "The Glaciation of the Arctic and Sub-Arctic Regions, visited by the U. S. S. *Corwin* in the year 1881," accompanies the report of Captain C. L. Hooper, U. S. R. M., published by the government printing office at Washington in 1885, and contains Professor Muir's observations and deductions upon the glaciation of the whole Pacific coast from California to the Arctic.

No attempt has yet been made to measure the rate of progress of the Muir glacier, although Captain Carroll has several times promised himself to stake off and mark points on the main trunk, and note their positions from month to month during the summer. Mr. Willoughby said that the Indians told him that two years previously the line of the ice wall was a half mile further down the inlet, and that in their grandfathers' time it extended as far as Willoughby Island, five miles below. The old moraine that forms the bar at the mouth of the bay is sufficient evidence to scientists that the ice sheet covered the whole bay within what Professor Muir calls "a very short geological time ago." The Hooniah goat-hunters told Mr. Willoughby that the first tributary glacier connected with the Davidson glacier in Lynn Canal, and that they often made the journey across it to the Chilkat country. Kloh-Kutz told Professor Davidson that it was a one day's journey on snowshoes—about thirty miles—over to this bay of great glaciers, and thirty days' journey thence, through a region of high mountains and snow fields, to the ocean at the foot of the Mount St. Elias Alps.

RIVER ON NORTH SIDE OF THE MUIR GLACIER.

The vast, desolate stretch of gray ice visible across the top of the serrated wall of ice that faced us had a strange fascination, and the crack of the rending ice, the crash of the falling fragments, and a steady undertone like the boom of the great Yosemite Fall, added to the inspiration and excitement. There was something, too, in the consciousness that so few had ever gazed upon the scene before us, and there were neither guides nor guide books to tell us which way to go, and what emotions to feel.

We left the stewards cutting ice from the grounded bergs near the ship, and, putting off in the lifeboats, landed in the ravine on the north side of the glacier. We scrambled over two miles of sand and boulders, along the steep, crumbling banks of a roaring river, until we reached the arch under the side of the glacier from which the muddy torrent poured. Near that point, on the loose moraine at the side, there was the remnant of a buried forest, with the stumps of old cedar-trees standing upright in groups. They were stripped of their bark, and cut off six and ten feet above the surface, and pieces of wood were scattered all through the debris of this moraine. The disforesting of the shores of Glacier Bay is the mystery that baffles Professor Muir, as on all this densely wooded coast, this one bay lacks the thick carpet of moss and the forests that elsewhere conceal the evidences of glacial action. Patches of crimson epilobium covered the ground in spots, and flourished among the boulders at the edge of the ice sheet, where only a thin layer of dirt covers buried ice.

Reaching the sloping side of the ice-field, we mounted, and went down a mile over the seamed and ragged surface towards the broken ice of the water front. The ice was a dirty gray underfoot, but it crackled with a pleasant mid-winter sound, and the wind blew keen and sharp from over the untrodden miles of the glacier field. The gurgle and hollow roar of the subterranean waters came from deep rifts in the broken surface, and in the centre and towards the front of the glacier, the ice was tossed and broken like the waves of an angry sea. The amateur photographers turned their cameras to right and left, risked their necks in the deep ravines and hollows in the ice, and climbed the surrounding points to get satisfactory views. Every one gathered a pocketful of rounded rocks and pebbles, and shreds of ancient cedar trees carried down by the ice flood, and then, having worn rubber shoes and boots to tatters on the sharp ice, and sunk many times in the treacherous glacier mud, we reluctantly obeyed the steamer's whistle and cannon-shot, and started back to the boats.

A nearer sweep towards the long ice-cliff showed that the line of the front was broken into bays and points, the middle of the glacier jutting far out into the water, and the sides sweeping back in curves, as the cliffs decreased in height, and finally sloped down to the level of the side moraines. At points along the front, subterranean rivers boiled up, and, in the deep blue crevasses, cascades ran down over icy beds. In the full sunlight the front of the glacier was a dazzling wall of silver and snowy ice, gleaming with all the rainbow colors, and disclosing fresh beauties as each new crevasse or hollow came in sight.

GLACIER BAY. FRONT OF MUIR GLACIER.

A magnificent sunset flooded the sky that night, and filled every icy ravine with rose and orange lights. At the last view of the glacier, as we steamed away from it, the whole brow was glorified and transfigured with the fires of sunset;

the blue and silvery pinnacles, the white and shining front floating dreamlike on a roseate and amber sea, and the range and circle of dull violet mountains lifting their glowing summits into a sky flecked with crimson and gold.

It was a chill, misty morning, a year later, when the watch again sighted "Scidmore Island, one mile off the starboard beam," and its long, green undulating shore was visible through the rain. Entering Muir Inlet, the *Ancon* went cautiously through the floating ice and anchored in the curve of the south end of the glacier's front, but a few hundred yards from a long shelving beach that would have shone with its golden sand in sunlight. There were the same deep soundings near the front, as on the other side of the inlet, but the *Ancon's* anchor was dropped nearer the moraine shore, where the lead gave only twenty-five fathoms.

Under the dull gray sky all dazzling effects of prismatic light were lost, but the fretted and fantastic front showed lines and masses of the purest white and an infinite range of blues. Avalanches of crumbling ice and great pieces of the front were continually falling with the roar and crash of artillery, revealing new caverns and rifts of deeper blue light, while the spray dashed high and the great waves rolled along the icy wall, and, widening in their sweep, washed the blocks of floating ice up on the beaches at either side. The ship's cannon was loaded and fired twice point blank at the front of the glacier. The report was followed by a second of silence, and then an echo came back that intensified the first ring many times, and was followed by a long, sharp roll as the echo was flung from cavern to cavern in the ice.

SECTION OF THE MUIR GLACIER (TOP.)

The small boats landed us on a beach strewn with ice cakes, and lines of stranded shrimps marked the wash of the waves raised by the falling ice. Some shrimps two and three inches long were found, but the most of them were delicate little pink things not an inch in length. The crimson epilobium blossoms nodded to us from every slope and hollow of the long lateral moraine that lay between the water and the high mountain walls. Over sand and boulders, and across a roaring stream that issued from the side of the glacier, the pilgrims crept to the foot of the slope, and then up a long incline of boulders and dirty ice to a first level where they could look out over the frozen waste and across the broken front. Deep crevasses seamed the ice plain in every direction, as on the north side of the frozen river; but, although the view is not so extended as on the other side, the level of the ice field is reached more easily, and it is a steep but only a short climb up over the buried ice to the top of the glacier. The treacherous gray glacier mud—"the mineral paste, and mountain meal" of Prof. Muir—engulfed one at every careless step, and rocks would sink under one, and land even the high-booted pilgrims knee-deep in the fine, sticky compound. A half-mile from what appeared to be the bank of the frozen river, there was clear solid ice underlying the rocks and mud, and occasionally caves in this side wall enticed the breathless ones to rest themselves in the pale shadows of the glacier ice. Fragments and rounded pebbles of red and gray granite, limestone, marble, schistose slate, porphyry and quartz were picked up on the way, and many of the bits of quartz and marble were deeply stained with iron. The Polish mining engineer with the party assured us that all Glacier Bay was rich in the indications of a great silver-belt, and held up carbonates, sulphates, and sulphurets to prove his assertion.

From this south-side landing we easily approached the base of the ice cliffs by following up the beach to the ravine that cut into the ice at the edge of the moraine. We got a far better idea of the height and solidity of the walls by standing like pigmies in the shadow of the lofty front, and looking up to the grottoes and clefts in the cobalt and indigo cliff. It was dry and firm on the beach, and the golden sand was strewn with dripping bergs of sapphire and aquamarine that had been swept ashore by the spreading waves. These huge blocks of ice on the beach, that had looked like dice from the ship, were found to be thirty and forty feet long and twenty feet high.

The nearer one approached, the higher the ice walls seemed, and all along the front there were pinnacles and spires weighing several tons, that seemed on the point of toppling every moment. The great buttresses of ice that rose first from the water and touched the moraine were as solidly white as marble, veined and streaked with rocks and mud, but further on, as the pressure was greater, the color slowly deepened to turquoise and sapphire blues. The crashes of falling ice were magnificent at that point, and in the face of a keen wind that blew over the ice-field we sat on the rocks and watched the wondrous scene. The gloomy sky seemed to heighten the grandeur, and the billows of gray mist, pouring over the mountains on either side, intensified the sense of awe and mystery. The tide was running out all of the afternoon hours that we spent there, and the avalanches of ice were larger and more frequent all of the time. When the anchor was lifted, the ship took a great sweep up nearer to the glacier's front, and as we steamed away there were two grand crashes, and great sections of the front fell off with deafening roars into the water. We steamed slowly down the inlet, and out into Glacier Bay, stopping, backing, and going at half speed to avoid the floating ice all around us, that occasionally was ground and crunched up by the paddle-wheels with a most uncomfortable sound. With each thump from the ice, and the recurrence of the noise in the paddle-box, and then the sight of some red slats floating off on the water, Dick Willoughby's concern was remembered; and the advantages of the screw propeller, and the merits of the favorite and original *Idaho*, were appreciated.

SECTION OF THE MUIR GLACIER (FRONT.)

While we cruised away in the mist and twilight, the children, who never could be made to keep ordinary bedtime in that latitude, celebrated the birthday of one of their number with high revel. While they danced around the cake on the cabin table, and blew out the eight candles one by one with an accompanying wish, the last boy wished that the happy youngster might "celebrate many more birthdays in Glacier Bay," and the elders applauded him.

After the *Idaho* had made its first visit to the Muir Glacier, and returned Dick Willoughby to his Hooniah home and his strawberry farm, we had a seven hours' enforced anchorage, on the succeeding day, in a narrow fiord on the north end of Chicagoff Island, which that same Willoughby had described as an unknown channel, "a hole in the mountain," and a short cut to the open ocean, that he had travelled many times himself. Following up his forty-fathom channel, the lead marked shoaling waters, and before we knew it the *Idaho* ran her nose on a sloping bank, and stayed there until the returning tide floated her off.

There had not been a canoe in sight, nor a sign of life along the shores all that morning, but the ship's officers had hardly settled the fact that they were hard aground before several canoes were seen in the wake, and the gangway was surrounded with bargaining Hooniahs, who held up furs, baskets, and trophies for us to buy. More and more of them came paddling down the narrow lane of emerald water, and family groups in red blankets were soon at home around blazing camp fires on the narrow ledges of the shore, and added greatly to the picturesqueness of the scene. Of all the little fiords we had been into, this one was the most beautiful, and even Naha Bay cannot surpass it. The narrow channel has steep, wooded hills on either side, and a rugged, snow-covered mountain stands sentry at the head of the fiord, and the clear, green water was so still that every tree and twig was clearly reflected; the ship rested double, and the breasts of the soaring eagles were mirrored in all the shadings of their plumage. The silence was profound, and every voice or sound on deck was echoed from the mountains, and could be heard for a long distance up the inlet. Had it not been for the Hooniah canoes following so promptly, we might have supposed ourselves explorers, who had penetrated into some enchanted region, or dreamers who were seeing this beautiful valley in a strange sleep. It was exploration to the extent that all our course up the inlet was across the dry land of all the charts then published, and the *Idaho* was aground in the woods according to the authorized maps.

This Idaho Inlet, as it is now put down, is the sportsman's long-sought paradise. The stewards, who went ashore with the tank-boats for fresh water, startled seven deer as they pushed their way to the foot of a cascade, and the young men who went off in an Indian canoe caught thirteen large salmon with their inexperienced spearing. Mr. Wallace, the first officer, took a party off in the ship's small boats, and we swept gayly up the inlet, over waters where the salmon and flounders could be seen darting in schools through the water and just escaping the strokes of the oar. At the mouth of the creek at the head of the inlet, the freshening current was alive with fish, and some of the energetic ones landed there, and, pushing ahead for exploration, were soon lost to sight in the high grass and the underbrush that fringed the forest. It began to rain about that time, and a dripping group remained by the boats, watching the rainbow fish playing in the waters, and enjoying the dry Scotch humor of the officer, who had led us off on this water picnic. Clouds rolled over our snow-capped mountain and blurred the landscape, and after an hour of quietly sitting in the rain, even the amphibious Scot began to wish, too, that the wanderers would return, lest the falling tide should leave us on the wrong side of the shallows at the mouth of the creek. As he took a less humorous view of the situation, all the rest joined in the strain and began to berate the Alaska climate with its constant downpour. Some one was impelled to ask the genial Scotchman if it was really true that the summit of Ben Nevis is never seen oftener than twice a year. He nearly upset the boat to refute that slander, and his emphatic "No!" may be still ringing and echoing around the north end of Chicagoff Island.

After the first officer had returned his boatloads of damp but enthusiastic passengers to the ship, the stories of fish, and boasts of the great bear-tracks seen on shore, disturbed the tranquillity of the anchorage. The captain of the ship took his rifle and was rowed away to shallow waters, where he shot a salmon, waded in, and threw it ashore. While wandering along after the huge bear-tracks, that were twelve inches long by affidavit measure, he saw an eagle flying off with his salmon, and another fine shot laid the bird of freedom low. When the captain returned to the ship he threw the eagle and the salmon on deck, and at the size of the former every one marvelled. The outspread wings measured the traditional six feet from tip to tip, and the beak, the claws, and the stiff feathers were rapidly seized upon as trophies and souvenirs of the day. A broad, double rainbow arched over us as we left the lovely niche between the mountains in the evening, and then we swept back to Icy Straits and started out to the open ocean, and down the coast to Sitka, having a glimpse, on the way, of the vast glacier at the head of Taylor Bay, that Vancouver and his men visited while his ships lay at anchor in Port Althorp, just west of our Idaho Inlet.

CHAPTER XI.

SITKA—THE CASTLE AND THE GREEK CHURCH.

At six o'clock in the morning the water lay still and motionless as we rounded the point from which Mount Edgecombe lifts its hazy blue slopes, and threaded our way between clearly reflected islands into this beautiful harbor, which is the most northern on the Pacific Coast. In the mirror of calm waters the town lay in shimmering reflections, and the wooded side of Mount Verstovaia, that rises sentinel over Sitka, was reflected as a dark green pyramid that slowly receded and shortened as the ship neared the shore. By old traditions the ravens always gather on the gilded cross on the dome of the Greek church when a ship is in sight, and one lone, early riser flapped his big black wings and croaked the signal before the ship's cannon started the echoes. A steam launch put out quickly from the man-of-war *Adams* to carry the mail bags to that ship, and a sleepy postmaster came down to look after his consignments. There were signs of life in the Indian village, or *rancherie*, further up shore, and one by one the natives assembled on the wharf with their baskets and bracelets for sale, or, wandering down with the blankets of the couch wrapped about them, and lying face downward with their heads propped on their hands, yawned and studied the scene. They sprawled there like seals, and some of the members of this leisure class remained on the wharf for hours and for nearly all day without stirring.

The queer and out-of-the-way capital of our latest Territory seemed quite a metropolis after the unbroken wilderness we had been journeying through, and the rambling collection of weather-beaten and moss-covered buildings that have survived from Russian days, and the government buildings, in their coats of yellow-brown paint, smote us with a sense of urban vastness and importance. At a first look Sitka wears the air and dignity of a town with a history, and can reflect upon the brilliant good old days of Russian rule, to which fifteen years of American occupancy have only given more lustre by contrast. It is a straggling, peaceful sort of a town, edging along shore at the foot of high mountains, and sheltered from the surge and turmoil of the ocean by a sea-wall of rocky, pine-covered islands. The moss has grown greener and thicker on the roofs of the solid old wooden houses that are relics of Russian days, the paint has worn thinner everywhere, and a few more houses tumbling into ruins complete the scenes of picturesque decay. Twenty years ago there were one hundred and twenty-five buildings in the town proper, and it is doubtful if a dozen have been erected since. The æsthetic soul can revel in the cool, quiet tones of weather-worn and lichen-stained walls, and never be vexed with the sight of raw boards, shingles, and shavings in this far northern capital. A gravelled road leads straight from the wharf to the front of the Greek church, the board walk beside it painted with lines of white on either edge, to guide the wayfarer's steps on the pitch-dark nights, that set in so early and last so long during the winter season.

SITKA.

The barracks, the custom house and the governor's castle form a group of public buildings on the right of the landing-wharf, and the small battery at the foot of the castle terrace is quite imposing. The castle is a heavy, plain, square building, crowning a rocky headland that rises precipitously from the water on three sides, and turns a bold embankment to the town on the other. According to Captain Meade, this eminence was called Katalan's Rock by the early Russian settlers, in memory of the chief who lived on it, and the governors made it a perfect fortress, with batteries and outer defences and sentries at all the approaches. This colonial castle is in latitude only 17′ north of Queen Victoria's summer home at Balmoral. Two buildings have crowned Katalan's Rock before the present one, the first rude block-house being destroyed by fire, and the second one by an earthquake. The castle is one hundred and forty feet long and seventy feet wide, built of heavy cedar logs, while copper bolts pierce the walls at points, and are riveted to the rock to hold it fast in the event of another earthquake. The Russian governors of the colony resided in the castle, and many traditions of social splendor hang to this forlorn and abandoned old building. The Russian governors were usually chosen from the higher ranks of the naval service and of noble families at home. These captain-counts, barons, and princes deputed to rule the colony maintained a miniature court around them, and lived and entertained handsomely. Lutke, Sir Edward Belcher, Sir George Simpson, and other voyagers of the early part of this century, give charming pictures of the social life at Sitka. State dinners were given by the governor every Sunday, and a round of balls and gayeties made a visitor's stay all too pleasant.

Baron Wrangell's wife was the first chatelaine of the castle who left a social fame. She was succeeded in her pleasant rule by the wife of Governor Kupreanoff, who accompanied her husband to Sitka in 1835, crossing Siberia on horseback to Behring Sea. It was Madame Kupreanoff who entertained Captain Belcher, and after a line of many charming women there came the second wife of Prince Maksoutoff, a beautiful chatelaine, who made the castle the abode of a gracious hospitality, and left many social traditions to attest her tact and charm. Society was more democratic in her days than it has been at any time since, and the noble Russian hostess overlooked rank and class, and welcomed all to the castle on an equality. The admiral of the fleet and the pilot were on the same social plane while under the governor's roof, and at a ball the governor made it his duty to lead out every lady, and the princess danced with every one who solicited the honor, no matter how humble his station. Caviare and strong punches marked every banquet board, and at the beginning of a ball the ladies were first invited out by themselves to partake of strong and pungent appetizers, and then the gentlemen gathered around the side tables and took their tonics. A big brass samovar was always boiling in the drawing-room, and day or night a glass of the choicest caravan tea was offered to visitors. Some beautiful samovars were brought out from Russia by the families of the higher officers, and after the brass foundry was established, they were manufactured at Sitka. Some of these old Sitka samovars are still to be found by the curio-hunters, and, as they grow rarer, they are the more highly prized.

The governors brought all their household goods with them from Russia; and surrounded themselves with comfort and luxury. The castle was richly furnished, the walls of the drawing-room were lined with mirrors, and its interior appointments were all that Muscovite ideas could suggest. When it was turned over to the United States as government property seventeen years ago, the castle was well furnished and in perfect condition, but after the troops left, it was neglected like everything else, and has been stripped, despoiled, and defaced. Every portable thing has been carried off, the curiously wrought brass chandeliers, the queer knobs and branching hinges on the doors, and all but the massive porcelain stoves in the corners of the large apartments. The lantern, and even the reflector, that used to send beacons to the mariner from the castle tower, have gone, and the place is little better than a ruin. The hall where the governors received and entertained the Indian chiefs is a rubbish hole; of the carved railing that fenced off a little boudoir in the great drawing-room, not a vestige remains; and not a relic is left of the old billiard-room to prove that it ever existed.

The signal officer has rescued two rooms on the ground floor for his use, but otherwise the only tenant of the castle is the ghost of a beautiful Russian, whose sad story is closely modelled on that of the Bride of Lammermoor. She haunts the drawing-room, the northwest chamber, where she was murdered, and paces the governor's cabinet, where the swish of her ghostly wedding-gown chills every listener's blood. Twice a year she walks unceasingly and wrings her jewelled hands.

At Easter time she wanders with sorrowful mien from room to room, and leaves a faint perfume as of wild roses where she passes. Innumerable young officers from the men-of-war have nerved up their spirits and gone to spend a solitary night in the castle, but none have yet held authentic converse with the beautiful spirit, and learned the true story of her unresting sorrow. By tradition, the lady in black was the daughter of one of the old governors. On her wedding night she disappeared from the ball-room in the midst of the festivities, and after long search was found dead in one of the small drawing-rooms. Being forced to marry against her will, one belief was that she voluntarily took poison, while another version ascribes the deed to an unhappy lover; while, altogether, the tale of this Lucia of the northwest isles gives just the touch of sentimental interest to this castle of the Russian governors. The Russian residents cannot identify this ghost with any member of the governors' families, and say that the whole thing has been concocted within a few years to keep sailors and marauders away at night, and to entertain the occasional tourist.

The room is pointed out in the castle that was occupied by Secretary Seward during his visit, and the same guest-chamber has an additional interest in the memory of Lady Franklin's visit. It is possible that with the arrival of a territorial governor the castle may again become an official residence; and if repaired and restored to its original condition, it could be made quite a pleasant place.

The Custom House building also shelters the postmaster, whose office, not being a salaried one, does not offer great temptations to any aspiring citizens as yet. His compensation was a little over one hundred dollars for the last year, and by the quarterly accounts, which all the Alaska postmasters are dilatory about sending to the department, the Sitka post-office has only about the same amount of business as the Juneau and Wrangell offices.

A detachment of marines from the man-of-war in the harbor was quartered in the old barracks at the opposite side of the steps leading down from the castle terrace. Every morning while we were there, about eight men went through guard mount and inspection with as much military precision and form as if a company or regiment were deploying on the parade ground. The houses that were used for officers' quarters during the time that a garrison was maintained were burned by the Indians, after the soldiers were withdrawn, and there is a blank on that side of the green quadrangle. The Indian village is reached through a gate in the stockade fence at one side of the parade ground, and in the Russian days the gate was closed every night, and the Indians obliged to remain outside until morning. Under United States rule they have been permitted to roam as they pleased, and during the time between the withdrawal of the troops and the arrival of a naval ship, they held the inhabitants at their mercy.

The buildings on the main street are all heavy log houses, some of them clapboarded over, and a few of them whitewashed, but decay has seized upon many, and their roofs are sinking under the weight of moss. Both at the Northwest Trading Company's store on the wharf, and in the large, rambling stores on this street, there were curios by the roomful, and everything from canoes to nose rings were to be seen. Though the prices were higher, as befits a capital, the Sitka traders had the most tempting arrays of carved and painted woodwork, and baskets, and bracelets in endless designs.

THE GREEK CHURCH AT SITKA.

At the end of the main street, fronting on the small square or court, stands the Russian Orthodox Church of St. Michael. It has the green roof, the bulging spire, the fine clock, and the chime of bells, that might distinguish any shrine in Moscow. In these days of its decadence, much of the glory has been stripped from the Sitka church, and the faded walls and roof, almost destitute of paint, tell a sad tale. It was once a cathedral, presided over by a resident bishop, and when dedicated in 1844, the venerable Ivan Venianimoff, Metropolite of Moscow, who had labored for years as priest and bishop at Ounalaska and Sitka, sent richest vestments, plate, and altar furnishings to this church. Since the purchase of Alaska by the United States, the richer and better class of Russians have left, and there are only three families of pure Russian blood to worship in the church. Of the Creoles, or half-breeds, the emancipated serfs, and the converted natives, who once crowded the church on Sundays and saints' days, not a third remain, and decreasing numbers bow before the altar of St. Michael's each year.

The Russian government, in its protectorate over the Greek church, assumes the expenses of the churches at Sitka, Ounalaska, and Kodiak, and about $50,000 are expended annually for their support. With the diminishing congregations, it is merely a question of time when the Alaska priests will be recalled, as the abandonment of the Russian chapel in New York is significant of the coming change.

After the transfer of the territory, the Russian bishop moved his residence to San Francisco, and, taking charge of the chapel there, made annual visits to the Sitka, Kodiak, and Ounalaska churches. The last incumbent of the office, Bishop Nestor, was lost overboard while returning from Ounalaska to San Francisco in May, 1883, and at Moscow no one has been found willing to be sent out to this diocese. Father Mitropolski, now in charge with one assistant, was formerly at the Kodiak church.

The exterior of the church is not imposing, as the paint has worn and flaked off the walls, and the panelled picture of St. Michael over the doorway is dim and faded. The chime of six sweet-toned bells in the tower were sent from Moscow as a gift, and they retain their clear and vibrant tones, and still ring out the hours. Our watches, that had been keeping Astoria or ship's time, were forty-five minutes ahead of the true local time indicated by the ornamental dial of the church clock, and for the first time we realized that the ship had veered to the westward considerably while apparently going due north. A more serious difference of time had to be contended with at the time of the transfer, as the Russian Sabbath, which came eastward from Moscow, did not correspond to the same day of the week in our calendar travelling westward. It took official negotiations to settle this difference and set aside the old Julian calendar.

INTERIOR OF THE GREEK CHURCH AT SITKA.

The interior of the cruciform church is richly decorated in white and gold. In either transept are side altars, and the main altar is reached through a pair of open-work bronze doors set with silver images of the saints. In this inner sanctuary no woman is allowed to tread, and on the smaller altars there the richest treasures of the church are kept. Over the bronze doors is a large picture of the Last Supper, the faces painted on ivory, and the figures draped in robes of silver. On either side are large paintings of the saints, covered with robes and draperies of the same beaten silver, and the halos, surrounding their heads, of gold and silver set with brilliants. Heavy chandeliers and silver lamps hang from the ceiling, and tall candlesticks and censers are before the pictured saints. There is a small chapel in the north transept, where services are held in winter, and on one of the panels of the altar there is an exquisite painting of the Madonna. The sweet Byzantine face is painted on ivory, and a silver drapery is wrapped about the head and shoulders. St. Michael, St. Nicholas, and the glorious company of apostles and angels on the same altars are robed in silver garments with jewelled halos. This chapel and the whole church still wore the lavish Easter decorations of wreaths, festoons, evergreen trees, and streamers of bright ribbons, both July weeks that I visited it.

On the Sunday morning that the *Idaho* lay at the Sitka wharf we all attended morning service at the church, and were seated on benches at one side while the congregation stood throughout the long service, which was chanted by a male chorus concealed behind a carved screen near the altar. The men stood on one side of the church, and the women on the other, and at places in the service they knelt and prostrated themselves until their foreheads touched the floor, and made the sign of the cross constantly. One aged man especially interested me with the devout manner in which he bowed and continually made the sign of the cross during the service. He was poorly clad, and in appearance he was one of Tourgénieff's serfs to the life, as one pictures them from the pages of his novels.

EASTER DECORATIONS IN THE GREEK CHURCH AT SITKA.

On the following Monday—July 16, 1883—we heard the church bells chiming in full chorus at an unwonted hour in the morning, and, hurrying to the square, we found that the Czar's manifesto was to be read, and a grand Te Deum sung in honor of the coronation of Alexander III. Although the Ruler of Holy Russia had donned his imperial coronet weeks before, the official papers notifying the priest of that event only came up with the mails of our steamer. The usual morning service was elaborated in many ways. The choir of male voices chanted all the Te Deums appointed for such special occasions, the priest wore his most sumptuous vestments of cloth of gold and cloth of silver, the incense was wafted in clouds through the wreathed and garlanded church, and the kneeling congregation rose one by one and went forward to kiss the richly-jewelled cross that the priest extended towards them. At the close, a joyous peal rang out from the six sweet-toned bells in the steeple, and the devout souls went about the church kneeling and crossing themselves before the altars, and kissing the silver and ivory bas-relief images of the saints. Having doffed his splendid robes and his purple velvet cap, Father Mitropolski came forth and greeted his visitors, and had his assistant bring out some of the ancient treasures and vestments to show us. There were jewelled crosses, chalices of silver and gold, jewelled caskets, and quaint illuminated books in precious covers. The bishop's cap shown us was a tall, conical structure lined with satin, and covered with pearls, amethysts, rubies, and enamelled medallions in filigree settings. The crowns held over the heads of the bride and groom during the marriage service were fine pieces of Russian workmanship, and the silver basin for holy water was well executed. Rich vestments of old damask, of heavy velvets embroidered with bullion and set with small stones, and robes of cloth of gold and cloth of silver, were displayed, together with the draperies used on the altar on various occasions, and the embroidered pall thrown over the coffin at funeral services. The choicest of the church treasures, including an enamelled cross set with diamonds and fine stones, and a book of the Scriptures with an elaborately wrought silver cover weighing twenty-seven pounds, were taken to the San Francisco church after the transfer. The bishop's robes and special belongings were taken there also, and after Bishop Nestor's death the richest of them were sent back to Russia. In 1869 the church was robbed of much of its plate and treasures, by some discharged soldiers of the garrison, it was thought, and only a few of the valuables were recovered.

During our first stay the assistant priest found a chest of old bronze medals, crosses, and enamelled triptychs in the garret of the church, and the visitors contributed well to the poor fund in order to obtain these relics. It was certified that all the small crosses and medals had been blessed at Moscow before being sent out to the colony, and these ikons or images were given to the soldiers and others on their saints' days. A small bronze medal with the image of St. Nicholas fell to my lot, with the head of Christ in one corner, that of the Virgin in another, and their names raised in old Slavonic characters above them. It has a loop to be hung by a ribbon, and St Nicholas' face is worn smooth by the reverent lips that have touched it. These medals,—common enough and to be bought for a few coppers in Russia,—were highly valued by us among our other Sitkan souvenirs.

The priest of the Sitka church, Father Mitropolski, is broad and liberal in his views, and quite astonishes some narrower sectarians by his mode of life and participation in ordinary amusements. His tolerance and liberal tendencies were proved by his recently reading the Episcopal marriage service before the altar of the Greek Church, uniting at the time a naval officer of Unitarian faith to a teacher at the Presbyterian mission. Father Mitropolski, a wife, and a family of little daughters—Xenia, Nija, and Alexandra—keep life and sunshine in the rambling, half-ruined house, which, as the bishop's residence, was formerly the finest dwelling after the castle. The roof was then bright emerald green, and this and the green dome and roof of the church showed well in the cluster of red roofs that covered the other buildings in the town. With diminished church revenues and a lessening congregation, the building has slowly fallen into sad decay, the galleries and porches have dropped off, and only a part of the house is now occupied. The drawing-room contains a few pieces of rich furniture as relics of its former days, and the portraits of the czars, and the shining samovar, declare it the home of loyal Russians. An ancient guitar, made of some finely grained wood that is hardly

known to modern makers of that instrument, was for a long time in the possession of Father Mitropolski, having descended with the residence from the line of
bishops and priests. It is very curious in its shape and details, one end of it being
rounded in a great curve, and the keyboard not resting on the body of the guitar
at all. It has a sweet, melancholy tone, and accompanies appropriately some of
the strange little Russian songs that are sung to it. There is a private chapel off the
drawing-room, which contains a beautifully decorated altar, and family service is
held there daily.

A Lutheran church, facing the Greek church on the square, was founded by
Governor Etolin, in 1844, for the Swedes and Finns employed by the fur company,
and in the foundries and shipyard at Sitka. During the stay of the United States
troops the Lutheran church was used by the post chaplain, a Methodist. The abandoned church is now in the last stage of ruin, the roof sunken in, and the walls
dropping apart. The pipe-organ, brought from Germany forty years ago, was rescued by a young officer of musical tastes, and by clever repairing it was put in
good condition, and found to be a very fine instrument.

Facing on this same church square is the warehouse and the office of the old
Russian-American Fur Company. The solid log buildings have stood the ravages
of time and the damp climate, and a mining-engineer and assayer has taken possession of it for his office. Quite appropriately the headquarters of the fur trade,
which constituted the most valuable interest of the early days, is now the labo-
ratory of an assayer, who tests the minerals upon which so much of the future
importance of the territory rests.

The officers' club-house, back of the Greek church, is still in a fair condition,
but the tea-gardens and the race-course have vanished in undergrowth. A sturdy
little fir-tree, rooted in the crevice of a great boulder or outcropping ledge of rocks
in front of the club-house, is one of the curiosities of Sitka, and has been growing
in that solid granite as long as anyone now living there can remember.

The sawmill, with its large water-wheel, is dropping to decay, the hospital
building was burned while used as a mission-school, and it is hard to trace the site
of the old shipyard, that was a most complete establishment in its day. For a long
time it was the only yard on the coast, and vessels of all nationalities put in there
for repairs. The Russians had one hundred and eighty church holidays during
the year, and observed them all carefully. English naval commanders, by keeping
their own Sabbath, and having the Russian Sabbath and holidays celebrated by
closing the shipyards and stopping work, used to have long stays in the harbor;
and the impatient navigators, in view of the whirl of social life that marked the
visit of a strange ship, fairly believed that the delays were managed by the governor's authority. At the foundries, ploughs were made and exported to the Mexican
possessions south of them, and the bells of half the California mission churches
were cast at the Sitka foundry.

At the end of the scattered line of houses that fringe the shore, the Jackson
Institute, a Presbyterian mission-school and home, occupies a fine site, facing the
harbor. The mission was founded in 1878, and named for the Rev. Sheldon Jack-

son, who has charge of the Presbyterian missions in Alaska, and the building is soon to be enlarged, to accommodate a larger number of pupils than were first gathered in it, under the care of Mr. and Mrs. Austin.

CHAPTER XII.

SITKA—THE INDIAN RANCHERIE.

The doorway of the Greek church, and the dial on its tower, face toward the harbor, and command the main street. Beyond the houses at the right there is a little pine-crowned hill, with the broken and rusty ruins of a powder-magazine on its slope, and on a second hill beyond is the graveyard where the Russians buried their dead. An old block house, that commanded an angle of the stockade, stands sentry over the graves, and the headstones and tombs are overgrown with rank bushes, ferns, and grasses. Prince Maksoutoff's first wife, who died at Sitka, was buried on the hill, and a costly, elaborately carved tombstone was sent from Russia to mark the spot. After the transfer and withdrawal of troops, the Indians, in their maraudings, defaced the stone, and attempted to carry it off. It was broken in the effort, and left in fragments on the ground. Lieutenant Gilman, in charge of the marines during the stay of the *Adams*, became interested in the matter, hunted for the grave in the underbrush, and undertook the work of replacing the tombstone. Beyond the Russian cemetery, on the same overgrown hillside, are the tombs of the chiefs and medicine-men of the Sitka *kwan*. The grotesque images and the queer little burial boxes are nearly hidden in the tangle of bushes and vines, and their sides are covered with moss.

The Russians had a special chapel out on this hill for the Indians to worship in, as shown in old illustrations of Sitka, but the building has disappeared. There was a heavy stockade wall also, separating the Indian cemetery and village from the white settlement, but it has nearly all been torn down and carried off by the Indians during the years of license allowed them after the troops left, and only fragments of it remain in places.

Entering through the old stockade gate, the Indian *rancherie* presents itself, as a double row of square houses fronting on the beach. Each house is numbered and whitewashed, and the ground surrounding it gravelled and drained. The same neatness marks the whole long stretch of the village, and amazement at this condition is only ended when one learns that the captain of the man-of-war fines each disorderly Indian in blankets, besides confining him in the guard-house, and that the forfeited blankets are duly exchanged for paint, whitewash, and disinfectants. Police and sanitary regulations both are enforced, and the Indians made to keep their village quiet and clean. When all the Indians are home from their fishing and trading trips, and congregated here in the winter, they number over a thousand, and all goes merry at the *rancherie*. There are no *totem* poles, or carved, grotesque-ly-painted houses to lend outward interest to the village, and the Indians themselves are too much given to ready-made clothes and civilized ways to be really picturesque.

Annahootz, Sitka Jack, and other chiefs have pine doorplates over their lintels, to announce where greatness dwells, but the palace of Siwash Town is the residence of "Mrs. Tom," a painted cabin with green blinds, and a green railing across the front porch. Mrs. Tom is a character, a celebrity, and a person of great authority among her Siwash neighbors, and wields a greater power and influence among her people, than all the war chiefs and medicine-men put together. Even savage people bow down to wealth, and Mrs. Tom is the reputed possessor of $10,000, accumulated by her own energy and shrewdness. We heard of Mrs. Tom long before we reached Sitka, and, realizing her to be such a potentate among her people, we were shocked to meet that lady by the roadside, Sunday morning, offering to sell bracelets to some of the passengers. The richest and greatest chiefs are so avaricious that they will sell anything they own.

Mrs. Tom invited us to come to her green-galleried chalet in Siwash town, "next door to No. 17," at any time we pleased. On the rainiest morning in all the week we set our dripping umbrella points in that direction, and found the great Tyee lady at home. It was raw and chill as a New York November, but Mrs. Tom strolled about barefooted, wearing a single calico garment, and wrapping herself in a white blanket with red and blue stripes across the ends. Her black hair was brushed to satiny smoothness, braided and tied with coquettish blue ribbons, and her arms were covered with bracelets up to her elbows. She is a plump matron, fat, fair, and forty in fact, and her house is a model of neatness and order. On gala occasions she arrays herself in her best velvet dress, her bonnet with the red feather, a prodigious necktie and breastpin, and then, with two silver rings on every finger, and nine silver bracelets on each arm, she is the envy of all the other ladies of Siwash town. When she came to the ship to be photographed by an admiring amateur, she had, besides her ordinary regalia, a dozen or more pairs of bracelets tied up in a handkerchief, and we began to believe her wealth as boundless as her neighbors say it is. Like all the Indians she puts her faith mostly in blankets, and her house is a magazine of such units of currency, while deep in her cedar boxes she has fur robes of the rarest quality.

Mrs. Tom has acquired her fortune by her own ability in legitimate trade, and each spring and fall she loads up her long canoe and goes off on a great journey through the islands, trading with her people. On her return she trades with the traders of Sitka, and always comes out with a fine profit. A romance once wove its meshes about her, and on one of her journeys it was said that Mrs. Tom bought a handsome young slave at a bargain. The slave was considerably her junior, but in time her fancy overlooked that discrepancy, and after a few sentimental journeys in the long canoe she duly made him Mr. Tom, thus proving that the human heart beats the same in Siwash town as in the Grand Duchy of Gerolstein.

This interesting bit of gossip, duly vouched for by some of the white residents, is opposed by others, who say that Mr. Tom is a chief of the Sitka *kwan* in his own right, and that he made the *mésalliance* when he wedded his clever spouse, and that he owns a profitable potato-ranch further down Baranoff Island. Any one would prefer the first and more romantic biography, but, anyway, Mr. Tom is a smooth-faced, boyish-looking man, and evidently well trained and managed by his spouse. In consideration of their combined importance, he was made one of the delegated policemen of Siwash town, and he makes malefactors answer to him, as he has learned to answer to his exacting wife.

On the occasion of another morning call, Mrs. Tom was meditating a new dress, and the native dressmaker who was to assist in the creation was called in to examine the cut of our gowns, when we called upon her that time. There was a funny scene when Mrs. Tom discovered that what appeared to her as a velvet skirt on the person of one of her visitors, was merely a sham flounce that ended a few inches under a long, draped overskirt. Her bewildered look and the sorry shake of her head over this evidence of civilized pretence amused us, and in slow, disapproving tones she discussed the sham and swindle with her dressmaker. She showed us her accordeons, and gave us a rheumatic tune on one of them, and we were afterwards told that she gives dancing parties in winter to the upper ten of Siwash town, who dance quadrilles to the accordeon's strains.

Sitka Jack's house is a large square one fronting directly on the beach, and during his absence at Pyramid Harbor the square hearthstone in the middle was being kept warm by the relatives he had left behind him. When this house was built, in 1877, it was warmed by a grand *potlatch*, or feast and gift distribution, that distanced all previous efforts of any rivals. An Alaska chief is considered rich in proportion as he gives away his possessions, and Sitka Jack rose an hundredfold in Siwash esteem when he gave his grand *potlatch*. All his relatives assisted in building the house, and this same community idea entitles them to live in it. Over five hundred blankets were given away at his *potlatch*, and the dance was followed by a great feast, in which much whiskey and native *hoochinoo* figured. Ben Holladay, Sr., with a large yachting party, was in the harbor at the time, and lent interest to the occasion by offering prizes for canoe races and adding a water carnival to the other festivities. Sitka Jack nearly beggared himself by this great house-warming, but his fame was settled on a substantial basis, and he has since had time to partly recuperate. He has aged rapidly of late years, and now he delights to crouch by his fireside in winter evenings and relate the story of his great *potlatch* of seven years ago, which was such an event that even the white residents date by it. Another great *potlatch* made the summer of 1882 historical, and the presence of the *Dakota*, with General Miles and his regimental band aboard, stirred the *rancherie* to redoubled efforts.

Jack and Kooska, the silversmiths of the Sitka *kwan*, are very skilful workmen, and one can sit beside their work benches and watch them fashion the bracelets that are in such demand. During the summer months they can sell their ornaments faster than they can make them, and in two hours after a steamer's arrival their stock is exhausted, and they work night and day on special orders while the vessel is at the wharf. If you give them the order in the morning the bracelets are ready in the afternoon, as carefully finished and engraved as any of the others of their make. In one doorway we saw a woman crouching or lying face downwards, and slowly engraving a silver finger ring. She had a broken penknife for an engraver's tool, and she held it in her closed hand, blade down, and drew it towards her as she worked. Her attitude, and the management of the steel, set the oriental theorists off into speculations again, and they decided that she herself must have come straight across from Japan, so identical were her proceedings with those of the embroiderers and art workers in the kingdom of Dai Nippon.

She was quite unconscious and self-possessed while we stood chattering about her, and continued to chew gum in the most nonchalant manner. Inside of this barred doorway, the other members of the family were sitting about the fire, taking their morning meal. For their ten o'clock breakfast they were enjoying smoked salmon with oil, and an unhealthy looking kind of dough, or bread, washed down by very bad tea, judging from the way in which the tin teapot was allowed to boil and thump away on the coals. They are none of them epicures, and even in the matter of salmon they make no distinction, and cure and eat the rank dog salmon almost in preference to the choicer varieties. Although they are expert hunters, and bring in all the venison and wild fowl for the Sitka market, they seldom eat game themselves. It takes away a civilized appetite to see them eat the cakes of black seaweed, the sticks and branches covered with the herring roe that they whip from the surface of the water at certain seasons, and the dried salmon eggs that they are so particularly fond of. They eat almost anything that lives in the sea, and the octopus, or devil-fish, is a dainty that ranks with seal flippers for a feast. Clams of enormous size, found on the beaches through the islands, and mussels are other staple dishes.

The Sitka Indians, we were assured by a resident, "are the sassiest and most rascally Siwashes to be found in the country," but outwardly they differed very little from the other tribes that we had seen. They have the same broad, flat faces, and from generations of canoe-paddling ancestors have inherited a magnificent development of the shoulders, chests, and arms. This development is at the expense of the rest of the frame, and, from sitting cramped in their canoes, the lower limbs are dwarfed and crooked, and their bodies affect one with the unpleasant sense of deformity. They are stumbling and shambling in their gait, and toe in to exaggeration; and these amphibious, fish-eating natives are as different as possible from the wild horsemen of the plains, or the pastoral tribes of the southwest. The Sitkans have the same mythology and totemic system as the rest of the Thlinket tribes, and reverence the spirits of the raven, the wolf, the whale, bear, and eagle; and their worship of the spirits and ashes of their ancestors is quite equal to the Chinese. They cremate their dead, with the exception of the medicine men, who are laid away in state, and the poles and fluttering rags set up around the village indicate the sacred spots where the ashes lie. They worship the spirits of the earth, air, and water; and the spirits of the departed ones, now occupying the bodies of the ravens that fly overhead, exempt those huge croakers from shot and snare. They show some belief in a future state by saying that the flames of the aurora borealis are the spirits of dead warriors dancing overhead. When a chief dies his wives pass to his next heir, and unless these relicts purchase their freedom with blankets, they are united to their grandsons, or nephews, as a matter of course. High-strung young Siwashes sometimes scorn these legacies, and then there is war between the totems, all the widows' clan resenting such an outrage of decency and established etiquette. Curiously with this subjection of the women, it is they who are the family autocrats and tyrants, giving the casting-vote in domestic councils, and overriding the male decisions in the most high-handed manner. Hen-pecking is too small a word to describe the way in which they bully their lords, and many times our bargain with the ostensible head of the family was broken up by the woman arriving on the scene, and insisting that he should not sell, or should charge us more. Woman's rights, and her sphere and influence, have reached a development among the Sitkans, that would astonish the suffrage leaders of Wyoming and Washington Territory. They are all keen, sharp traders, and if the women object to the final price offered for their furs at the Sitka stores, they get into their canoes, and paddle up to Juneau, or down to Wrangell, and even across the border to the British trading posts. They take no account of time or travel, and a journey of a thousand miles is justified to them, if they only get another yard of calico in exchange for their furs. All the Thlinkets are great visitors, and canoe loads of visiting Indians can always be found at a village. The Sitka and the Stikine *kwans* seem to affiliate most, but visits from members of all the tribes make the Sitka *rancherie* an aborigine metropolis. Busybodies and cosmopolitans, like Sitka Jack, live all over the archipelago, and it was this roaming propensity that gave the military forces so much trouble during garrison days at Sitka. The land forces could do nothing with the scornful Indians in their light *kanims*, and when the order was given to let no Indian leave the *rancherie*, they snapped their fingers at the challenging and forbidding sentries, and paddled away at their pleasure. They have a great respect for a gun-boat with its ceremony, pomp, and strict discipline, and its busy steam launches, that can follow their canoes to the most remote creeks and hiding-places in the islands. The Indians employed on the *Adams* were diligent and faithful servitors, and were much pleased with their sailors' caps and toggery, and the official state surrounding them.

Indian legends and traditions can be had by the score at Sitka, but it is hard to verify any of them, and the myths, rites, and folk-lore of the people are not to be gathered with exactness during the touch-and-go excitement of a summer cruise. Bishop Veniaminoff mastered their language, and translated books of the Testament, hymns, and catechism, and published several works on the Koloshians. Baron Wrangell also wrote a great deal concerning them, and abstracts from these two writers have been given by Dall and Petroff. No ethnologists have made studies among the Thlinkets since Veniaminoff and Wrangell, a half century ago, and the field lies ready for some northern Cushing.

CHAPTER XIII.
SITKA—SUBURBS AND CLIMATE.

Enthusiasts who have seen both, declare that the Bay of Sitka surpasses the Bay of Naples in the grandeur and beauty of its surroundings. The comparison is instituted between these two distant places, because the extinct volcano, Mount Edgecumbe, rears its snow-filled crater above the bay, as Vesuvius does by the curving shores of the peerless bay of the Mediterranean. Nothing could be finer than the outlines of this grand old mountain that rises from the jutting corner of an island across the bay, and in the sleepy, summer sun, Edgecumbe's slopes are bluer than lapis lazuli or sapphire, and the softest, filmiest gray clouds trail across the ragged walls of the crater. It is more than a century since it poured forth its smoke and lava, but jets of steam occasionally rise from it now, and if an exploration of its unknown slopes is ever made, some signs of active life will doubtless be found. Great patches of snow lie within the crater's rim, and, standing as a sentinel on the very edge of the great Pacific, Edgecumbe is perpetually wreathed with the clouds that float in from the sea. The Indians have fastened many of their legends and myths to it, and the Creator and the original crow are supposed to have come from its depths and to still dwell therein, while Captain Cook, the great navigator, gave it the name which it now bears.

A hundred little islands lie in the harbor of Sitka, within the great sweep of the Baranoff shores, whose curve is greater than a semicircle at this point. Each one is a tangled bit of rock and forest, and their dense, green thickets and grassy slopes are bordered with mats of golden and russet seaweeds, that at low tide add the last fine tone to a landscape of the richest coloring. Every foot of island shore off Sitka is sketchable, and a picture in itself; and the clear, soft light, the luminous transparent tones, would be the rapture of a water-color artist. Japonski, which is the largest of this group of little islands, lies directly abreast of Sitka, and the Russians maintained an observatory on it during their ownership. At the time of the transfer, all of the larger islands of the harbor were marked off as government reservations, but during these seventeen years nothing has been done to maintain the government's claim, and settlers have lived on, cleared, and cultivated the land without molestation. The old observatory on Japonski Island has dropped to ruins, the last vestige of it has disappeared under the dense cover of vegetation, and the squatter who now occupies it raises fine Japonski potatoes for the Sitka market.

During the time that the Russians kept their careful meteorological records at the Japonski Observatory and on shore, the thermometer went below zero only four times, and the variation between the summer and winter temperature is no greater than on the California coast. It is the warm current of the Kuro Siwo, or Black Stream of Japan, pouring full on this shore, that modifies the temperature, and brings the fogs and mists that perpetually wreath the mountains, so that Fort Wrangell, though south of Sitka, is colder in winter and warmer in summer on account of its distance from the ocean current. The Sitka summer temperature of 51° and 55° pleases the fancy of dwellers in the east, quite as much as the even and temperate chill of 31° and 38° in midwinter. Ice seldom forms of any thickness, and skating on the lake back of the church at Sitka is a rarity in the winter amusements. While St. John's in Newfoundland is beleaguered by icebergs in summer, and its harbor frozen solid in winter, Sitka, ten degrees north of it, has always an open roadstead. As compared with the climate of Leadville, or some of the torrid spots in Arizona, the miners at Sitka and Juneau have nothing to complain of, and never have to contend against the fearful odds that opposed the miners during the first rush to the Cœur d'Alène region.

The mean temperature of the air and of the surface sea water, and the precipitation for each month of the year at Sitka, as given in the tables in the Alaska Coast Pilot for 1883, are as follows:—

Month.	Temperature of the air.	Temperature of surface sea water.	Precipitation.
January	31.4	39	7.35
February	32.9	39	6.45
March	35.7	39.5	5.29
April	40.8	42	5.17
May	47.0	46.5	4.13
June	52.4	48	3.62
July	55.5	49	4.19
August	55.9	50	6.96
September	51.5	51.5	9.66
October	44.9	48.9	11.83
November	38.1	44.4	8.65
December	33.3	41.7	8.39
Year	43.3	45.0	81.69

The only drawback to this cool and equable climate is the heavy rainfall, which even a Scotchman says makes it "a wee hair too wet." One soon gets used to it, and goes around unconcernedly in a panoply of rubber and gossamer cloth, and rejoices that Sitka is not Fort Tongass, where the rainfall was 118.30 inches a year, for the time that the drenched and half-drowned officers kept the records. With all this downpour there is little dampness in the air, and, contradictory as this may seem, it is proven by the fact that clothes will dry under a shed during the heaviest rains. Boots and shoes do not mould, clothing does not get musty as in other climates, and on shipboard it is noticeable that kid gloves and shoes show no reluctance at being pulled on on the wettest mornings. The snow lies on the mountain tops and sides all the year through, though in a warm, dry summer it retreats to the summits and higher ravines. In winter the snow seldom lasts long on the level, and mist and rain, coming after each snowfall, soon reduce it to slush. These contradictions of climate are quite at variance with the accepted ideas of Alaska, and although its enemies say that it can never be made to support a population since grain and vegetables will not grow there, vegetables continue to be raised in this part of the territory, as they have for more than fifty years, and wild timothy and grasses grow three and four feet high in every clearing. No very intelligent methods of cultivating the soil have ever been attempted, and drainage is an unknown science. Vancouver found the Indians cultivating potatoes and a kind of tobacco, and there are little plantations back in sheltered nooks of the archipelago, where the Indians go each year to plant and gather their potatoes. The Siwash sows his potatoes as a farmer does his grain, and very fine tubers cannot be expected from such farming. So far the residents of the territory have been like those dwellers on western cattle ranches, who count their cattle by thousands and use condensed milk and imported butter, and the tin can is oftener seen than the hoe or garden tools among them.

Although hay cannot be cured in the natural way in this rainy region, scientific farmers think it feasible to cut and salt in trenches all the hay that will be needed for the cattle for many years. Sleek cows are grazing in the streets and open places around Sitka, and the residents point with pride to two venerable mules that were left by the quarter-master, when the garrison was abandoned, and that for seven years ran wild and "rustled" for themselves summer and winter. They weathered all the wet seasons, foraged for themselves in the winters, and rioted in sweet grasses as high as their ears during the perfect, luxuriant summers, and are good mules now.

The fine little sponges and the delicate coral branches that are occasionally found in the harbor puzzle one with another hint of the tropics in this high latitude. Great fronds of seaweed and kelp as large as banana leaves drift on the rocks with the rushing tides, and the long, snaky *algæ* that float on the water are often found eighty and one hundred feet long. It is of these tough, hollow pipes that the Indians make the worms for their rude *hoochinoo* distilleries, or, splitting and twisting it, make fishing lines many fathoms in length. The same little *teredo* that eats up ship timbers and piles in southern oceans is as destructive here in the harbor of Sitka as anywhere in the tropics. The piles of the wharf only last five years at the longest, and the merciless borers eat up the timbers of the old wrecks and hulks with which the first foundations for a wharf were begun, and nothing but the yellow cedar of the archipelago is said to withstand the *teredo*.

Among other things that Sitka can boast of as an attraction is a promenade, a well-gravelled walk that the Russians built along the curving line of the beach, and through the woods, to the banks of the pretty Indian River. Up and down this walk the Russians used to stroll, and during the stay of the mail steamer the walk to Indian River is taken once and twice a day by the passengers, who are enraptured by the scenery, and given such an opportunity to see the heart of the woods and the mysteries of the forest growth. In seasons past, many primitive and picturesque little bridges have spanned the rushing current of this crystal clear stream, but high waters have swept them away season after season. Lieut. Gilman, in charge of the marines attached to the *Adams*, who rescued Princess Maksoutoff's tombstone, and was general director of public works and improvements, took his men and a force of Indians belonging to the ship's crew, and cleared a new pathway from the beach to the river, in 1884. He led paths up either side of the stream for a half mile or more; bridged the stream twice, and threw two picturesque bridges across the ravines on the river bank. A great deal of taste and ingenuity was shown in choosing the route along the river, so as to bring in view all the best points of scenery, and the rustic bridges in fantastic designs add greatly to many of the glimpses from under the greenwood trees. All along Indian River the ferns run riot, covering the ground in every clearing, and curling their great fronds up with the huge green leaves of the "devil's club," that would make parasols for people larger than elfs or fairies. The moss covers everything under foot with a close, springy carpet six inches deep, and moss and lichens, ferns and grasses envelop every fallen log and twig, and convert them into things of beauty. Giant firs and pines rise above the prostrate trunks of other large trees, whose wood is still sound at the heart, although the roots of a tree seventy feet high are arched and knotted over them. These overgrown trunks of prostrate trees are scattered all through the woods, and on one side of the river there is a fallen tree that would excite wonder even in the groves of California. Where the upturned roots are exposed, they are matted into a broad flat base on which the tapering trunk without tap-roots once stood like a candle on a candlestick. The fallen trunk is over ten feet in diameter, and a man six feet high is dwarfed when he stands beside the root. A second forest of ferns, bushes, and young trees has sprung up on top of this overturned tree, and its giant outlines will soon be lost in the tangle of vegetation.

The size of the cedar-trees in the archipelago has long been a matter of record. Army officers tell that cedars eight feet in diameter were cut down when they built the post at Fort Tongass, and Mr. Seward often boasted of the great planks, four and five feet wide, hewn by stone hatchets, that he measured in Kootznahoo and Tongass villages.

One bridge hangs its airy trestles over Indian River at a point where the main branch comes tumbling down in cascades, and a side stream pours in its sparkling, clear waters. Beyond that bridge, the path winds out into a clearing, and past an old brewery that flourished and made fortunes for its owners under Russian rule. The United States has prevented the manufacture and importation of all kinds of liquors in Alaska, and the brewery has been abandoned for many years. All the acres of the clearing in which it stands are covered thickly with blueberry bushes and rose bushes, while white clover lies like snow-drifts on either side of the corduroy road that leads into the town. The salmon berries, that wave their clusters of golden and crimson fruit in the woods and along the steep river bank, disappear at the edge of this clearing, and the blueberries are thicker than anything else that can grow on a bush. Big ravens croak in the tall tree-tops in the woods, inviting a shot from a sportsman, but, when hit, they fall into such thickets that the most experienced bird dogs could never retrieve one. Tiny humming-birds, with green and crimson throats, nest in the woods along the river, and the drumming of their little wings is the first warning of their presence. All that woodland that borders Indian River is a part of an enchanted forest, and more lovely than words can tell.

Where the path again reaches the beach and brings in view the harbor and its islands, a large square block of stone lies beside the path. It is popularly known as the Blarney Stone, and dowers the one who kisses it with a charmed tongue. All the men-of-war and revenue cutters that have visited the harbor have left their names and dates cut in the rock, and some strange old Russian hieroglyphs ante-date them all and give a proper touch of mystery to it. Captain Meade speaks of this Blarney Stone as a favorite rock "on which Baranoff, the first governor, used to sit on fine afternoons and drink brandy, until he became so much overcome that his friends had to take him home." There are several improbable and man-ufactured legends attached to it, but since the Indians have taken to gathering around it and sitting on it in groups, faith in the miraculous power of the stone has decreased among the white people.

In connection with this woodland walk along Indian River, a tragic little sto-ry was told, to a company sipping tea around a shining samovar one night, that invests even the garrison days that succeeded the transfer with something of ro-mantic incident. The captain and a lieutenant of one of the companies stationed at Sitka in the first year of United States possession fell desperately in love with the same beautiful Russian. She was a most charming woman, with soft, mysterious eyes, a pale, delicate face, and a slow, dreamy smile that set the two warriors wild. All the garrison knew of their fierce rivalry, so marvelled not a little when their old friendship appeared to be restored, and the two suitors started off on a hunting expedition together. One haggard man returned two days later, and said that his companion had been attacked and gored to death by an enraged buck in the forest. He was gloomy and strange in his manner, and at nightfall went to the house of the Russian lady to break the news of his rival's death. The friends of the lost offi-cer talked the thing over, and, suspecting that a duel had been fought, decided to go out the next day and search for the body. In the morning the surviving rival was found dead in bed, with a look of agony and horror on his face. One story was that his victim had appeared to him, and he had died of fright and terror; the other was that some unknown and subtle poison had been administered to him in a cup of tea, and the official report ascribed his death to heart-disease. The body of the lost rival was found at the foot of a steep bank on the shore of Indian River, where a tangle of ferns, bushes and grasses shaded and almost covered the clear, still pool in which he lay. His rifle was near him, and a bullet-hole in the heart told the sad truth, that his friends had suspected. His death was officially attributed to the acci-dental discharge of his own rifle while hunting, and under these two verdicts the real truth was concealed. The family of the Russian beauty disappeared from Sitka in a few months, and the story had been half forgotten until the recent opening of a path along Indian River recalled it to some of those who lived at Sitka at the time.

All around Sitka and its beautiful bay there are sylvan spots where the sports-man and the angler rejoice. The late Major William Gouverneur Morris, who lived at Sitka for several years, and was collector of customs at the time of his death, was an enthusiastic fisherman, and could tell tempting tales of his exploits with the rod. A small lake, a few miles back from the town, was his favorite resort, and on one occasion the Major's party caught four hundred and three trout in three hours. At Sawmill Creek a party of visiting anglers hooked sixty pounds of trout one morning, and the little Indian boys land salmon-trout from any place along Indian River.

At old Sitka, nine miles north of the present town, a salmon cannery was established in 1879 by the Messrs. Cutting of San Francisco. The Sitka Indians offered great objections to the landing of the Chinamen who were sent up to start the work in the cannery, and their spirit was so hostile at first, that the agent feared he would have to abandon the Chinamen or the whole project. The chiefs were finally pacified by being assured that the Chinese had only been brought to teach them a new process of salmon-canning, and after a short time all but a few of the Chinamen were sent back, and over one hundred Indians were employed at the cannery. After four years the cannery was moved to a point further north, and the Bay of Starri Gavan settled into its old deserted way. Over twenty-one thousand cases of canned salmon were shipped from the new cannery in 1884, and the owners felt justified in following the prospectors' advice to go further north.

South of Sitka the bay is indented with many inlets, and ten miles below the town are the Hot Springs, destined to again become a resort and sanitarium, when Sitka regains the size and importance of old. The springs are situated in a beautiful bay, and the waters, impregnated with iron, sulphur, and magnesia, are efficacious in cases of rheumatism and skin diseases. The Russian Fur Company erected a hospital there for its employees, but in late years only the Indians, occasional hunters, and prospectors have patronized the springs to any extent. An eccentric old lady, who writes blank-verse letters to the President and the Secretary of the Navy when things go wrong in Sitka, spent some weeks in solitude at the springs one summer, and was highly indignant when the naval commander sent down and insisted upon her return to the settlement, as they were all alarmed for her safety. The lazy Indians who go to the springs are said to sit in the pools of warm water all night, rather than gather the wood for a camp-fire, and they have great faith in the powers of the medicated waters. Some of the enthusiasts, who have the glory of the territory at heart, foresee the day when the Hot Springs will be famous, and a summer hotel, with all civilized accompaniments, draw visitors from all parts of the globe. Professor Davidson, in an article in "Lippincott's Magazine," of November, 1868, tells of a glacier hidden away near the bay, which will, of course, add to the attractions of this summer resort of the next century.

At Silver Bay, nearly south of Sitka, the earliest indications of gold were found in the archipelago. Soon after the California discoveries of 1848, the Emperor of Russia became convinced that there must be mineral wealth in his possessions in America. The directors of the fur company ignored all his first suggestions about undertaking a search expedition, and, as they did not want their own business interfered with, gave the hostility of the natives always as an excuse for not making any attempts. Their course was quite the same as that followed later by the Hudson Bay Company's agents, when gold was discovered on the Frazer River and in the

Cariboo regions of British Columbia. The Emperor, persisting in his notion, sent out from St. Petersburg, in 1854, a promising and adventurous young mining engineer, named Dorovin, who, beginning at Cook's Inlet, searched the coast down to Sitka without making any great discoveries. Arrived at Sitka, the gay northwest capital, he plunged into all the social dissipations, and, after a year's idleness, sent back a report condemning the country. He made no attempt to search for minerals on Baranoff Island, and some years later, when a Russian officer found a piece of float gold in Silver Bay, the governor quieted the interest without resorting to the knout, as old Baranoff did. Years afterwards a United States soldier found float gold in the same place, and, getting help from the garrison, discovered the quartz ledge of Baranoff Island.

On Round Mountain, southeast of Sitka, are situated the Great Eastern, the Stewart, and other mines, that attracted great attention at the time of their discovery in 1871 and 1872. The pioneers in this mining district were Doyle and Haley, two soldiers, who had lived in the mining districts of California and Nevada. Nicholas Haley is the most energetic of miners, and has carefully prospected the region about Sitka. He has found stringers of quartz on Indian River, and has more valuable claims at the head of Silver Bay than on the long ledge cropping out on the slopes of Round Mountain. The mines on this ledge have had many vicissitudes, have changed hands many times, have been involved in lawsuits, while no one could hold a valid title to a foot of mineral land in Alaska; and finally, through unfortunate management, the work was stopped, and the mills have stood idle for years. The want of civil government, or adequate protection for capitalists, has prevented the owners from risking anything more in the development of these mines, although the assays and the results of working proved these Sitka mines to be valuable properties.

CHAPTER XIV.
SITKA—AN HISTORICAL SKETCH.

For a town of its size, strange, old, tumble-down, moss-grown Sitka has had an eventful history from first to last. Claiming this northwestern part of America by right of the discoveries made by Behring and others in the last century, the Russians soon sent out colonies from Siberia. The earliest Russian settlements were on the Aleutian Islands, and thence, moving eastward, the fur company, whose president was the colonial governor, and appointed by the Crown, established its chief headquarters at Kodiak Island in 1790. Kodiak still lives in tradition of the Russian inhabitants of the archipelago as a sunny, summery place, blessed with the best climate on this coast.

Tchirikoff, the commander of one of Behring's ships, was the first white man to visit the site of Sitka, and two boatloads of men were seized and put to death by the savage Sitkans, July 15, 1741.

The first settlement was made in 1800 at Starri Gavan Bay, just north of the present town, and the place was duly dedicated to the Archangel Gabriel and left in charge of a small company of Russians. In the same year, when the rest of the world was shaken with the great battles of Marengo and Hohenlinden, the Indians rose and massacred the new settlers and destroyed their buildings. Baranoff was then governor of the colony, a fierce old fellow, who began life as a trader in Western Siberia, and was slowly raised to official eminence. He established the settlement at Kodiak before he made the venture at Sitka, and when he heard of the destruction of his new station, immediately arranged to rebuild it. In 1804 he tried it over again, building the chief warehouse on the small Gibraltar of Katalan's Rock where the castle now stands, and dedicating the place to the Archangel Michael. Baranoff was ennobled, and, moving his headquarters to Sitka, remained in charge until 1818. He opened trade and negotiations with the United States and many countries of the Pacific; he welcomed John Jacob Astor's ships to this harbor in 1810, and made with them contracts for the Canton trade, that were sadly interrupted by the war of 1812 between our country and England.

In Washington Irving's "Astoria" there is a life-like sketch of this hard-drinking, hard-swearing old tyrant, and the picture does not present an attractive view of life at New Archangel, or Sheetka. In 1811 Baranoff sent out the colony under Alexander Kuskoff, and established a settlement at Fort Ross, in California, in the redwood country of the coast north of San Francisco. Grain and vegetables were raised there in great quantities for the northern settlements for the space of thirty years, when the Czar ordered his subjects to withdraw from Mexican territory.

Baranoff ruled the colony with a rod of iron, and his absolute power of life and death over those under him, and the free use of the knout, kept the turbulent Indians, Creoles, and Siberian renegades in good order. He died at sea on his way home to Russia, and succeeding him as governor came Captain Haguemeister, and then a long line of noble Russians, generally chosen from among the higher officers of the navy.

Under Russian rule the colony ran along in pleasant routine; the southeastern coast was for a time leased to the Hudson Bay Company, and their proximity and the slow encroachments of the English in trade soon aroused Russia to a realization of the danger that threatened this distant colony in the event of a war. Russian America was first offered for sale to the United States during the Crimean war in 1854, by Baron Stoeckl, who afterwards concluded the treaty of purchase in 1867. In 1854 the English threatened the town of Petrapaulovski on the Kamschatkan coast, and the Russians foresaw the blockading and bombarding of their towns on the American side. This first offer was declined by President Pierce, and later negotiations came to naught in President Buchanan's day, when an offer of $5,000,000 was declined by Russia. Robert J. Walker, who assisted in drawing up the legal documents of transfer when we did finally buy the territory, stated once that during Polk's administration the Czar offered Russian America to the United States for the mere payment of government incumbrances and cost of transfer. Wily old Prince Gortschakoff had to tell it, too, when his envoy made such a shrewd sale for him, that his master was for years anxious to get rid of this distant and unprotected colony at any sacrifice, provided, always, that it did not fall into the hands of the English, who wanted it so badly.

In 1861 Russia and the United States held council in regard to establishing a telegraph line from this country to Europe, via Russian America, Behring Straits, and Siberia. Four years later an expedition was sent out by the Western Union Telegraph Company, and several ships and a large corps of engineers, surveyors, and scientists, were engaged in exploring the coast from the United States boundary line northward to the Yukon country, and along the Asiatic coast to the mouth of the Amoor River. Over $3,000,000 were expended in these surveys, and a telegraph line was erected for some hundred miles up the British Columbia coast, reaching to a point near the mouth of the Skeena River, that brought Sitka within three hundred miles of telegraphic communication instead of eight hundred and fifty miles, as has been its condition since the scheme was given up. After two years' work, the company abandoned the undertaking and recalled its surveying parties. The demonstrated success of the Atlantic cable, and the difficulty of maintaining the line through the dense forest regions of the coast and the uninhabited moors of the North, induced the company to give up the plan. Prof. Dall, of the Smithsonian Institute; Whymper, the great English mountain climber; Prof. Rothrocker, the botanist, and Col. Thomas W. Knox, who accompanied different parties of the Western Union Telegraph Company expedition, have written interesting books of their life and travels while connected with this great enterprise.

As the time approached for the expiration of the lease by which the Hudson

Bay Company held the franchise of the Russian-American Fur Company, great desire was manifested by citizens on the Pacific coast that the United States should purchase the colony. The legislature of Washington Territory sent a memorial to Congress in January, 1866, urging the purchase of the Russian possessions, and it was followed by earnest petitions from all parts of the Pacific coast. A syndicate of fur traders even proposed to buy the country of Russia on their private account, and sent a representative to Washington to consult with Secretary Seward in regard to having the United States establish a protectorate over their domain in that case. The Hudson Bay Company's lease was to expire in June, 1867, and in the spring of that year the plan of purchase by the United States government assumed definite shape. Negotiations were entered into by Secretary Seward and Baron Stoeckl, the Russian minister, and, though conducted with great secrecy, were soon rumored about. At that time President Johnson was plunging into the most stormy part of his career, threats of impeachment were in the air, and the articles had even been discussed by the House of Representatives before its adjournment, March 4, 1867. All of the preceding winter Washington had been full of rumors of great schemes, looking to a drain on the Treasury, and the House had grown wary and vigilant. Mexican patriots, from three different camps, were beseeching the aid of Congress and the State Department. The Juarez and Ortega factions were imploring loans of from $50,000,000 to $80,000,000, and Maximilian's emissaries were doing their best in the way of diplomacy to aid the fortunes of their imperial master, who had just taken the field against the insurgents. With such discords at home, Secretary Seward projected a brilliant stroke of foreign policy, and counted upon drawing off some of the hostile fires, and thrilling patriotic breasts by this purchase of Russian America, which should carry the stars and stripes to the uttermost limits of the north, and extend our dominion 3,000 miles west of the Golden Gate of California to that last island of Attu in the Aleutian chain, "o'er which the earliest morn of Asia smiles."

On the evening of the 29th of March, Baron Stoeckl went to Secretary Seward's residence on Lafayette Square, joyfully waving the cable message that gave the Czar's approval to the plan, as then outlined. Baron Stoeckl proposed that they should draw up the treaty on the following day, but the Secretary said, "No! we will do it now, and send it to the Senate to-morrow."

There were no telephones at the capitol then, and messengers were sent in every direction to summon Secretary Seward's assistants, and open and light the building at Fourteenth and S Streets, then occupied by the State Department. Baron Stoeckl hunted up his secretaries and chancellor, and at midnight the company assembled, including Senator Charles Sumner, Chairman of the Senate Committee on Foreign Relations. Leutze has preserved the scene in a painting owned by Hon. Frederick W. Seward, of Montrose, N. Y. Secretary Seward and his assistants, Messrs. Hunter and Chew, and M. Bodisco, Secretary of the Russian Legation, form a central group. Baron Stoeckl stands beside the large globe of the world, and the lights of the chandelier overhead fall full upon Russian America, to which Baron Stoeckl is pointing his hand. Senator Sumner and Mr. Frederick Seward occupy a sofa in a corner back of this group, holding a school atlas before them.

The signatures were affixed to the treaty at four o'clock on the morning of March 30. The illumination of the State Department at that unusual hour attracted suspicious attention, and it was known that something of import was going on. It was intended to keep the matter wholly secret until the Senate had ratified the treaty, but journalistic enterprise ran high, and a New York reporter shadowed the Secretary of State, and, hanging on to the back of his carriage as he drove home with Baron Stoeckl that night, caught an inkling of the terms of the treaty and gave them to the world.

On the same day the treaty was sent to the Senate, then convened in extra session, and, discussed in secret conclaves, was confirmed on the 10th of April, chiefly through the agency of Charles Sumner, who, although not favorable to the measure at first, arose on the tenth day and delivered a speech, which was one of the finest efforts of his life, and an epitome of all that was known and had been written up to date concerning Russian America. Every chart, every narrative of the old discoverers, every scientific work and special report, was consulted by that great scholar, and his speech "on the cession of Russian America" is still a work of authority and reference to those who would study the question.

There was great surprise when the terms of the treaty were made known. The wits went to work with their jokes on the "Esquimaux Acquisition Treaty," and Sir Frederick Bruce, the British Minister, was so chagrined at the news, that he telegraphed to the Earl of Derby for instructions to protest against the acceptance of the treaty. It was ratified by the Senate by a vote of thirty yeas and two nays, the opposing twain being Senators Fessenden and Ferry.

While the matter was pending there were many conclaves and dinner councils at the residence of the Secretary of State. The "polar bear treaty" and the "Esquimaux senators" were common names at the capital, and of the Secretary's dinner parties one scribe wrote: "There was roast treaty, boiled treaty, treaty in bottles, treaty in decanters, treaty garnished with appointments to office, treaty in statistics, treaty in military point of view, treaty in territorial grandeur view, treaty clad in furs, ornamented with walrus teeth, fringed with timber, and flopping with fish." Other menus gave "icebergs on toast," "seal flippers frappee," and "blubber au naturel."

It was a great puzzle for a while to know what name should he given to the new territory, as Russian America would no longer do. The wits suggested "Walrussia," "American Siberia," "Zero Islands," and "Polaria," but at Charles Sumner's suggestion it was called "Alaska," the name by which the natives designated to Captain Cook the great peninsula on the south coast, and which, translated, means "the great land." The articles were exchanged and the treaty proclaimed by the President, June 20, 1867. Secretary Seward was more than delighted with the success of his efforts, and the day after the proclamation said: "The farm is sold and belongs to us." He felt sure that he had the advantage of his enemies this time, and had gone far enough north to counteract any leaning or sentiment toward the South, that he had been accused of harboring. He proposed to make General Garfield, then fresh in his military honors, a first Governor of the Territory, and later he intended to divide the country into six territorial governments.

The President and his premier lost no time in clinching the bargain, and immediately set about to receive and occupy the Territory, without waiting for the House of Representatives to appropriate the $7,200,000 of gold coin to pay for it with. Brigadier-General Lovell H. Rousseau was furnished with a handsome silk flag and many instructions by Secretary Seward, and left New York the same August in company with Captain Alexis Pestchouroff and Captain Koskul, who acted as Commissioners on the part of Russia. Gen. Jefferson C. Davis, in command of 250 men, was ordered to meet him at San Francisco, and left there at the same time as the Commissioners, on September 27. Gen. Rousseau and his colleagues were taken on board the man-of-war *Ossipee*, then in command of Captain Emmons, and when they reached Sitka, on the morning of October 18, 1867, found the troop ships already at anchor there. Three United States ships, the *Ossipee* under Captain Emmons, the *Jamestown* under command of Captain McDougall, and the *Resaca* under Captain Bradford, were flying their colors in the harbor that gay October morning, and the Russian flag fluttered from every staff and roof-top. At half past three o'clock in the afternoon the United States troops, a company of Russian soldiers, the group of officials, some citizens and Indians, assembled on the terrace in front of the castle. The ceremony of transfer was very simple, the battery of the *Ossipee* starting the national salute to the Russian flag, when the order was given to lower it, and the Russian water battery on the wharf returning, in alternation of shots, the national salute to the United States flag, as it was raised. The Russian flag caught in the ropes coming down, wrapped itself round and round the flagstaff, and although the border was torn off, the body clung to the staff of native pine. The Russian soldiers could not reach it until a boatswain's chair was rigged to the halyards, and then one of them untwisting the flag, and not hearing Captain Pestchouroff's order to bring it down, flung it off, and it fell like a canopy over the bayonets of the Russian soldiers.

The rain began then, and the beautiful Princess Maksoutoff wept when the Russian colors finally fell. The superstitious affected to find an omen in this incident, but the American flag ran up gayly, and when the bombardment of national salutes was over, Captain Pestchouroff said: "By authority of his Majesty the Emperor of Russia, I transfer to the United States the Territory of Alaska!" Prince Maksoutoff handed over the insignia of his office as governor, and the thing was done. There was a dinner and a ball at the castle, an illumination and fireworks that night, and the bald eagle screamed on all the hill tops. The Russian citizens began to leave straightway, and in a few months fifty ships and four hundred people had sailed away from Sitka, and the desolation of American ownership began. Only three families of the educated class and of pure Russian blood now live there, to remember and relate the tales of better days. After this formal transfer, garrisons of United States troops were established at Fort Tongass, near the southern boundary line, at Fort Wrangell, at Sitka and Kodiak, under orders of the Department of the Columbia; but the ship carrying the troops to establish a fort on Cook's Inlet struck a rock and went to pieces when near its destination. All the lives were saved, and the project of a fort at that point was then abandoned.

Immense sums were paid by the government for the transportation of troops and freight in the few months after the occupancy, and, by the time Congress met, the United States had a firm hold on the new possession. There were exciting times at Sitka for a few months, and the first rush of enterprising and unscrupulous Americans quite astonished the departing Russians, who were unused to the tricks of the adventurers, who always hurry to a new country.

Professor George Davidson was sent with eight assistants to make a report on the general features and resources of the country, and from July to November he cruised along the coast on the revenue cutter *Lincoln*. He was mercilessly cross-examined by the special committee of Congress during the exciting winter that followed at Washington.

Secretary Seward trod a thorny pathway, and he and his newly-acquired Territory were the theme of every wit and joker in the public prints. Congress was in an ugly frame of mind, and even the party leaders in the House of Representatives felt dubious about getting an appropriation to pay for Alaska. The wildest reports of the country and its resources were current, and while one sage represented it as a garden of wild roses, and a place for linen dusters, the next one said the only products were icebergs and furs, and the future settlers would cultivate their fields with snow-ploughs.

The irrepressible Nasby wrote: "The dreary relic of diplomacy to the south of the North Pole is a land reservation for the Blair family," and he advised President Johnson to "swing around the circle," and visit "this land of valuable snow and merchantable ice."

In a less humorous vein a Democratic editor said: "Congress is not willing to take $10,000,000 from the Treasury to pay for the Secretary of State's questionable distinction of buying a vast uninhabitable desert with which to cover the thousand mortifications and defeats which have punished his pilotage of Andrew Johnson through his shipwrecked policy of reconstruction. The treaty has a clause binding us to exercise jurisdiction over the Territory and give government to forty thousand inhabitants now crawling over it in snow-shoes. Without a cent of revenue to be derived from it, we will have to keep regiments of soldiers and six men-of-war up there, and institute a Territorial government. No energy of the American people will be sufficient to make mining speculation profitable in 60° north latitude. Ninety-nine one-hundredths of the territory is absolutely worthless."

In this spirit the thing went on through all of that stormy winter. The impeachment trial was held, and President Johnson acquitted May 17, 1867. On the following day General N. P. Banks introduced a bill appropriating $7,200,000 to pay for Alaska, and as it hung uncertain for weeks, it was determined to get the appropriation through in a deficiency bill, if the Banks bill failed. At a night session on the 30th of June, with the House in committee of the whole, and General Garfield in the chair, General Banks made a most eloquent speech, painting Alaska in glowing colors and luxuriant phrase, and winning the suffrages of the disaffected ones on his own side by the audacity of his genius. Judge Loughbridge, of Iowa, opposed the bill, and three Democrats (Boyer of Pennsylvania, Pruyn of New York, and Johnson of California), made ringing speeches in its favor. The next day C. C. Washburn made a severe speech against it, and Maynard, of Tennessee, spoke for it. Then the grand "old commoner," Thaddeus Stevens, made an oration in its favor, ending up with a fish story of the skipper who ran his ship aground on the herring in Behring Sea, and ran it so high and so dry on the wriggling fish, that it broke in two. On the 14th of July the bill passed by ninety-eight yeas, forty-nine nays. Fifty-three members not voting, endangered its success, but the House showed its temper by a clause insisting that hereafter it should take part in the consideration of treaties, as well as the Senate. Two weeks later the Czar was chinking his bags of American gold, when dust again rose from the State Department. The cost of the cable messages sent by the two governments, in regard to the negotiations and the transfer, amounted to nearly $30,000. When their share of the bill was presented to the Russian government, they refused to pay it, claiming that the treaty provided that the United States should pay $7,200,000 and all the expenses of transfer. There were polite messages between the diplomats, but at last the cable company reduced the bill, and our State Department paid for all of it.

In the end many statements and prophecies concerning the Territory have been disproved, but we received a country of 580,107 square miles, equal in area to one sixth of the whole United States, and for this great empire we paid at the rate of one and nineteen-twentieths of a cent per acre. The Alexander archipelago itself, comprising 1,100 islands, and an area of 14,142 geographical square miles, will soon prove itself worth the purchase-money alone, when it is explored, developed, and settled. Of the strip of main land, thirty miles wide and three hundred miles long, off which the islands are anchored, Sir George Simpson, Governor-in-Chief of the Hudson Bay Company, once said that all the British possessions in the interior, adjacent to it, were useless, if this coast strip were not leased to them. For years Great Britain made overtures to buy this strip, and hordes of its mining adventurers made threats to drive the Russians away; yet, by the hooks and crooks of diplomacy, it came into the possession of the United States, while the southern border of this strip is distant six hundred and forty miles from our once northern boundary, the forty-ninth parallel. By leasing those tiny Seal Islands, in Behring Sea, to the Alaska Commercial Company, the government has derived a revenue of over $300,000 per annum, and the Territory has, in this way, paid a fair percentage of interest on the purchase-money, since it has been virtually at no expense to protect it, or keep up a form of government. In view of the later mineral discoveries, it is said that Douglass Island alone is worth all that the United States gave for the Territory, and events are slowly proving the foresight and wisdom of Mr. Seward in acquiring it.

The Russians knew almost nothing of the topography or resources of the country when they passed it over to us, as the directors of the fur company, having absolute control, had made everything subservient to their interests and trade. A clause in their lease provided that the government should have the right to all mineral lands discovered, so that they took good care to discourage explorers and prospectors. Baranoff is even said to have given thirty lashes to a man who brought in a specimen of gold-bearing quartz, and warned him of worse punishment if he found any more ore. All the records and papers of the fur company were turned over to the United States, and the archives at St. Petersburg were searched for any documents or reports pertaining to Russian America. Two shelves in the State Department Library at Washington are filled with these manuscript records of early Alaskan events. They are written in clear Russian text, as even as print, and forty of the volumes are archive reports of the directors and agents of the fur company. Fifty of them are office records and journals, and one bulky volume contains the ships' logs that were of sufficient value and interest to warrant their preservation. None of them have been translated, except as students and specialists have made notes from them for their own use. Mr. Ivan Petroff gave these archives a thorough inspection in gathering the materials for his valuable Census Report of 1880.

CHAPTER XV.

SITKA.—HISTORY SUCCEEDING THE TRANSFER.

A great event in the history of Sitka after the transfer was the visit of Ex-Secretary Seward and his party, and their stay was the occasion of the last gala season that the place has known. Mr. Seward and his son had gone out to San Francisco by the newly-completed lines of the Union and Central Pacific Railroad, intending to continue their travels into Mexico. He casually mentioned before Mr. W. C. Ralston, the banker, that he hoped some time to go to his territory of Alaska. Within a few hours after that Mr. Ralston wrote him that there were two steamers at his service, if he would accept one for a trip to Alaska. The fur company offered their steamer, the *Fideliter*, and Mr. Ben Holladay put the steamer *Active* at the disposal of Mr. Seward and his party. Mr. Holladay's offer was accepted, and his best and favorite commander, Captain C. C. Dall, was given charge of the *Active*, and everything provided for a long yachting trip. The others invited by Mr. Seward to partake of this magnificent hospitality were his son Frederick W. Seward and his wife, Judge Hastings, of San Francisco, Mr. and Mrs. Smith, of St. Louis, Hon. W. S. Dodge, revenue collector and mayor of Sitka, Hon. John H. Kinkead, postmaster and post trader at Sitka, and Captain Franklin of the British Navy, a nephew of the lamented Sir John Franklin. They left San Francisco on the 13th of July, 1869, and, touching at Victoria, reached Sitka July 30. The Ex-Secretary was received with a military salute on landing, and went to the house of Mayor Dodge. He kept the Russian Sabbath by attending service in the Greek church on our Saturday, and the American Sabbath, by listening to the post chaplain in the Lutheran church on the following day. Like many visitors since then, Mr. Seward said, at the end of his second day, that he had met every inhabitant, and knew all about them and their affairs. On another day General Davis gave a state reception at the castle, and Mr. Seward being dissuaded from his original plan of going up to Mount St. Elias, lest, after the voyage across a rough sea, he should find the monarch of the continent hidden in clouds, made up a party for the Chilkat country instead. General Davis and his family, two staff officers, and a few citizens, were invited to join them, and they went in by Peril Straits to Kootznahoo, and then up to the mouth of the Chilkat River. The incidents of their visit to Kloh-Kutz in his village have been related in a preceding chapter. Adding Professor Davidson and his assistants to their party, the *Active* returned to Kootznahoo, and visited the coal mine near Chief Andres village, and spent another day on a fishing frolic in Clam Bay. On his return to Sitka Mr. Seward was the guest of General Davis at the castle, and on the evening before his departure he addressed the assembled citizens in the

Lutheran church. He took leave with regret, and sailed away with a military salute on a clear and radiant day. They touched at the Takou glacier and Fort Wrangell, went up the Stikine River to the mining camps on the bars near the boundary line, and last visited Fort Tongass. The adjoining village of Tongass Indians, with its many fine *totem* poles and curious houses, was very interesting to them, and the old chief Ebbitts paid great honors to the Tyee of all the Tyees. Mr. Seward carried away a large collection of Alaska curios and souvenirs, and his lavish purchases quite shook the curio markets of those days. By the etiquette of the country the fur robes laid for him to sit on in the chief's lodges were his forever after, and the exchange of gifts consequent upon such hospitalities made his visits memorable to the chiefs by the *potlatches* left them. Mr. Seward carried home a dance cloak covered with Chinese coins, that the Russians had probably gotten during the days of their large trade with China, and sold to the Indians for furs. When the Chinese embassy visited Mr. Seward at Auburn, they gave him the names of the coins, and some of them dated back to the twelfth and fifth centuries, and to the first years of the Christian era. A quantity of Alaska cedar was taken east, and, in combination with California laurel, was used in the panellings and furnishings of the Seward mansion at Auburn.

A year later Lady Franklin went to Sitka on the troop-ship *Newbern*, and for three weeks was entertained at the castle, and occupied the same corner guest-chamber already made historic by Mr. Seward. At that time, 1870, she was nearly eighty years of age, but she was a most active and wonderful woman. She was accompanied by her niece, Miss Cracroft, who was her private secretary, and her object in visiting Alaska was to trace rumors that she had heard of the finding of relics of her husband. It was a fruitless search, and the widow of Sir John Franklin only lived for five years after this second trip to the Pacific coast in quest of tidings of the lost explorer.

With the exception of these incidents, Sitka grew duller and more lifeless by a slow-descending scale, with every year that succeeded the transfer of the territory to the United States. The officers of the garrison chafed under the isolation from even the remote frontiers of Washington Territory and Oregon, and the soldiers kept tumult rising in the Indian village. After ten years' occupation the military sailed away one day in 1877, and as no civil government was established to succeed their rule, the inhabitants were in despair. In a short time the Indians began to presume upon their immunity from punishment, and distilling their *hoochinoo* openly and without hindrance, soon had pandemonium raging in the *rancherie* and overflowing into the town. They burned the deserted quarters and buildings on the parade ground, killed and mutilated cattle, and the Russian priest was powerless to prevent the defilement of his church by crowds of lazy, indolent Indians, who lay on the church steps and gambled on any and every day. Trouble was precipitated by the Indians murdering a white man in November, 1878. The murderers were arrested by some friendly Indians and put in the guard-house, and immediately the whole village was in arms. The white citizens, who had been appealing for the protection of their own government before this, were virtually in a state of siege and at the mercy of the enraged Siwashes. The murderers were sent to Oregon for trial, but still their people raged. The three hundred white people were outnumbered two and three times by the Indians, and all winter they were in momentary dread of a final uprising and a massacre. The Russians arranged to gather at the priest's house at any sign of disturbance, and the collector of customs prepared to send his family below.

When all hope of help from their own government was gone, the citizens made a last, desperate appeal for protection to the British admiral at Victoria. Without waiting for diplomatic fol-de-rol, Captain A'Court, of H. M. S. *Osprey*, made all haste to Sitka on his humane errand. He reached there in March, 1879, and quiet was immediately restored. Three weeks later the little revenue cutter *Oliver Wolcott* came in, and anchored under the protecting guns of the big British war ship. The Indians laughed in scorn, and the British captain himself felt that it would be wrong to leave the people with such small means of defence at hand. Early in April the United States steamer *Alaska* came, and then the *Osprey* left. The captain of the *Alaska* declared his presence unnecessary, the Indian scare groundless, and, cruising off down the coast and back to more attractive regions, left the people again at the mercy of the Indians. The naval authorities, after receiving the report and recommendations of Captain A'Court, had the grace to order the *Alaska* back, and it remained in the harbor of Sitka until relieved by the sailing ship *Jamestown*, June 14.

The *Jamestown* was commanded by Captain Lester A. Beardslee, who instituted many reforms, cruised through all parts of the archipelago, kept the Indians under control, and finally made an official report, which is one of the most valuable contributions to the recent history of Alaska. He was succeeded in command of the *Jamestown* by Captain Glass, an officer who displayed marked abilities in his management of the charge entrusted to him. He exhibited a firmness that kept the natives in check, and exercised justice and humanity in a way to win the approval of those cunning readers of character. He made the Indians clean up their *rancherie*, straighten out the straggling double line of houses along shore, and then he had each house numbered, and its occupants counted and recorded. By his census of Sitka, taken Feb. 1, 1881, there were 1,234 inhabitants; 840 of these were in the Indian village, and only 394 souls composed the white settlement. He had a "round-up" of the native children one day, and each little redskin was provided with a tin medal, with a number on it, and forthwith ordered to attend the school, at peril of his parents being fined a blanket for each day's absence. Aside from this benevolent and paternal work, the big Tyee of the *Jamestown* used to terrify the natives by his sudden raids upon the moonshiners, who made the fiery and forbidden *hoochinoo* with illicit stills.

He supervised treaties of peace between the Stikine and Kootznahoo tribes, between the Stikine and Sitka tribes, and kept a naval protectorate over the infant mining camp at Juneau, until he was relieved by Commander Lull, with the steamer *Wachusett*, in 1881. The fascination of the north country brought Captain Glass back, in command of the *Wachusett*, in three months' time, and he remained at the head of Alaskan affairs for another year.

In October, 1882, Captain Merriman was detailed for the Alaska station, in command of the *Adams*, and for a year he and his ship played an important part in local history. He visited all the points in the archipelago, fought the great naval battle of Kootznahoo, and cruised off to the settlements on the Aleutian Islands. Peace and order reigned in the rancherie at Sitka, the Indians and miners of Juneau were chastised when they deserved it, and protected in what few rights they or any one had in the abandoned territory, and crooked traders and distillers of *hoochinoo* had an unfortunate time of it.

The *Adams* was the only visible sign of the nation's power for which the Indians had any great respect, and the nation's importance was advanced tenfold when the "big Tyee" silenced the unruly Kootznahoos. He was called upon to act as umpire, referee, probate and appellate judge, and arbiter in all vexed questions, in addition to his general duties as protector and preserver of the peace. With the Naval Register and the United States Statutes for code and reference, Captain Merriman exercised a general police duty about the territory. He maintained a paternal government and protectorate over the Indians, and the judgment of Solomon had often to be paralleled in deciding the issues of internecine and domestic wars. He had often to put asunder those whom Siwash ceremonies or the missionaries had joined together, to protect the young men who refused to marry their great-uncles' widows, to interfere and save the lives of those doomed to torture and death for witchcraft, to prevent the killing of slaves at the great funerals and *potlatches*, and to look after the widows' and orphans' shares in the blankets of some great estate. For these delicate and diplomatic duties Captain Merriman was well fitted. The dignity and ceremony that marked all his intercourse with the natives raised him in their esteem, and his firm and impartial judgment, his kindness and consideration, so won them, that there were wailing groups on the wharf when he sailed away from Sitka, and they still chant the praises of this good Tyee, who will always be a figure in history to them.

Captain J. B. Coghlan succeeded him in command of the *Adams*, and the Indians having been in the main peaceful, and the mining camp all quiet, Captain Coghlan gave a great deal of time to careful surveying of the more frequented channels of the inside passage. He marked off with buoys the channel through Wrangell Narrows, marked the more dangerous rocks and the channel in Peril Straits, corrected the erroneous position of several bays and coves, examined and reported new anchorages, and designated unknown rocks and ledges in Saginaw Channel and Neva Strait. In addition to this practical part of his profession, Captain Coghlan looked to the other interests confided to him. He visited all the Indian settlements, looked up their abandoned villages, encouraged prospectors and kept a keen eye on all mineral discoveries. An especial want in Alaska is a good coal mine, and although there are seams of it all through the islands, none of it is valuable for steaming purposes, and the Nanaimo coal has to be relied upon. Early voyagers discovered coal a half century ago, and a vein on Admiralty Island has been regularly discovered and announced to the world by every skipper who has touched there since. Captain Coghlan was keenly alive to the importance of finding good coal in this favored end of the territory, and he told the story of the latest discovery in a way to make his listeners weep from laughter.

While out on a survey trip one day, an Indian came to him mysteriously and said: "Heap coal up stream here," at the same time stealthily showing a lump of the genuine article. Quietly, and so as to attract as little attention as possible, the captain, two sporting friends, and the Indian started off, ostensibly duck-hunting. After they left the harbor of Sitka the Indian led the way up a narrow channel, and turned into St. John the Baptist's Bay, where careful and extensive surveys had been conducted but a short time before. The officers began to look amazed, but the Indian led on until he beached his canoe and triumphantly showed them a pile of anthracite coal stored under the roots of the tree. The coal-hunters recognized it as some of the anthracite coal that had been sent from Philadelphia, and this lot had been stored there for the convenience of the steam launches, on their trips between the ship and points where they were surveying in Peril Straits. Securing the quiet of the Indian, the officers went back to the ship, and after a few days gave specimens of coal to different experts on board. Tons of the same article lay in the bunkers under them, but the experts went seriously to work with their clay pipes and careful tests. None of them agreed about it. One of them declared it good coal, of good steaming quality and pure ash. Another one said it was lignite, and of no value, and never could be used for steaming. Rumors of the discovery of a coal mine soon spread through Sitka, and one man started out to follow up what he supposed had been the course of the coal-hunters, with the evil intent of jumping that mine. The ship was just starting off on a cruise, so followed the jumper, and overtaking him in his lone canoe at Killisnoo, the coal-hunter turned pale and nearly died with fright lest he should be punished with naval severity for his wicked designs. The joke on the coal-hunters, the coal experts, and the would-be jumper of the coal mine made the ship ring when it was told.

In August, 1884, the *Adams* sailed away from Sitka, and its place was taken by the *Pinta*, under the command of Captain H. E. Nichols, who for several years did most valuable work in the southern part of the archipelago while in command of the coast-survey steamer *Hassler*. His surveys were the basis for many of the new charts of that region that accompanied the Alaska Coast Pilot of 1883, compiled by Prof. W. H. Dall, and his return with the *Pinta* allows him to continue his surveys.

The *Pinta* is one of fifteen tugs or despatch boats built during the war for use at the different navy yards. It did service for many years at the Brooklyn yard, but became notorious about two years ago while undergoing repairs at the Norfolk yard. An unconscionable sum was spent in repairing; a local election was helped on, or rather off, by this means, and the board of officers called to survey and report upon the *Pinta* when the work was completed unhesitatingly condemned it, and declared it unseaworthy. A second survey was called in this awkward dilemma, and on the trial trip the much-tinkered ship made about four knots an hour. It went up to Boston, ran into the brig *Tally-Ho* that lay at anchor there, and more of its officers were brought up before a court of inquiry. A daring officer was at last found willing to peril his life in taking the *Pinta* around the Horn, and to attempt this hazardous exploit the armament was dispensed with until it should reach the Mare Island navy yard in California. It started the latter part of November, and reached San Francisco at the end of May, where more repairs were made, its guns mounted, and it then cleared for its new station. Its detail comprises seven officers and forty men, and a detachment of thirty marines quartered at Sitka for shore duty.

These naval officers connected with Alaska affairs have received great commendation for the course pursued by them in the Territory, and the history of the naval protectorate is in bright contrast to the less creditable operations of military rule. As the character of the country has become known, the uselessness of a land force has been appreciated, and it is most probable that a man-of-war will always be stationed in this growing section of the territory. Several naval officers, enjoying and appreciating the beautiful country, have made special requests to be returned to the Alaska station, and are enthusiastic over the region that knows neither newspapers nor high hats. They have many compensations for the larger social life they are deprived of, and are envied by all the tourists who meet them. For the sportsmen there are endless chances for shooting everything from humming-birds to ducks, eagles, deer, and bear. The anglers tell fish stories that turn the scales of all the tales that were ever told, and the lovers of nature feast on scenes that ordinary travellers cannot reach, and but dimly dream of in this hurried touch-and-go of an Alaskan cruise. In the curio line they have the whole Territory wherefrom to choose, and the stone, the copper, and the modern age yield up their choicest bits for their collections. A practical man has told me that there is the place where the officers can save their money, wear out their old clothes, and learn patience and other Christian virtues by grace of the slow monthly mail. Some few amuse themselves with a study of the country and its people; and the origin, tribal relations, family distinctions, and mythology of the Indians open a boundless field to an inquiring mind. They come across many odd characters and strange incidents among the queer, mixed population, and gather up most astonishing legends. One frivolous government officer, stationed for a long time in the Territory, once electrified some Alaska enthusiasts in a far-away city by putting out his elbows, and drawling with Cockney accent: "Ya-as! Alaska is all very well for climate, and scenery, and Indians, and that sort of thing, but a man loses his grip on society, you know, if he stays there long!"

It took seventeen years to date from the signing of the treaty until the Congress of the United States grudgingly granted a skeleton form of government to this one Territory that has proved itself a paying investment from the start. Every year the President called the attention of Congress to the matter, and once the commander of a Russian man-of-war on the Pacific coast announced his intention of going up to Sitka to examine into the defenceless and deplorable condition of the Russian residents, to whom the United States had not given the protection and civil rights guaranteed in the treaty. He never carried out his intentions, however, and the neglected citizens had to wait.

After innumerable petitions and the presentation in Congress of some thirty bills to grant a civil government to Alaska, the inhabitants were on the point of having the Russian residents of the Territory unite in a petition to the Czar, asking him to secure for them the protection and the rights guaranteed in the treaty of 1869. The Russian government would doubtless have enjoyed memorializing the

United States in such a cause, after the way the republic has taken foreign governments to task for the persecutions of Jews, peasants, and subjects within European borders.

Senator Harrison's bill to provide a civil government for Alaska was introduced on the 4th of December, 1883, and, with amendments, passed the Senate on the 24th of January, 1884. It was approved by the House of Representatives on the 13th of May, and, receiving President Arthur's signature, Alaska at last became a Territory, but not a land district of the United States, anomalous as that may seem.

Hon. John H. Kinkead, ex-Governor of Nevada, and who had once resided at Sitka as postmaster and post trader, was made the first executive. The other officers of this first government were: John G. Brady, Commissioner at Sitka; Henry States, Commissioner at Juneau; George P. Ihrie, Commissioner at Fort Wrangell; Chester Seeber, Commissioner at Ounalaska; Ward MacAllister, jr., United States District Judge; E. W. Haskell, United States District Attorney; M. C. Hillyer, United States Marshal for the District of Alaska; and Andrew T. Lewis, Clerk of Court. These officers reached their stations in September, 1884, and the rule of civil law followed the long interregnum of military, man-of-war, and revenue government in the country that was not a Territory, but only a customs district, and an Indian reservation without an agent.

The most sanguine do not expect to see Alaska enter the sisterhood of States during this century, but they claim with reason that southeastern Alaska will develop so rapidly that it will become necessary to make it a separate Territory with full and complete form of government, and skeleton rule be confined to the dreary and inhospitable regions of the Yukon mainland.

The citizens who have struggled against such tremendous odds for so many years were rather bitter in their comments upon the tardy and ungracious action of Congress in giving them only a skeleton government; and the Russians and Creoles are more loyal to the Czar at heart, after experiencing these seventeen years in a free country. To a lady who tried to buy some illusion or tulle in a store at Sitka, the trader blurted out, "No, ma'am, there's no illusion in Alaska. It's all reality here, and pretty hard at that, the way the government treats us."

The dim ideas that the outside world had of the condition of Alaska was evinced by the stories Major Morris used to tell of dozens of letters that were addressed to "The United States Consul at Sitka." Governors of States and more favored Territories regularly sent their Thanksgiving Proclamations to "The Governor of Alaska Territory," long before the neglected country had any such an official as a governor, or any right to such a courteous appellation as "Territory."

CHAPTER XVI.
EDUCATION IN ALASKA.

Although the pride of this most advanced and enlightened nation of the earth is its public school system, the United States has done nothing for education in Alaska. According to Petroff's historical record, from which the following *resumé* is made, the Russian school system began in 1874, when Gregory Shelikoff, a founder and director of the fur company, established a small school at Kodiak. He taught only the rudiments to the native Aleuts, and his wife instructed the women in sewing and household arts. Through Shelikoff's efforts the empress, Catherine II., by special ukase of June 30, 1793, instructed the metropolite Gabriel to send missionaries to her American possessions. In 1794 the archimandrite, Ivassof, seven clergymen, and two laymen reached Kodiak. Germand, a member of this party, established a school on Spruce Island, and for forty years gave religious instruction and agricultural and industrial teachings to the natives.

In 1820 a school was established at Sitka, and instruction given in the Russian language and religion, the fundamental branches, navigation, and the trades; the object in all these schools maintained by the government and the fur company being to raise up competent navigators, clerks, and traders for the company's ranks.

In 1824 Ivan Veniaminoff landed at Ounalaska, and began his mission work among the Aleuts. He translated the Scriptures for them, and compiled a vocabulary of their language, and in 1838 he went back to Irkutsk and was made bishop of the independent diocese of Russian America. Returning to Alaska, he established himself at Sitka, founded the Cathedral church, and undertook the conversion of the Koloschians, or Thlinkets. He studied their language, translated books of the Testament, hymns, and a catechism, and wrote several works upon the Aleuts and Thlinkets, which are still the authority upon all that relates to their peculiar rites, superstitions, beliefs, and customs.

In the year 1840 Captain Etolin, a Creole, educated in the colonial school at Sitka, became governor and chief director of the fur company, and, during his administration of affairs, educational matters received their full share of attention. A preparatory school was founded by Etolin, who adopted the wisest measures for its success. Religious teachings were given in all the schools, and arithmetic, astronomy, and navigation were considered important branches. Etolin himself was a fine navigator, and, while in command of the company's ships, he made a survey of the coast, and a map which is still considered authority. His wife established a school for Creole girls, educating them in the common branches and household duties, and furnishing them with dowries when they married the company's officers or employees. In 1841 Veniaminoff founded a theological seminary at Sitka, and it was maintained until the transfer of the territory and the removal of the bishop's see to Kamschatka. In 1860 the school system was reorganized by a commission, the scope and efficiency of the institution increased, and thorough training in the sciences and higher branches afforded.

In 1867 the territory passed into the possession of the United States, the Russian support was withdrawn from the schools, and educational affairs have been at a standstill ever since. No rights were reserved for the Indians in the treaty of 1867, so that there is no real "Indian Question" involved. The Treasury regulations forbidding the importation or sale of intoxicating liquors makes the whole Territory an Indian reservation in one sense; but there have never been any treaties with the tribes; there are no Indian agents within the boundaries; and, uncontaminated by the system of government rations and annuity goods, the parties have been left free, with but one exception, to work out their own civilization.

In leasing the Seal Islands to the Alaska Commercial Company, the government bound the company "to maintain a school on each island, in accordance with said rules and regulations, and suitable for the education of the natives of said islands, for a period of not less than eight months in each year." Government agents have seen that the company kept its promises for "the comfort, maintenance, education, and protection of the natives of said islands," and having provided carefully for these essentials on those few square miles of land, the general government omitted to do anything for the rest of the great country and its 33,246 native inhabitants, who are certainly as much entitled to educational aid as the inhabitants of the nearer Territories and the Southern States. The Alaska Commercial Company has maintained schools on St. Paul's and St. George's islands as agreed, and, becoming interested in the rapid progress made by one very bright and clever young Aleut at St. Paul's, the company sent him to Massachusetts to complete his studies. They paid all his expenses for five years, and he left the Massachusetts State Normal School with credit, and is now in charge of the schools at the Seal Islands, an intelligent and highly esteemed young man, in whom the company takes a natural pride.

According to the census report of 1880, the native population of Alaska numbers 33,246. Of this number 7,225 are Thlinkets and Haidas, inhabiting the southeastern part of the Territory, and Petroff gives the following enumeration of the tribes:—

Tribes.

Chilkat	988
Hooniah	908
Kootznahoo	666
Kake	568
Auk	640
Taku	269

Stikine	317
Prince of Wales Id. (West Coast)	587
Tongass	273
Sitka	721
Yakutat	500
Haida	788
	— — —
Total	7,225

While the military garrison was at Sitka, the wives of the officers taught classes of the natives every Sunday, and when General O. O. Howard's attention was directed to the matter, during a trip through the country, he reported the condition of affairs to the mission boards. The Presbyterian Board was the first to enter the field, Mrs. McFarland establishing the school at Fort Wrangell in 1877. In 1878 a school was started at Sitka; in 1880 one was established at Chilkoot Inlet, and after that, one among the Hooniahs of Cross Sound, and at Howkan and Shakan, among the Haidas. A school for Russian and Creole children was maintained at Sitka in 1879, under the protection of Captain Glass, U.S.N., whose efforts in the cause of Indian education have already been recorded.

The Indians are quick to learn and anxious to be taught, and, appreciating the practical advantages of an education, they unceasingly beg for teachers and schools. The only drawback to their upward progress is their want of all moral sense or instincts. The missionary teachers sent out by the Presbyterian Board have been well received by the Indians, but, on account of a few unfortunate instances, are not popular with the white residents. The native chiefs have often given up the council-houses and their own lodges to them for school-rooms, and taken the instructors under their special protection.

Recognition was at last given to the rights and the wants of these people in 1884, and in section 13 of the "Act providing a civil government for Alaska," an appropriation of $25,000 was made for the education of all children of school age, without reference to race. The public schools contemplated in this act are yet to be established, as the civil officers have first to inspect, and make their reports and suggestions as to the wisest disposal of the fund.

At the same session of the forty-eighth Congress, the Indian appropriation bill made this provision: "For the support and education of Indian children of both sexes at industrial schools in Alaska, $15,000." The Presbyterian Board of Missions, through the Rev. Dr. Kendall, made application for a portion of this fund in 1884, and the Commissioner of Indian Affairs, in his letter recommending that it should be granted, said:—

"In the total neglect of the government (since Alaska was purchased) to provide for the educational needs of Alaska Indians, they have been indebted for such schools as they have had solely to religious societies, and for most of these schools they are indebted to the society which Dr. Kendall represents. For the establishment and support of its schools that society, last year, expended over $20,000, and also expended nearly $5,000 for mission work. In the enlargement of their educational work in Alaska, they have therefore the first claim to assistance from the appropriation recently made by government for the support of schools in Alaska. Moreover, they have now on the ground officers and employees who can carry on the work."

A contract was therefore made with the mission authorities at Sitka for the education and care of one hundred pupils, at an expense to the government of $120 per capita per annum, the expenditure to be made in quarterly payments from the appropriation named above. It was estimated that for the first year the whole expenditure would not exceed $9,000 or $10,000. The contracts are temporary, and can be annulled at two months' notice should a different policy prevail at headquarters; and the original intention of establishing a government industrial school after the plan of the successful institution at Carlisle Barracks, Pa., will probably not be carried out for some time.

The Roman Catholics built a chapel at Fort Wrangell some years ago, but it has been closed for a long time, and there are no missions of that church now maintained in southeastern Alaska at least. It would seem as though this were a field particularly adapted to the efforts of the Jesuits, who have always been so successful among the native tribes of the Pacific coast.

Two Moravian missionaries from Bethlehem, Pa., the Rev. Adolphus Hartman and the Rev. William Weinland, were taken up to the Yukon region by the U. S. S. *Corwin* in the spring of 1884, and will devote themselves to mission work among the Indians of the interior.

CHAPTER XVII.
PERIL STRAITS AND KOOTZNAHOO.

When the steamer gets ready to leave Sitka, there is always regret that the few days in that port could not have been weeks. There are always regrets, too, at not seeing Mount St. Elias, when the passengers realize that the ship has begun the return voyage. Mr. Seward was most desirous of seeing Mount St. Elias from the sea, but was deterred from carrying out his plan by the stories of the rough water to be crossed, and the certainty of fogs and clouds obscuring his view when he reached the bay at the base of the great mountain. There are seldom any passengers or freight billed for Mount St. Elias, and the mail contract does not require the steamer to run up that three hundred miles to north-westward of Sitka and call at the mountain each month. The U. S. S. *Adams* carried some prospectors up to Yakutat Bay in 1883, and its officers took that opportunity of visiting the great glacier that fronts for seventy miles on the coast at the foot of the giant peak of North America. One of the officers made a series of admirable water-color sketches, but no angles were taken to determine the exact height of the mountain, and the elevation of the untrodden summit is not yet determined with precision.

In June, 1884, the *Idaho* went up to the mouth of Copper River to land Lieutenant Abercrombie, U. S. A., and his exploring party, and the pilot's story of the radiantly clear sky, and the view of Mount St. Elias, one hundred and fifty miles away, added poignancy to the regrets of the July passengers. From a height of 17,500 feet, the mountain has now risen to 19,500 feet, according to the latest "Coast Pilot," and somewhere it has been given an elevation of 23,000 feet above the sea. Fame and glory await the mountain-climber who reaches its top, and every American who rides up the Righi, or has a guide pull him up other Alpine summits, should blush that a grander mountain in his own country, the highest peak of the continent, too, has never yet been accurately measured, or explored, or ascended.

When, as the log says, "the ship lets go from Sitka wharf," there are two routes to choose in starting southward. One leads out through the beautiful Sitka Sound, and past Mount Edgecumbe, to the open sea, and then the course is down the shore of Baranoff Island and around Cape Ommaney to the inside waters. The mountain outlines of the Baranoff shore are particularly fine from the ocean, but a landsman finds more beauty in the peaks and ranges as seen from the quiet waters of Chatham Strait on the other side of the island. Cape Ommaney, in rough weather, is more dreaded by mariners than the Columbia River bar, and wits and punsters take liberties with its name when they round Cape Ommaney in a head wind and chop sea. The Pacific raises some mighty surges off that point, and there are small islands and hidden rocks on all sides of it. Vancouver had to anchor for several days in a little bight before he could venture around the cape, and in later times it has been a place of peril and anxiety to the navigators of the coast.

The other route from Sitka leads around the north end of Baranoff Island, and through Peril Straits across to Chatham Strait. Peril Straits is a narrow gorge or channel between the two mountainous islands of Chicagoff and Baranoff, and is strewn through all of its tortuous way with rocks and ledges over which the rushing tides pour in eddies and rapids. Several wrecks have occurred in this dangerous passage, and in May, 1883, the freight steamer *Eureka* struck a rock, and was beached near shore in time to save it from complete destruction. All lives were saved, and the crew and salvage corps had a camp near the wreck for three weeks, before the ship was raised and taken to San Francisco for repairs.

It was aptly named Peril, or Pogibshi, Strait, by the Russians, though Petroff says that it was called that on account of the death of one hundred of Baranoff's Aleut hunters, who were killed by eating poisonous mussels there, rather than on account of its reefs and furious tides. It takes a daring and skilful navigator to carry a ship through that dangerous reach, and it is something fine to watch Captain Carroll, when he puts extra men at the wheel and sends his big steamer plunging and flying through the rapids. The yard-arms almost touch the trees on the precipitous shores, and the bow heads to all the points of the compass in turn, as "the salt, storm-fighting old captain" stands on the bridge, with his hands run deep in his great-coat pockets, and drops an occasional "Stab'bord a bit!" "Hard a stab'bord!" or "Port your helm!" down the trap-door to the men at the wheel. Aside from its evil fame, it is a most picturesque and beautiful channel, the waters a clear, deep green, and the shores clothed with dense forests of darker green.

Captain Coghlan made a survey of Peril Straits before leaving Alaska, and marked off the channel with buoys. He found so many rocks and reefs that had been unsuspected, that the mariners said that they would never dare to venture through Peril Straits again, after learning how rock-crowded and dangerous it was.

Down Chatham Strait,green and snow-covered mountains rise on either side, and on the shores of Admiralty Island marble bluffs show like patches of snow on the long shore line of eternal green. The old Indian village of Kootznahoo, the "Bear Fort" of the natives, lies in a cove on the Admiralty shore, and, from first to last, the Kootznahoo tribe have proved an unruly set. They made hostile demonstrations to Vancouver's men when they explored the strait, and in 1869 the authorities had to deal severely with them, destroying a village and carrying the chief away as hostage, or prisoner, on the U. S. S. *Saginaw*. In October, 1882, the shelling of this Kootznahoo village by Captain Merriman, U. S. N., made a great stir, and editors six thousand miles away heaped vituperation and invective upon the head of that officer, without waiting to know of anything but the bare fact of the shelling. The docility of the Indians since then, and the expressed approval of the Tyee's action by the chiefs of the tribe, prove how efficacious his course was at the battle of Kootznahoo. In Alaska, where the history of that bombardment is still fresh, and the survivors are walking about in paint and nose rings, the whole thing wears a different aspect, and fragments that one remembers of those blazing editorials appear now as most laughable. Every scribe brought in a ringing sentence about the "eternal ice and snows of an arctic winter;" but they don't have arctic winters in this part of Alaska, as a study of the Japan Current and the isothermal lines will show, and while the battle raged the thermometer stood higher than it did in New York. Other errors were bound to creep in where the fires of enthusiasm were kindled with so little information, and to the officers and people of Sitka the newspapers were a source of unending entertainment when the bombardment of Kootznahoo began to reach their columns.

As related on the spot, that Kootznahoo story of the torpedo and the whale is Homeric in its simplicity. Some Indians went out in a canoe with the white men employed by the Northwest Trading Company at Killisnoo. While paddling towards a whale, one of the bombs attached to a harpoon exploded and killed an Indian. If it had been a common Indian, nothing would ever have been heard of the incident, but when the natives saw their great medicine man laid low, they raised an uproar. Going back to first causes, they demanded two hundred blankets from the trading company as compensation for their loss. The company naturally ignored this tax levied by the coroner's jury, and straightway there were signs of war.

The Indians' demand for blood or ransom was made stronger by their capturing one of the white men and holding him as hostage, but when they found that he was one-eyed they tried to send him back for exchange. They claimed that he was *cultus* (worthless), and demanded a whole and sound man for their dead shaman. They made ready to murder all the white men at the adjoining station, intending, however, to spare the agent's wife and children, as they afterwards confessed. As the signs of the coming trouble were more apparent, the little steamer *Favorite* was sent to Sitka with the agent's family, and an appeal made for help to the *Adams*. Captain Merriman returned in the *Favorite*, accompanied by the revenue cutter *Corwin*.

A great *wa-wa* was held with the ringleaders and marauders, and to their bold demand for the two hundred blankets, Captain Merriman responded with a counter-demand, that the Indians should bring him four hundred blankets, and forever after keep the peace, or he would shell their village. Mistaking his word for that of a common Indian agent, the red men went their riotous way, and at dusk of a November afternoon the *Corwin* anchored outside the reef and sent the shot hurtling through the village. The Indians gathered up their blankets and their stores of winter provisions, and took to the woods, but the bombardment was not so severe, but that a few rascally Kootznahoos stayed in the village and plundered the abandoned houses. The tribute of blankets was paid, the Kootznahoos humbled themselves before the big Tyee, or their "good father," and a more docile, penitent, and industrious community does not exist than those same obstreperous Indians.

The liquor that the Hudson Bay Company and the Russian traders furnished to the Indians was very weak and very expensive, and the Kootznahoos rest some of their claims to distinction on the fact that the native drink, or *hoochinoo*, was first distilled by their people. A deserter from a whaling-ship taught them the secret, and from molasses or sugar, with flour, potatoes, and yeast, they distil the vilest and most powerful spirit. An old oil can and a musket barrel, or a section of the long, hollow pipe of the common seaweed (*nereiocistum*) furnish the apparatus, and the *hoochinoo*, quickly distilled, can be used at once. After any quantity of it has been made, its presence is soon declared, and the Indians are frenzied by it. *Hoochinoo* is the great enemy of peace and order, and the customs officers can much easier detect a white man smuggling whiskey than catch the Indians in the distilling act. It is apparent enough when they have imbibed the rank and fiery spirit, but it is impossible to watch all the illicit stills that they set up in their houses, or hide in lonely coves and places in the woods. The man-of-war is always on the lookout for indications of *hoochinoo*, and at the first signs a raid is made on a village, the houses and the woods searched, and the stills and supplies destroyed. With the cunning of a savage race they have wonderful ways of hiding it in underground and up-tree warehouses, and many exciting stories are told by the naval officers of the great *hoochinoo* raids they have taken part in.

Lumme or rum, these children of nature sometimes call the forbidden fluid, as, like their Chinese cousins, the Thlinkets are unable to pronounce the letter *r*, and give the *l*-sound as its equivalent in every case. There are many points of resemblance between the Kootznahoos and the Orientals; and in writing of the origin of these Thlinket tribes of the archipelago, Captain Beardslee, in his official report, says:—

"All of the tribes mentioned except the Kootznahoos seem to have sprung from a common origin; they speak the same language and have similar customs and superstitions, and from these the Kootznahoos differ so slightly that a stranger cannot detect the difference. Their legend is that originally all lived in the Chilkat country; that there came great floods of ice and water, and the country grew too poor to support them, and that many emigrated south; that the Auks are outcasts from the Hoonah tribes, and the Kakes from the Sitkas, and both tribes deserve to be still so considered; that the Kootznahoos came from over the sea, and the Haidas, who live on Vancouver's Island, from the south. I have imbibed an impression, which, however, I could not obtain much evidence to support, that all of the tribes except the Haidas are Oriental,—in every respect they resemble the Ainos of Japan far more than they do our North American Indians,—and that the Kootznahoos are of Chinese origin; while the Haidas, who are superior to all of the others in intelligence and skill in various handicrafts, are the descendants of the boat-loads whom Cortez drove out of Mexico, and who vanished to the north."

All this part of Admiralty Island is a coal field, and veins and outcroppings of lignite have been found on every side of it, and along the inlets and creeks leading to the interior. A good coal mine would be worth more than a gold mine, in Alaska, and though seams have been discovered with regularity since 1832, none of the explorers seem to have found just the thing yet. In 1868 Lieutenant-Commander Mitchell explored Kootznahoo Inlet, leading into the heart of Admiralty Island, and at the head of the perilous channel opened a coal seam. In the following year, Mr. Seward's party went up to the Mitchell mine, and they were enthusiastic over its promises. The coal burned beautifully in the open air, but when the real tests were put to it, and it was tried in the boiler-room of the ship, it was found to contain so much crude resin that it was destruction to boiler iron. Geologically, the country is too young to have even any very good lignite beds, but the archipelago is now swarming with coal prospectors and coal experts, and there is such a general craze for coal that it may yet be forthcoming. At present the Nanaimo coal is depended upon entirely for steaming purposes, and the mail-steamer has to carry its own supply for the whole round trip, and take as freight the coal needed for the government ships at Sitka.

After Captain Hooper's mine of true coal at Cape Lisburn, on the Arctic coast, the most promising indications are at Cook's Inlet and around the Kenai peninsula. Although irrelevant in this connection, it perhaps naturally follows in this lignite vein to mention a coal mine accidentally discovered by an English yachtsman, Sir Thomas Hesketh, while cruising about Kenai. He treed an eagle on a hunting trip, and, other means failing to dislodge it, the sportsman set fire to the tree. The roots ran down into a coal seam, that, taking fire, was burning two years later, when the last ship touched there. Another escapade of the yachting party was to set a dead monkey adrift in a box, and when it washed ashore near Kodiak, the Indians, who had had a tradition that the evil spirit would come to earth in the shape of a little black man, fled that part of the island in terror and never went back.

CHAPTER XVIII.

KILLISNOO AND THE LAND OF KAKES.

Around the point from Kootznahoo, a sharp turn leads through a veritable needle's eye of a passage to Koteosok Harbor, made by the natural breakwater of a small island lying close to the Admiralty shore. This island was named by Captain Meade as Kenasnow, or "near the fort," as the Kootznahoos designated it to him. It is a picturesque, fir-crowned little island, and its dark, slaty cliffs are seamed with veins of pure white marble. Its ragged shores hold hundreds of aquariums at low tide, and in the way of marine curios there are, besides the skeletons of whales, myriads of star fish and jelly fish and barnacles strewing the beach; the acres of barnacles giving off a chorus of faint little clicking sounds as they hastily shut their shells at the sound of any one approaching.

On this little island of Kenasnow, the Northwest Trading Company has its largest station, Killisnoo, where codfish are dried, herring and dogfish converted into oil, and the air weighted with the most horrible smells from the fish guano manufactured there. The company has extensive warehouses, works, and shops on Kenasnow, and around the buildings there are gathered quite a village of Kootznahoo Indians, who are employed at the fishery. This station represents an investment of over \$100,000, the oil works alone having cost \$70,000, and extravagant management having doubled all the necessary expenses of the first plant. As there was no water supply on the solid rock of Kenasnow, a reservoir with a storage capacity of 90,000 gallons of water was constructed; and, with cedar forests on every side, every bit of lumber used was brought by freight from below.

Killisnoo was first established as a whaling station, but many causes decided the company to abandon that branch of fishery. There is a tradition that the Indians once regarded their great totemic beast, the whale, with such veneration that they would never kill it, nor eat of its flesh and blubber. The Kootznahoos have grown skeptical in many ways, and they made no objections to harpooning the whale, until the bomb exploded in 1882; and after the troubles following upon that impious adventure, the company decided that whaling was not a profitable business, and began to fish for cod and smaller fry.

The codfish are caught in the deeper waters of Chatham Strait around the island, the Indians going out in the fleet of small boats to fish, and turning their catch into large scows, which are towed in by the two steam launches that are kept constantly busy. Connoisseurs pronounce this cod remarkably fine, firm, and white, and as neither hake nor haddock are ever found there, the Killisnoo codfish is not open to the same suspicions as rest on so many Eastern fish. They average in weight from three to five pounds, and the Indians are provided with boats and paid two cents apiece for every codfish caught. A difficulty in the way of drying in the open air in this moist climate has been solved by building a drying-house, where the process is accomplished artificially. There seems to be no limit to the quantity of fish that can be caught, and during one visit at Killisnoo a scow was towed in from Gardner Point loaded with eight thousand fine large cod, and 1,576 boxes of the dried fish were ready to be shipped south.

From the end of August into January, the waters of Chatham Strait are black with herring. The Indians used to catch them with primitive rakes, made by driving nails through the end of a piece of board, and with this rude implement they could quickly fill a canoe with herring, each nail catching two and three fish. Seines have supplanted the aborigine's hand-rake, and a thousand barrels of silver herring have been taken at a single haul, although the average haul is about half as many barrels, and requiring eleven men to each net then. Each barrel of fish yields about three gallons of oil at the oil works, which are managed by men who have had charge of menhaden fisheries on the Atlantic coast. As the result of the first year's work, 82,000 gallons of herring oil were shipped below in 1883, selling at the rate of thirty cents per gallon. Within the year an attempt was made towards supplying the cod-liver oil of pharmacy, and five cases of it sent below for trial received the highest indorsement from physicians.

More picturesque and less fragrant than the buildings of the company were the log and bark houses of the Indians, who have abandoned their old village and fort of Kootznahoo, and settled around the Killisnoo station. The local celebrity is the famous old head chief of the Kootznahoos, Kitchnatti or Saginaw Jake, who, for the iniquities of his tribe, was carried off as a hostage in the man-of-war *Saginaw* in 1869. He was a prisoner for a long time on board that ship at the Mare Island Navy Yard in California, and when he was afterward returned to his people, he became an apostle of peace and the greatest friend of the white man. He is a crooked, bow-legged old fellow, and he superintended the tying up of the ship in a most energetic way. He lurched and tacked across the dock, waving his cane wildly to his underlings, and giving hoarse, guttural words of the fiercest command. He wore a derby hat with a gold band, and the uniform coat of a captain of the navy, while two immense silver stars on his breast gave his name and rank as the Killisnoo policeman, and a dangerous-looking billy was suspended from his shoulder by a variegated sash.

Besides being a hostage of war, Kitchnatti was once denounced by a terrible shaman, who had an incurable patient on hand. The chief was found bound and tied for torture, and barely rescued in time by naval friends. He has now no respect for his own medicine-men, and proved it once by telling one of the curio collectors that he knew where there was a shaman's grave full of beautiful carvings and trophies. He was bidden to get them, and offered a price for his grave-robbing. In a few days Jake reappeared, looking sad and despondent. He mentioned the name of a sub-chief, and, with a tone of severe disapproval, said:—

"Heap bad Indian. He rob medicine-man's grave. Sell curios to trader. Bad man."

When Jake spied the photographers on shore, he made wild signals, ran off to his cabin, and reappeared clad in fuller regalia; then, drawing an old cutlass, braced himself up in a "present-arms" attitude before the camera, and nodded for the operator to go on. He then led them to his neatly whitewashed house, and showed them a cigar-box full of letters of credentials and testimonials of character given him by naval officers, ship captains, traders, and missionaries. All of these Indians have a great fancy for these letters. They beg them from every one in power, and carry them around tenderly wrapped in paper, to show them as certificates of their worth, character, and importance. Some of Jake's letters were profusely sealed with great splotches of red wax, and there is a story that he for a long time innocently showed a testimonial, which ran: "The bearer of this paper is the biggest scoundrel in Alaska. Believe nothing that he says, and look out, or he will steal everything in sight." These poor old men of letters have many funny jokes played on them in this way, and it is really touching to see the innocent pride with which they display these insignia.

Jake pointed with pleasure to a row of illuminated posters and portraits of theatrical celebrities that decorated one wall of his cabin, and explained that they were pictures of his friends. The faces were those of Nat Goodwin, Gus Williams, John McCullough, Thomas Keane, and others, and the high colors and grand attitudes much pleased the old chief. In quite another vein Jake pointed to a small box tomb on the other side of the channel, where he had buried his little daughter a few days before. A flag-pole, with a small United States flag at half-mast, gave mute testimony to Jake's ideas of patriotism and mourning etiquette. His wife betrayed her state of grief by wandering about in a black dress, with a black umbrella held down closely over her head all of the time.

AN ALASKA "LADY"; AND BASKET WEAVERS AT KILLISNOO.

At Killisnoo blackened faces were almost the rule, and every other native woman had her face coated with a mixture of seal oil and soot. A group of these blackamoors made a picture, as they sat inside a cabin door weaving their pretty baskets of the fine inside bark and roots of the cedar. One younger woman wore a silver pin sticking out through her under lip, another had a large wooden labrette in her lip; and when the photographer tried to take the group, their neighbors ran up and joined in the tableau.

At Killisnoo, once, the anglers baited their lines and hung them overboard, as inducements to the codfish. The lunch-gong summoned them below, but they tied their lines and trusted to some fish swallowing the hooks while they were gone. When the first angler came up and touched his line, his face glowed, and he began pulling in the weighty prize. When the line left the water a bottle was dangling on the end of it, tied with a sailor's knot, and hook and bait intact. The second angler drew up a dried codfish, and then, when they looked around for the captain of the ship, he was nowhere to be found.

There are a few Kake Indians among the fishermen and workmen at Killisnoo, and their old home or proper domain is on Kouiu Island, further down Chatham Straits. The Kakes are outcasts and renegades among the tribes, and, from early days, there has been reason for the bad name given them. They were hostile, treacherous, and revengeful, and were dealt with warily by the old traders. In 1857 a war party paddled a thousand miles down to Puget Sound, and at Whidby Island murdered Mr. Ebey, a former collector of customs at Port Townsend, in retaliation for an indignity put upon their men in the preceding year. They carried his head back with them, and great war dances followed the return of the avenging Kakes.

At the north end of Kouiu Island are the ruins of the three villages destroyed during the Kake war, in 1869. The origin and incidents of this war are thus sketched in a private letter by Captain R. W. Meade, U. S. N., who commanded the U. S. S. *Saginaw*, at that time in Alaskan waters:—

"The war was due originally to the killing of a Kake Indian at Sitka by the sentry on guard at the lower end of the town. There had been some trouble with the Indians outside the stockade, and General Jeff C. Davis, who commanded the department, with headquarters at Sitka, had given orders to prevent all Indians from leaving Sitka during the night—I think it was New Year's night. He had asked me to co-operate with him, and my patrol-boats sent several canoes back to the Indian village. About daylight a canoe was discovered leaving the village. The soldier nearest the canoe hailed and ordered the canoe back, and as it did not go back after a third or fourth hail, fired, killing a Kake Indian. The canoe still continued to paddle off, and, though pursued by the boats of the *Saginaw*, that had seen the firing, escaped. Subsequently, in revenge for this, the Kake Indians murdered two Sitka traders, Messrs. Maugher and Walker, and General Davis determined to punish them by destroying their villages. I was asked to co-operate, and, although I think the trouble could have been avoided in the first place, yet, after the wanton murder of two innocent men, I felt it my duty to give the Kake tribe—a very ugly one—a lesson. We therefore took on board some twenty-five soldiers from the garrison at Sitka, and went to the Kake country. The Indians abandoned their villages on our approach, and three villages were destroyed by fire and shell. A stockaded fort was also destroyed by midshipman, now Lieutenant Bridges, of the *Saginaw*. The Indians were dismayed, and no further trouble, I believe, has occurred with them. There was no loss of life on either side—it was a bloodless war."

The Kakes have never returned to these villages, and in diminished numbers they roam the archipelago, creating trouble and disturbances wherever they draw up their canoes. Their visits are dreaded equally by the natives and whites, and Captain Beardslee peremptorily ordered them out of Sitka when several war canoes, filled with a visiting party, came abreast of the *rancherie*, shouting and singing their peculiar songs. Their unpleasant reputation has, doubtless, kept settlers away from Kouiu Island, and there is not yet as much as a salmon cannery or packing house on its shores. The island is over sixty miles long, with an irregular, indented shore, and wherever the surveyors have followed its lines they have seen forests of yellow cedar. This timber will, in time, make Kouiu and the adjoining island of Kuprianoff the most valuable land sections in this part of the Territory. The yellow cedar is said to be the only good ship timber on the Pacific coast, and is the only wood that can resist the teredo, which eats up the pine piles under wharves in two years from the time they are driven. The trees are found five and seven feet in diameter, and attain the height of one hundred and fifty feet, and the fine, closely grained, hard, yellow wood was once exported to China in large quantities by the Russians. The Chinese valued it for its fine, hard texture, and they carved it into chests and small articles, and exported it as camphor wood. Its odor is by some said to resemble sandal wood, and, by others, garlic, but it takes a beautiful satiny polish, and will be as valuable as a cabinet wood as for ship timber. Some of it that has been sent to Portland has been sold at seventy-five dollars a thousand feet, and Mr. Seward prized very highly the fine cedar that he carried home with him. As there has always been complaint of the quality of the Oregon timber, and vessels built of its pine could not be insured as A 1 but for three years, it may seem strange that no attempts have been made to utilize the vast forests of cedar scattered through the archipelago. Seven years ago a bill was introduced in Congress asking that one hundred thousand acres of timber land on Kouiu Island should be sold to a company, that guaranteed to establish a shipyard and build a vessel of twelve hundred tons burthen within two years. The same inscrutable reasons that for a long time prevented anything being done for the development of Alaska prevented the bill from becoming a law. Even the present act establishing a form of civil government does not make the Territory a land district, and nothing could seem more perverse than this action. Timber lands can neither be bought nor leased, and as settlers can in no way acquire an acre, there are few saw mills in the Territory, and their owners are guilty of stealing government timber, and liable to prosecution if the new officials press things to the finest point. Want of lumber has been a serious hindrance and obstacle to settlers, and the miners at Juneau had to pay freight on, and await the monthly consignments of, Oregon pine that were shipped to a country crowded with better timber.

CHAPTER XIX.

THE PRINCE OF WALES ISLAND.

Like Kouiu and Kuprianoff islands, the Prince of Wales Island is another home of the yellow or Alaska cedar. It was named by Vancouver, and when the Coast Survey changed his name of the George III. Archipelago to the Alexander Archipelago, this largest island of the group retained its former designation. It is from one hundred and fifty to two hundred miles long, and from twenty to sixty miles wide, but the surveys have never been complete enough to determine whether it is all one island or a group of islands. Great arms of the sea reach into the heart of the island, and dense forests of cedar cover its hills and dales. The salmon are found in the greatest numbers on every side of it, and the pioneer and most successful cannery and packing houses are on its shores. On account of its timber and its salmon, it was once proposed to declare the island a government reservation of ship timber for the use of the navy yards on the Pacific coast, and to lease the valuable fisheries. The very mention of Alaska has been provocative of roars of laughter in the houses of Congress, and though the reservation would have been larger than the State of New Jersey, and its value incalculable, the wits took their turn at the measure and nothing was done. A citizen of Alaska, who has chafed under the neglect and indignities put upon this Territory, made scathing comments upon the debates of both House and Senate, brought about by these cedar reservation bills and the bill for a Territorial government. His final shot was this: —

"If those Senators and Congressmen don't know any more about the tariff, and the other things that they help to discuss, than they do about Alaska, the Lord help the rest of the United States. Their ignorance of the commonest facts of geography would disgrace any little Siwash at the Fort Wrangell School. What have they paid for all these special government reports for, if they don't ever read them when they get ready to speak on a foreign subject, to say nothing of what can be found in the encyclopædias and geographies?"

These Alaskans are keenly critical of all that is written about their Territory, and they scan newspaper accounts with the sharpest eyes for an inaccuracy or a discrepancy. The statesmen who have assailed the Territory in speeches and debates in Congress are condemned with a certain thoroughness and sweep; and to introduce a copy of *The Congressional Record*, containing such efforts, causes even worse explosions than the one quoted. It was one of these revengeful jokers who laid the scheme for having an eminent senator introduce a bill to build a wagon road from Fort Wrangell to a point on the Canadian Pacific Railroad on the eastern slope of the Rocky Mountains. An appropriation of $100,000 was asked for, and every married citizen was to receive six hundred and forty acres of agricultural or grazing land in the Territory. As the contemplated highway would lead for a thousand miles across British Columbia, through the densest woods and over the roughest country, and from the island town of Fort Wrangell only ten leagues of the route would be within the Alaska boundaries, some of the joke can be discovered.

On the west shore of Prince of Wales Island there is a large salmon cannery and saw-mill at Klawak, belonging to Messrs. Sisson, Crocker, & Co., of San Francisco. It was established in 1878, and the shipments of salmon are made direct by their own schooners to San Francisco, or by their steam launch, which makes frequent trips to Kaigahnee and Fort Wrangell, the nearest post offices and landings of the mail steamer. In 1883 the Klawak cannery shipped 10,000 cases of salmon to San Francisco, and in 1884, 8,000 cases were sent below. The Klawak settlement is off the regular line of the steamer, and rarely visited by it, now that the cannery is well established and furnished with its own boats; but it is described as one of the many beautiful places in the archipelago where the silver salmon run in greatest numbers.

For salmon fisheries and salmon canneries there exists a perfect craze all along the Pacific coast, and from the Columbia River to Chilkat such establishments are projected for every possible place. At the most northern point of our cruise we picked up a piratical-looking man, in flannel shirt and tucked-up trousers, who had been sent to Alaska "to *prospect* for salmon," by the owners of one of the large canneries at Astoria, Oregon. This piscatorial prospector had for years been a pilot on the Columbia River, and this fact, together with his buccaneer air, made him quite a character on deck. The prospector was the kindest and best-natured man that ever lived, with a bushy head and beard, and a mild, twinkling blue eye. Months of strolling in the mud and moisture of Alaska soil had taught him to roll his trousers well up at the heel, and he continued that cautious habit after he came on board, often pacing the dry and spotless decks of the *Idaho* with his checked trousers rolled halfway to his knees, and the gay facings of red leather streaking his nether limbs like the insignia of the knightly order of the garter. Confidentially he said to the mate one day, "Did you notice the terrible cold I had when I came up with you? Well, it was all because my wife made me wear that — — white shirt." The sincerity and earnestness with which he said this sent his accidental listeners off convulsed, and the prospector's latest remarks passed current in the absence of daily papers and humorous columns.

Not all of the "salmon prospectors" are as worthy and reliable as this shipmate, and in their solitary quests they have time to gather and manufacture some fish stories that leave all the Frazer River yarns far behind. At every place that we touched we were shown or told about "the biggest liar in Alaska." These great prevaricators and embroiderers of the truth were not always in the salmon business, and quite as often were searching for coal or the precious metals. One pretty bay was famous as the residence of such a man, who had beguiled capitalists below into letting him sink $10,000 in a fishery. When the ship anchored off his lodge in the wilderness early one rainy morning, a hirsute man on shore ran down the beach, and, making a trumpet of his hands, conversed with the officers on deck. He had sent word previously that he had eighty barrels of salmon ready for shipment, but when the inquisitive men from the steamer went off to his packing house, not more than four hundred salmon lay pickling in the vats, with not a barrel ready. This Mulberry Sellers followed them back to the small boats, talking volubly all the way, and the last that we saw, as the anchor chains rattled in and the ship moved off, was the mendacious fisherman standing in the rain, and talking through his hand trumpet. "Captain! can't you wait a while?" was the farewell plea that we heard wafting over the water, and all of that afternoon in the cabin, while the rain pelted overhead, we were entertained with anecdotes of this same celebrity and other champion prevaricators of the Territory.

When we left Sitka on the *Ancon*, and went out over the rolling main and around Cape Ommaney, the first stopping-place was at the north end of the Prince of Wales Island, where a narrow winding channel, not more than twice the width of the ship's beam, leads into the beautiful basin of Red Bay.

This intricate little place was known to the Russian traders long ago, and called Krasnaia Bay, but it was only in 1884 that a packing-house was built and the shining silver salmon decoyed into seines. It is a beautiful little place, hidden away on the edge of the great island, and its air must be restful to the nerves. The beating of the ship's paddle-wheels could be heard for miles in such quiet landlocked waters, and the steamer's whistle gave warning of its presence long before it rounded the last bends of the bay. Nevertheless, there were no signs of life or excitement about the fishery, and the two men in sight and at work on the beach did not even turn their heads to look at the large ocean steamer bearing down towards them. No freight seemed ready, neither boats nor canoes put out, and the passengers longed to be listeners when the captain and purser went ashore in the first gig and held parley with the easy-going fishermen on the beach. When we followed in the next boats the spicy part of the interview was over, and we simply found that Red Bay was the most awful smelling place in Alaska, the beach a dirty quagmire covered with kelp and heads and tails of salmon, and the Indians a hard and fierce-looking set. The captain had only the pleasure of the scenery and the excitement of some skilful pilot practice for going in there, as the lone fishermen had no salmon ready to ship after all the requests for the steamer to call on the July trip.

Once out of the tortuous channel and along the shore some miles, we anchored at the mouth of Salmon Creek, where a lighter lay ready loaded at the packing-house, and three hundred and twenty-five barrels of salted salmon were towed out to the ship and put on board as the result of the first catch of the first year of this new fishery. There was an energetic proprietor running that establishment, and he welcomed the boat-load of visitors on shore and led them over a half-acre of shavings into the side door of the packing-house. A prying man of the party spied a great string of salmon trout on the floor and raised hysterical shrieks. "Oh! that's nothing," said the proprietor coolly, "a little mess that I caught for the captain of the ship. The creek is full of them out here. This Injun will get you some lines." A veritable war-whoop followed the announcement, and the anglers broke into a war-dance, circling at all hands round, doing the pigeon-wings and chains in such a frenzied manner that the astonished Indians crept up on the barrels and sat gaping and trembling in their blankets at the sight of their uncivilized white brethren.

The Indians brought the fish lines, with common hooks and small stones tied on for sinkers, and the anglers were rowed out in an old scow and anchored not fifty feet from the front of the packing-house. It was not artistic fishing with fancy flies, and anglers with patent reels and nets would have looked scorn at the little group steadily pulling in all the hungry trout that snapped at the bits of salmon or salmon eggs hung out to them. An old Indian and a small boy came paddling around in a leaky canoe, and were pressed into service to cut bait for the busy fishermen. As the trout flopped into the scow faster than one a minute, wild shouts rent the air, and the Siwash adjutants joined in the yells that would have frightened off anything else in scales but these untutored Alaska trout. The flapping fish splashed and spoiled the clothes of the fishermen, but they never heeded that, and a tally-keeper was installed on the flour bags and barrels at the end of the scow. The excitement was communicated to the idlers who had stayed on the ship, and soon a second boat put out for the fishing ground, full of wild-eyed anglers anxious to join in the carnival. They anchored near the scow, and their efforts were received with shouts of derision as they began pulling in devil-fish, toad-fish, sculpin, skate, and marine curios enough to stock a museum, before a single trout was hooked. The Indians came down and sat in solemn rows on the logs on shore to watch the crazy white fishermen, and they made picturesque groups that were repeated in the glassy mirror of water before them. One old fellow in a red blanket made a fine point of color against the thick golden-green wall of spruce-trees on the shore, and children and dogs gave a characteristic fringe to all the groups. When the last lighter put out for the ship the lines were wound up, and the tally-keeper on the flour bags read the record written on the barrel tops. The two men, one small boy, and the brave creature in six-button gloves who baited and tended her own hook, caught altogether one hundred and ten trout in the hour and a quarter at anchor in the old scow. The weight was sixty pounds, and the fishermen were wild with glee. The one fair angler and the tally-keeper having mopped the slimy boat and the pile of fish with their dresses, and then seated themselves on flour bags, had full view of the fishing scene photographed on every breadth of their gowns. "What shall I do with my dress?" asked one of them when she reached the calm and well-dressed company on deck, and a cheerful woman said briskly: "I guess you'd better fry it, now that it is dipped in batter."

Sailing southward through Clarence Straits, a trader long resident in the country told us of many Indian superstitions, among others repeating that of their belief that the aurora flames are the shadows of the spirits of dead warriors dancing in the sky, and that a great display of northern lights portends a war between the tribes.

The folders of the Pacific Coast Steamship Company head the notice of the Alaska route with the inspiring line; "Glaciers, Majestic Mountains, Inland Seas, Aurora Borealis, and Nightless Days." All of this official promise had come to pass according to schedule, with the exception of the aurora, and although the sky never grew dark, even at midnight, we clamored for one display of northern lights. The captain told us to wait and take the trip in December if we wanted to see the arches of flame spanning the sky, and jets of brilliant color flashing to the zenith like spray from a fountain. He further wrought our fancies to the highest pitch by his descriptions of the marvellous auroras that he had seen on his mid-winter cruises, and the dazzling moonlight effects, when each snow-covered peak and range shone and glistened like polished silver in the flood of light, and the still waters repeated the enchanted scene. Bright as the midnight sky was with the lingering twilight of the long day, we had an aurora that night as we steamed down along the shores of the Prince of Wales' Island. The pilot roused the enthusiasts to see the promised display in the northern sky, and the arches and rays of pale electric light were distinct enough to maintain the word of the steamship company. The stars twinkled in the ghostly gray vault overhead, and the wan, white light flashed and faded in fitful curves, broad rays and waving streamers, that rested like a vast halo above the brows of the grand mountains lying in black shadows at our left.

The inexorable law of ship's duty only permits it to linger at a harbor for the time necessary to load or unload cargo, or for the time specified in the mail contract, and in this same hard practical vein it makes little difference whether a place is reached by night or day. It is light enough these summer nights to carry on all outdoor work, and the rare visits of the steamer are enough to set all the inhabitants astir at any hour, while the constant excitement of the trip, and the strange spell of the midnight light, makes the tourist indifferent to his established customs. Once on the *Idaho* we were at anchor in Naha Bay only from five to six o'clock in the morning, but it was barely two o'clock on a clear, still morning when the rattling of the *Ancon's* anchor chains again broke the silence of Naha Bay. Although we lay there for five hours, few passengers could be roused to watch the sunrise clouds, the leaping salmon, and the brilliant green and gold of the sun-touched woods and water. In the dew and freshness of the early morning, Naha Bay was more lovely than ever, and the little black canoes seemed to float in emerald air, so clearly green were the calm waters under them.

For another perfect summer afternoon the *Ancon* lay at the wharf in Kasa-an Bay, and, in the mellow, Indian summer sunshine, we roamed the beach, buying the last remaining baskets, bracelets, pipes, and spoons of the Indians, and pulling hard at the amateur's oar as we trailed across the bay in small boats to watch the fishermen cast and draw the net. The huge skeleton wheels on which the nets are dried had raised many comments at every fishery, but we had never been lucky enough to catch the men doing anything but winding the nets on these reels to dry. The fishermen had dropped the weighted net when we reached the cove on the opposite shore, and the line of bobbing wooden floats showed how this fence in the water was being gradually drawn in, and the area limited as it crept toward the beach. The sun was hot on the water, and the far away peal of the lunch gong, sounding in the stillness of the mountain bay, caused us to turn back to the ship before all the shining salmon were drawn up and thrown into the scows. The fascination of the water was too great to resist, and in the warmer sun of the afternoon we followed the shores of Baronovich's little inlet, rowing close in where the menzie and merton spruce formed a dense golden-green wall and threw clear shadows and reflections upon the water. We dipped into each little shaded inlet, posed in the boat for the amateur's camera to preserve the scene, and floated slowly over the wonderland that lay beneath the keel. It was with real regret that we saw the last barrel of salmon dropping into the hold, and, steaming down the beautiful bay in full sunshine, had a glimpse of the inlet where the village of Karta and its *totem* poles lies, before we turned into Clarence Strait.

INDIAN PIPE.

CHAPTER XX.
HOWKAN OR KAIGAHNEE.

Thus in its commercial mission the steamer wandered among the islands, touching at infant settlements and trading posts, and anchoring before Indian villages with traditions and *totem* poles centuries old. Rounding the southern end of the Prince of Wales Island to Dixon Entrance, the fog and mist crept upon us as we neared the ocean. It was a wet and gloomy afternoon when the *Idaho* anchored in the little American Bay on Dall Island, not more than a mile from Howkan, an ancient settlement of the Kaigahnee Haidas and a place of note in the archipelago. Howkan has more *totem* poles than any other village, and is one of the most interesting places on the route; but as Kaigahnee Strait before the village is thickly set with reefs, and swift currents and strong winds sweep through the narrow channel, it is dangerous for vessels to go near. The fur traders used always to anchor in the little bays on the opposite shore, and to one of them, American Bay, the Northwest Trading Company was about to move its stores. Only a small clearing had been made, and two buildings put up, at the time of that first visit, and it looked a very dreary and forlorn place, as we picked our way about in the rain, climbing over logs and sinking in the wet moss.

After the cargo had been discharged, the captain obligingly took the ship over to the nearest safe anchorage off the village, and we had a warm welcome on shore from the five white residents. For two years the missionary's wife and sister had met but one white woman, until the boatload of ladies went ashore from the *Idaho*, and overwhelmed them with a superfluity. We all gathered in the trader's house and store at first, and these two white residents of Howkan were none other than the Russian Count Z—— and his pretty black-haired Countess, a couple interesting in themselves and their history, and all the more extraordinary in their being found in this remote end of the world. The Count is a man of fascinating address and appearance, polished manners and cultivated tastes, and, being exiled for Nihilistic tendencies, he chose Alaska in preference to Siberia, and made his way across the friendly chain of islands to "the home of the free and the land of the brave." He married a charming Russian lady at Sitka, and, with the calm of a philosophic mind and the patience of a patriotic heart, he waits the time when amnesty or anarchy shall permit his return to holy Russia. Adversity and years in the savage wilderness have not robbed these people of their ease and grace of manner, and the handsome Count had all the charm and spirit that must have distinguished him in the gay world of his native capital. The little Countess was unfeignedly glad to see a few fellow creatures, and in the dusk of that dreary, wet night welcomed us to her simple home, and showed us her treasures, from the big blue-eyed baby to a wonderfully painted dance blanket. When we expressed curiosity at the latter, the pretty Russian seized the great piece of fringed and painted deerskin, and, wrapping it about her shoulders, threw her head back with fine pose, and stood as an animated tableau in the dusk and firelight of her Alaska chalet. "This was a *cultus potlatch*," she said, with a dainty accent, as she explained the way it came into her possession, and we all laughed at the way the Chinook jargon interprets that *dilettante* word as meaning "worthless." The Countess told us a better one about her asking a trader what had become of a man who used to live at Sitka, and the trader answering her that he was "*cultusing* around here somewhere." This Russian family was most interesting to us, and, setting aside all traditions of his rank, the Nihilist Count talked business with the captain in a most American manner, and, but for the inherent accent and air, a listener might have taken him for the most practical of business men, whose whole life had been spent in commercial marts, or as agent for a great trading company.

All of these kind people helped to show us about the place, and give us bits of local history on the way, and from them we learned that the Indian name Howkan means a fallen stone, and this village was called so on account of a peculiar boulder that lay on the beach. Like other places in Alaska, it has several names, and several ways of spelling each of them. The traders call it oftener Kaigahnee than Howkan, although old Kaigahnee, the original village of that name, is many miles distant from this place of the fallen stone. The missionaries named it "Jackson" in honor of the Rev. Sheldon Jackson, the projector and manager of Presbyterian missions in Alaska, and the Post Office Department recognized it as "Haida Mission" when the blanks and cancelling stamps were sent out for the small post-office. A request was made by the mission people to have the place put down as Jackson on the new charts, since issued by the Coast Survey, but the commander of the surveying steamer opposed it as an act of vandalism, and on the maps it still retains the harsh old Indian name by which it has been known for centuries.

The village fronts on two crescent beaches, and a long, rocky point running out into the water fairly divides it into two villages, so separate are their water fronts. A fleet of graceful Haida canoes was drawn up on the first and larger beach, all of them carefully filled with grass and covered over, and their owners joined in receiving the visitors, and accompanied us on our sight-seeing tour. The houses at Howkan are large and well built, and the village is remarkably clean. Some of the chiefs have weatherboarded their houses and put in glass windows and hinged doors, but before or beside nearly every house rises the tall, ancestral *totem* poles that constitute the glory of the place.

TOTEM POLES AT KAIGAN OR HOWKAN.

Skolka, one of the great chiefs, has a large house guarded by two *totem* poles, and at his offer the house had been occupied for two years as a school-room by the mission teacher. A flagstaff and a skeleton bell-tower were added to the exterior decorations of his house in consequence, and Skolka was the envy of all the Kaigahnees. Skolka is a wise and liberal chieftain, and a member of the Eagle family. Effigies of that totemic bird surmount the poles before his house, and on one pole appears the whiskered face of a white man, capped by an eagle, and finished with the images of two children wearing the steeple-crowned mandarin hats of the Tyees. Skolka explains these images as telling the story of one of his ancestors, who was a famous woman of the Eagle clan. She went out for salmon eggs one day, and when she drew up her canoe on the beach upon her return, she had several baskets filled. Not seeing her two little children, she called to them, but they ran and hid. Later she called them again, and they answered her from the woods with the voices of crows. Her worst fears were realized when she found that a white man, "a Boston man," had carried them off in a ship. These two orphans never returned to their people. Such is the simple kidnapping story that has been handed down in Skolka's family for generations, and this whiskered face on the *totem* pole is said to be almost the only instance of a Boston man attaining immortality in these picture-writings.

THE CHIEF'S RESIDENCE AT KAIGAN, SHOWING TOTEM POLES.

"Mr. John" is another fine-looking chief, who dresses in civilized style, and is rather proud of his advanced ways of living and thinking. He lives in a large house near Skolka, and has a grand old *totem* pole before his doorway. In his queer idiom he tells one, "I am a Crow, but my wife is a Whale;" and as Mrs. John is of generous build, there is lurking sarcasm in his statement.

The deceased chief, Mr. Jim, left some fine *totem* poles behind him, and on the second beach of the village there is a semicircle of ancient moss-grown *totem* poles standing guard over ruined and deserted houses. The mosses, the lichens, and the vines cling tenderly to these strange old monuments of the people, and, in the crevices of the carvings, grasses, ferns, and even young trees have taken root and thrive. Back in the dense undergrowth rise the mortuary poles, the carved *totems* and emblems that mark the graves of dead and gone Haidas. Skolka's father and uncles have fine images over their burial boxes, and from the head of the Eagle on one of these mortuary columns, a small fir-tree, taking root, has grown to a height of eight or ten feet. In this burying ground there are large boxes filled with the bones and ashes of those said to have died when the great epidemics raged among the islands a half century ago.

We found the Howkan ship-yard under a large shed, and the canoe builder showed us two cedar canoes that were nearly completed. The high-beaked Haida canoes are slender and graceful as Venetian gondolas, and the small, light canoes that they use in hunting sea otter are marvels of boat-building. The shapely skiffs that the boat builder showed us had been hewn from single logs of red cedar, and were ready to be braced and steamed into their graceful curving lines. Our admiration of the work caused him to offer a light, otter-hunter's canoe for fifty dollars, but not one of the company made a purchase. In one house we found a paralyzed man lying on a couch in the middle of the one great room, and the relatives gathered about him soon brought out their treasures and offered them for sale.

HALIBUT HOOK.

Like all of their tribe, these Kaigahnee Haidas are an intelligent and superior people, skilled in the arts of war and the crafts of peace, and their carvers have wrought matchless *totem* poles, canoes, bowls, spoons, halibut clubs and hooks, from time immemorial. These carvings show finer work and better ideas than the art relics of the other tribes, and in silver work they quite surpass the rest of the Thlinkets; although it is now claimed that they are not Thlinkets, differing from them materially in their language and traditions, while they have the same totemic system, familiar spirits, and customs. The Haida women were all adorned with beautifully made bracelets, and the superiority of Haida workmanship and designs is proven by the way that the Indians, even at Sitka, boast of their bracelets being Haida work. Kenowin is the chief silversmith, and his daughter wore a pair of broad gold bracelets carved with the Eagle *totem*. Gold is very rarely worn by the Indians, and they hardy seem to value the yellow metal, although some Haida silversmiths have worked in jewellers' stores in Victoria successfully, and learned the processes of acid treatments. The Haida rules of art, by which they conventionalize any animal they depict, are very exact, and on the large bracelet, shown in a previous illustration, the cinnamon bears represented as advancing in profile are joined in one full, grinning face which is recognized as the Haida crest. Their totemic Eagle has now degenerated into a base copy of the bird on American coins, but otherwise their art rules and traditions are unperverted. The key and original idea in many of their designs is the strange marking like a peacock's eye found on the back of the skate fish or sculpin, and besides carving it on all their solid belongings, they tattoo the emblem on their bodies.

These Kaigahnees have a curious tradition, related to us by the resident teacher, that quite resembles the biblical story of the ark and the flood. One old Indian now claims to have the bark rope which held the anchor of the big canoe when it rested on the high mountain back of Howkan. They have also a story resembling that of Lot's wife, only Sodom and Gomorrah were on Forrester Island, and a brother and sister, fleeing from a pestilence, were turned to stone, because the woman looked back while crossing the river. Their houses were petrified as well, and the petrified bodies of the disobedient ones still stand in the river to tell the tale.

When Wiggin's storms were being promised to the whole North American continent, in March, 1882, a white man at Kasa-an Bay read the prophecies, and explained them to the Indians. The warning spread rapidly from island to island, and at Howkan the natives began moving their things to the high ground, and were carrying up water and provisions for one whole afternoon. They believed that the promised tidal wave was coming, and at the time set for the storm, began to say, "Victoria all gone." There was a heavy storm outside that March night, and the agent of the trading company, returning from the Klinquan fishery in a whale-boat, was drowned by a wave upsetting the boat as he let go the tiller to furl the sail.

It was at Port Bazan, across Dall Island, that one of the Kaigahnees, whom we saw, found the remains of Paymaster Walker, who was lost with the steamer *George S. Wright*, in February, 1873. The loss of the *Wright* was one of the tragedies of the sea, and is still a current topic in Alaska. The steamer left Sitka on its return trip to Portland with several army officers and their families and residents on board. It was last seen at Cordova Bay, on the south end of Prince of Wales Island, and, in the face of warnings, the captain put out to sea in a heavy storm,—as he was hurrying to Portland for his wedding. It is supposed that the ship foundered, or struck a rock in Queen Charlotte Sound. The most terrible anxiety prevailed as week after week went by, with no tidings of the *Wright*, and the feeling was intensified when the rumor was started that it had been wrecked near a village of Kuergefath Indians, and that the survivors had been tortured and put to death. Two years after the disappearance of the *Wright*, the body of Major Walker was found in Port Bazan, recognizable only by fragments of his uniform, that had been held to him by a life-preserver. Other remains and fragments of the wreck were then found in the recesses of the ocean shores of the island, and the mystery of the *Wright* was at last solved.

Further up this coast, beyond the Klawock cannery, the mission has a branch station and a saw-mill, and, in time, will establish a school in this Shakan Island.

On my second visit to Kaigahnee Straits, the *Ancon* dropped anchor at two o'clock in the morning, and it was up and off again before five o'clock. A few enthusiasts did manage to row over to Howkan and back, but the rest of us were contented with one sleepy glance at the little settlement that, in a year's time, had surrounded the Northwest Trading Company's stores in American Bay. It was with great regret that we woke again to find the ship sailing over the most placid of waters, as it coursed up Dixon Entrance. It touched at Cape Fox, where we enjoyed the last of our delights and experiences on Alaska shores, stopped in a twilight rain at Tongass, and then slipped across the boundary line at night, and gave us all over again those enchanting days along the British Columbia coast.

CHAPTER XXI.

THE METLAKATLAH MISSION.

On occasional trips the steamer anchors off Metlakatlah, the model mission-station of the northwest coast, and an Arcadian village of civilized Indians, built round a bay on the Chimsyan Peninsula, in British Columbia. Metlakatlah is just below the Alaska boundary line, and but a little way south of Fort Simpson, the chief Hudson Bay Company trading post of the region, where the great canoe market, and the feasts and dances of the Indians, enliven that centre of trade each fall.

It was a rainy morning when the *Idaho* anchored off Metlakatlah, and the small boats took us through the drizzle and across a gentle ground-swell to the landing wharf at the missionary village. We were met there by Mr. Duncan, one of the noblest men that ever entered the mission field. He left mercantile life to take up this work, and was sent out by the English Church Missionary Society in 1857. He spent the first four years in working among the Indians at Fort Simpson, but the evils and temptations surrounding such a place quite offset his efforts, and he decided to go off by himself and gather the Indians about him at some place where they would be safe from other influences. Fifty Chimsyans started with him to found the village of Metlakatlah, and, in the twenty-odd years, they have built up a model town that they have reason to be proud of. When they first went there, a strip of the land was marked off for church purposes, and the rest of it divided among the Indians. It was considered a doubtful experiment at first, but Mr. Duncan put his whole heart and soul into the enterprise, and every Indian who went with him signed a temperance pledge, agreed to give up their medicine-men as advisers in sickness, and to do no work on the Sabbath. His faith has been proven in the results attained, and the self-respecting, self-supporting community at Metlakatlah proves that the Indian can be civilized as well as educated in one generation, if the right man and the right means are employed.

At the end of twenty-three years there is a well-laid-out village, with two-story houses, sidewalks, and street lamps. A large Gothic church has been built, with a comfortable rectory adjoining, and around the village green a school-house, a public hall, and a store are prominent buildings. All of these structures have been built by the Indians, and, with their own saw-mill and planing-mill, they have turned out the lumber and woodwork required for the public buildings and their own houses. Mr. Duncan has taught them all these necessary arts, working with them himself, and dividing the profits of their labors among the Indians. Under his management the Indians have established their cannery and store as a joint-stock company, and these once savage islanders understand the scheme, and draw their dividends as gravely as if their ancestors had always done so before them. The cannery is a model of neatness, the salmon being headed and cleaned on an anchored boat far off shore, and brought to the cannery all ready to be cut and fitted into tins. Everything is done by the Indians themselves, from making the cans to filling, soldering, heating, varnishing, labeling, and packing, and the Metlakatlah salmon bring the highest price in the London market, and each year handsome dividends are paid to the islanders. An average of six thousand cases are shipped every year, and each visitor that morning bought a can of the Skeena River salmon to carry off as a souvenir of Metlakatlah.

The women have been taught to spin and weave the fleece of the mountain goat into heavy cloths, shawls, and blankets. Boots, shoes, ropes, and leather are also made at Metlakatlah, and there is a good carpenter shop in the town. A telephone connects the village store with the saw-mill a few miles distant, and the Indians ring up the men at the other end of the wire, and "hello" to their brother Chimsyans in the most matter-of-fact manner. The steam-launch belonging to the cannery is engineered by one of their number, and the village compares favorably with any of the small saw-mill settlements of whites on Puget Sound.

While we wandered about the village under the escort of Mr. Duncan and his faithful David, the members of the brass band gathered themselves together and played "Marching Through Georgia," "Yankee Doodle," and other of our national anthems in honor of the American visitors. Twenty stalwart Indians comprise the full band, and, although nearly half of the musicians were off salmon fishing, those left did some most excellent playing on horn, cornet, and trombone, and sent farewell strains over the water as we got into the small boats and were pulled away to the ship. The Indians keep a visitors' house at the landing for the entertainment of friends in the adjoining tribes, and on the night preceding our arrival there had been a grand banquet and ball in honor of some canoe-loads of Haidas, who had come to pass a few days at these guest-houses of Metlakatlah. We found the Haidas looking much dilapidated on the morning after the ball, and among the picturesque groups sitting about the great square fireplace there was the most beautiful Indian maiden seen on the coast. The Haida beauty had a warm, yellow skin, with a damask bloom on her cheeks, a pair of large, soft, black eyes, and dazzling teeth. She gave a shy smile, and dropped her eyes before the admiring gaze and the exclamations of the party, and the susceptible young men from the ship immediately offered to stop off and stay with Mr. Duncan for a while. The Haidas had many curious things with them, and evinced a proper desire to make trade. One woman wore a pair of wide, gold bracelets, engraved with the totemic eagle and the Haida crest, and, putting her price at eighty dollars, sat stoical and silent through all the offers of smaller sums. They had fine silver bracelets, horn spoons, and carved trifles of copper and wood with them, but the desirable things were some miniature *totem* poles carved out of black slate stone, and inlaid with pieces of abalone shell to represent green and glistening eyes for each heraldic monster. These little *totem* poles are made of a soft slate found near Skidegate on the Queen Charlotte Islands. When first quarried it is very soft and easily worked, but hardens in a short time, and will crack if exposed to the sun or heat. It takes a fine polish, and for the small slate columns, fourteen and eighteen inches high, the Indians asked seven and ten dollars. We afterwards saw dozens and scores of these slate *totems* at the curio stores in Victoria, and though there seemed to be a sufficient supply of them for all the tourists of a season, the prices ranged from twenty to eighty dollars, and for plaques and boxes of carved slate the demand was proportionately higher.

It was with real regret that we parted with Mr. Duncan at the wharf, and it was not until we were well over the water that we learned of the serpent or the skeleton in this paradise. Though Metlakatlah might rightly be considered Mr. Duncan's own particular domain, and the Indians have proved their appreciation of his unselfish labors by a love and devotion rare in such races, his plainest rights have been invaded and trouble brewed among his people. Two years ago a bishop was appointed for the diocese, which includes Fort Simpson, Metlakatlah, and a few other missions. Fort Simpson is the older and larger mission settlement, and the higher officers of the church have always resided there, but Bishop Ridley, disapproving of Mr. Duncan's Low Church principles, went to Metlakatlah and took possession as a superior officer. Mr. Duncan moved from the rectory, and the bishop took charge of the church services. In countless ways a spirit of antagonism was raised that almost threatened a war at one time. The bishop informed the Indians that their store and warehouse was situated on ground belonging to the church. Instead of compromising, or leaving it there under his jurisdiction, the matter-of-fact Metlakatlans went in a body, pulled down the building, and set it up outside the prescribed limits. In endeavoring to prevent this, the bishop was roughly handled, and as he appreciated the hostile spirit of the greatest part of the community he sent to Victoria, asking the protection of a British man-of-war. The whole stay of the bishop has been marked by trouble and turbulence, and these scandalous disturbances in a Christian community cannot fail to have an influence for evil, and undo some of the good work that has been done there. Mr. Duncan made no reference to his troubles during the morning that we spent at Metlakatlah, and his desire that we should see and know what his followers were capable of, and understand what they had accomplished for themselves, gave us to infer that everything was peace and happiness in the colony. One hears nothing but praise of Mr. Duncan up and down the coast, and can understand the strong partisanship he inspires among even the roughest people. His face alone is a passport for piety, goodness, and benevolence anywhere, and his honest blue eyes, his kindly smile, and cheery manner go straight to the heart of the most savage Indian. His dusky parishioners worship him, as he well deserves, and in his twenty-seven years among them they have only the unbroken record of his kindness, his devotion, his unselfish and honorable treatment of them. He found them drunken savages, and he has made them civilized men and Christians. He has taught them trades, and there has seemed to be no limit to this extraordinary man's abilities. When his hair had whitened in this noble, unselfish work, and the fruits of his labor had become apparent, nothing could have been more cruel and unjust than to undo his work, scatter dissension among his people, and make Metlakatlah a reproach instead of an honor to the society which has sanctioned such a wrong. An actual crime has been committed in the name of Religion, by this persistent attempt to destroy the peace and prosperity of Metlakatlah and drive away the man who founded and made that village what it was. British Columbia is long and broad, and there are a hundred places where others can begin as Mr. Duncan began, and where the bishop can do good by his presence. If it was Low Church doctrines that made the Metlakatlah people what they were a few years since, all other teachings should be given up at mission stations. Discord, enmity, and sorrow have succeeded the introduction of ritualism at Metlakatlah, and though it cannot fairly be said to be the inevitable result of such teachings, it would afford an interesting comparison if the Ritualists would go off by themselves and establish a second Metlakatlah as a test.

A later expression of opinion on the troubles of Metlakatlah appears in the last annual report (1884) to the Dominion Government, by Colonel Powell, Superintendent of Indians in British Columbia. He writes as follows: —

"I am exceedingly sorry to state that serious trouble and the most unhappy religious rancor still exists at Metlakatlah, dividing the Indians, and causing infinite damage to Christianity in adjacent localities, where sides are taken with one or other of the contending parties. The retirement of either or both would seem the only true solution of the difficulties, and if the latter alternative is not desirable, and as fully nine tenths of the people are unanimous and determined in their support of Mr. Duncan, the withdrawal of the agents of the society to more congenial headquarters would, I think, be greatly in the interests of all concerned. Since the schism has occurred, the larger following of Mr. Duncan have resolved themselves into an independent society, with that gentleman as their guide and leader. The forms of the Anglican Church have been discarded, and they have designated themselves 'The Christian Church of Metlakatlah,' each member of which subscribes to a declaration pledging themselves to exclusively follow the teachings of the Bible as the rule of faith, and that they will, to the utmost of their power, prevent any divisions among the villagers, and do their utmost to promote the spiritual and temporal prosperity of the community. This association includes all the young and active residents of the village, hence they are all enthusiastic and determined in their desire for success. In addition to the large store, which, I was told, belonged to the Indians, and was a co-operative arrangement, Mr. Duncan has devoted his spare energies to the establishment of a salmon cannery, which, he informed me, was placed upon the same footing. This has afforded employment for a great majority of the inhabitants, and has kept them so busy for the last few months that happily they have had no time to give to contention. The secret of Mr. Duncan's great popularity with the Indians at Metlakatlah is his desire and fondness for inaugurating industries, which, after all, is the strongest bond that can be made to unite these people. The present difficulties, however, at Metlakatlah cannot continue much longer without culminating in serious consequences, means to avert which, of whatever nature they may be, should be promptly and effectually enforced."

CHAPTER XXII.
HOMEWARD BOUND.

Life on the waveless arms of the ocean has a great fascination for one on these Alaska trips, and crowded with novelty, incidents, and surprises as each day is, the cruise seems all too short when the end approaches. One dreads to get to land again and end the easy, idle wandering through the long archipelago. A voyage is but one protracted marine picnic and an unbroken succession of memorable days. Where in all the list of them to place the red letter or the white stone puzzles one. The passengers beg the captain to reverse the engines, or boldly turn back and keep up the cruise until the autumn gales make us willing to return to the region of earthly cares and responsibilities, daily mails and telegraph wires. The long, nightless days never lose their spell, and in retrospect the wonders of the northland appear the greater. The weeks of continuous travel over deep, placid waters in the midst of magnificent scenery might be a journey of exploration on a new continent, so different is it from anything else in American travel. Seldom is anything but an Indian canoe met, for days no signs of a settlement are seen along the quiet fiords, and, making nocturnal visits to small fisheries, only the unbroken wilderness is in sight during waking hours. The anchoring in strange places, the going to and fro in small boats, the queer people, the strange life, the peculiar fascination of the frontier, and the novelty of the whole thing, affect one strongly. Each arm of the sea and the unknown, unexplored wilderness that lies back of every mile of shore continually tempt the imagination.

Along these winding channels in "the sea of mountains," only the rushing tides ever stir the surface of the waters where the surveyor's line drops one hundred, two hundred, and four hundred fathoms without finding bottom, and the navigator casts his lead for miles without finding anchorage. All piloting is by sight, and when clouds, fogs, or the long winter nights of inky darkness obscure the landmarks, the fog whistle is kept going according to regulation, and the ship's course determined by the echoes flung back from the hidden mountains. Such feats in time of fog gave zest to ship life, and Captain Carroll, who performed them, was accused of being the original of Mark Twain's man, who made a collection of echoes. At every place in Alaska he had a particular echo that he brought out with the cannon's salute. At Fort Wrangell the hills repeated the shot five times; and at Juneau it came back seven times, before dying away in a long roll. At Sitka there was the din of a naval battle when the cannon was fired point blank at Mt. Verstovaia, and up among the glaciers, the echoes drowned the thunder of the falling ice.

Captain Carroll, for so many years in command of the mail steamer on this Alaska route, is a genius in his way, and a character, a typical sea captain, a fine navigator, and a bold and daring commander, whose skill and experience have carried his ships through the thousand dangers of the Alaska coast. He is a strict disciplinarian, whose authority is supreme, and the etiquette of the bridge and quarter-deck is severely maintained. When he leaves the deck and lays aside his official countenance, the children play and tumble over him and cling to him, and he is a merciless joker with the elders. He is possessed of a fund of stories and adventures that would make the fortune of a wit or *raconteur* on shore, and their momentary piquancy, as of salt water and stiff winds, makes it impossible for one to repeat them well. His fish stories are unequalled, and the despair of the most accomplished anglers. He leaves nothing undone to promote the pleasure and comfort of his passengers, who are in a sense his guests during the three or four weeks of a summer pleasure trip, and gold watches and several sets of resolutions have expressed appreciation of his courtesy and attentions to travellers. He is deeply interested in the welfare of the region that he has seen slowly awakening to the march of progress, and, being so identified with these early days and the development of the territory, is destined to live as an historic figure in Alaskan annals.

The pilot, Captain George, is everyone's friend, and his patience and good nature have to stand the strain of a steady questioning and cross-examination from the beginning to the end of a cruise. He is appealed to for all the heights, depths, distances, and names along the route; and finally, when everyone has bought a large Hydrographic Office chart of Alaska, Captain George is asked to mark out the ship's course through the maze of island channels. He has been pilot for twenty years on the northwest coast, and Mr. Seward and many others who saw the country under his guidance speak of him as a Russian. As his early home in "the States" was at Oshkosh, one can understand how that foreign-sounding name misled people. He, as well as all of the ship's officers, keeps a log of each cruise, and Captain George has furnished many notes and notices for the Coast Survey publications, and helps the memory of the tourists, who keep some of the most remarkable journals and diaries for the first few days of the cruise.

A character in the lower rank on one trip was the captain's boy, "John," a faithful henchman and valet, whose devotion and attachment to his master were quite wonderful. John is a Swede by birth, and his pale-blue eyes, fair complexion, and light hair were offset by a continuous array of spotlessly white jackets and ties. In the most Northern latitudes John would trip about the deck with his spry and jaunty tread, clad in these snowy habiliments of the tropics, and after a ramble among Indian lodges on shore, John would appear to our enraptured eyes as the very apotheosis of cleanliness and starchy perfection. At luncheon one day John set two pies before the captain, and announcing them as "mince and apple," withdrew deferentially behind his master's chair. "Which is the apple pie, John?" asked the captain, as he held a knife suspended over a disk of golden crust. "The starboard pie, sir," said John respectfully, and with a seriousness that robbed the thing of any intention.

Two deck passengers that enlivened the return trip of the *Idaho* were small black bear cubs four or five months old. There was always high revel on the hurricane deck during the "dog watches" when the bears were fed, and cakes and lumps of sugar from the cabin table enticed them to play pranks. The treacherous young bruin bought at Chilkat grew fat on the voyage, and was twice the size of a little stunted cub bought of a trader at Fort Wrangell. The Chilkat cub climbed the rigging like a born sailor after a fortnight's training, but much teasing made him surly and suspicious, and he would run for the ratlines at sight of a man. For the ladies, who fed them on sugar and salmon berries, both bears showed a great fondness, and the two clumsy pets would trot around the deck after them as tamely as kittens, and stand up and beg for sugar plainly. The little Fort Wrangell bear would crawl up on a bench beside one, and make plaintive groans until it was petted, and it would sun itself contentedly there for hours. They were amiable playfellows together, but they were puzzled and bewitched by the agile little toy-terrier "Toots," who lived on an afghan in the captain's cabin. That aristocratic little mite of a dog delighted to caper around and bewilder the bears with his quick motions, and it was a funny by-play to watch these young animals together. One evening in the Gulf of Georgia, we lingered on deck to watch a stormy, crimson sunset, and after that, when the moon rose like a fiery ball from the water, and faded to pale gold and silver in the zenith, the company grew musical and sang in enthusiastic chorus all the good old sea songs. With the first notes of the music the bears came pattering out, and, circling gravely before the singers, lay down, folded their forepaws before them in the most human attitude and listened attentively to "Nancy Lee" and "John Brown." Two young fawns, caught as they were swimming the channel near Fort Wrangell one morning, were quartered on the lower deck. In captivity their soft black eyes were sadly pathetic, and they were visited daily and fed on all the dainties for deer that could be gathered on shore. Foxes, strange birds, Esquimaux dogs, and other pets have been passengers on the return trips of the steamer, and the officers of the ship have done their share in presenting animals to different city gardens and parks.

As the end of Vancouver Island drew near, the scenery of the British Columbia coast gained in beauty, with the prospect of so soon losing our wild surroundings. After leaving Metlakatlah there was not a sign of civilization for two days, and in spite of Buffon and Henry James, Jr., we grew the more enthusiastic over the "brute nature" that so offends those worldlings. The days were clear, but one night the fog promised to be so dense that the ship made an outside run from the Milbank to Queen Charlotte Sound, over waters so still that none suspected that we had left the narrow inside channels.

We never met the oulikon, or "candle fish" of this coast, except as we saw the piscatorial torch at grocers' stores in Victoria; but we sailed for four hours through a school of herring one afternoon, as we neared the Vancouver shore. Sharks were following them by dozens, and sea-gulls flew overhead, ready to swoop upon the unlucky herring that jumped to the enemy in the air to escape the one in the water. Both times on the return voyage we slipped through Seymour Narrows without knowing it, so smoothly was the water boiling at the flood tide, and so absorbed were we once in the soft poetic sunset that finally left a glowing wall of orange in the west, against which the ragged forest line of the summits and the mountain masses were as if carved in jet. Looking upwards, even the masts and spars were sharply silhouetted against the glorious amber zenith, and it was hours before it faded to the pure violet sky of such midsummer nights.

Besides Mt. St. Elias, the Alaska passengers always beg for a view of Bute Inlet, which opens from the network of channels there at the head of the Gulf of Georgia, and runs far into the heart of the mountain range that borders the mainland shore. We hung over the captain's charts of the inlet with the greatest interest, and, with his explanations, imagination could picture that grand fiord, not a quarter of a mile in width, and with vertical mountain walls that rise from four thousand feet at the entrance, to eight thousand feet above the water's level at the head of the inlet. Soundings of four hundred fathoms are marked on the chart, and with cascades and glaciers pouring into the chasm, little is left for a scenic artist to supply. A trail was once cleared from the head of the inlet to the Cariboo mining district on the Frazer river, and surveys were made looking to a terminus of the Canadian Pacific Railroad, but both have been abandoned, and Bute Inlet is not accessible by any established line of boats. Lord Dufferin and the Marquis of Lorne visited it on British men-of-war, and carried its fame to England, by extolling its scenery as the grandest on any coast. When Lord Dufferin had gone further up and into Alaska, he made his prophecy that this northwest coast, with its long stretch of protected waters, would in time become one of the favorite yachting grounds of the world.

If the beautiful Gulf of Georgia is wonderland and dreamland by day, it is often fairyland by night, and there was an appropriate finale to the last cruise, when the captain came down the deck at midnight and rapped up the passengers. "Wake up! The whole sea is on fire" said the commander. We roused and flung open stateroom doors and windows to see the water shining like a sheet of liquid silver for miles on every side. The water around us was thickly starred with phosphorescence, and at a short distance, the million points of lights mingled in a solid stretch of miles of pale, unearthly flame. It lighted the sky with a strange reflection, and the shores, which there, off Cape Lazro, are twenty miles away, seemed near at hand in the clear, ghostly light. A broad pathway of pale-green, luminous water trailed after us, and the paddle-wheels threw off dazzling cascades. Under the bows the foaming spray washed high on the black hull, and cast long lines of unearthly, greenish white flame, that illuminated the row of faces hanging over the guards as sharply as calcium rays. A bucket was lowered and filled with the water, and the marvel of the shining sea was repeated in miniature on deck, each time the water was stirred. It was a most wonderful display, and many, who had seen this glory of the seas in the tropics, declared that they had never seen phosphorescent waters more brilliant than those of the Gulf of Georgia.

With such an illumination and marine fireworks we brought the last cruise virtually to an end, and another morning found the ship tied to the same coal wharf in Departure Bay. The pleasure travellers laid their plans for other trips, and in a few days the company was scattered.

Those who went up the Frazer River to its cañons said later: "The best of the Frazer only equals Grenville Channel, and the dust and heat are intolerable after the northern coast."

Those who went down past Mt. Tacoma, Mt. Hood, and Mt. Shasta, and into the Yosemite, said: "If we had only seen these places first, and not after the Alaska trip."

All agreed in the summing up of an enthusiast, who had travelled the fairest scenes of Europe and his own country, and wrote: "Take the best of the Hudson and the Rhine, of Lake George and Killarney, the Yosemite and all Switzerland, and you can have a faint idea of the glorious green archipelago and the Alaska coast."

My first journey on the *Idaho* in 1883 ended with our staying by the ship, and going around outside from Puget Sound to the Columbia River, and then we were tied up for three days at the government wharf at Tongue Point, near Astoria, while three hundred tons of Wellington coal was slowly unloaded. The smoke of forest fires and the summer fogs hid all the magnificent shores and headlands at the mouth of the great river, and the hundreds of little fishing-boats, with their pointed sails, that set out at sunset, soon vanished in the opaline mists. After dark a thousand tiny points of flame could be dimly seen on the water, as the fishermen lighted the fires in their boats to cook their suppers, or set their lanterns in the bows as they sailed slowly back to the canneries with their loads of salmon. Five days after we crossed the Columbia River bar, the ship reached Portland, and the journey was over.

The second cruise, which was blessed with clear sunshiny weather from beginning to end, was concluded at Port Townsend, where for three weeks we enjoyed such perfect summer days as are known nowhere but on Puget Sound. With Mt. Baker on one side as a snowy sentinel, and the broken range of the Olympic Mountains a violet wall against the western sky, it needed only the foreground of water and the immaculate silver cone of Mt. Tacoma rising over level woodlands, to make the view from Port Townsend's heights the finest on Puget Sound. When a great full moon hung in the purple sky of night, miles of the waters of the bay were pure, rippling silver; and, like a vision in the southern sky, glistened a faint, ethereal image, the peak of Mt. Tacoma, sixty miles away.

Appreciating all that was overhead and around us, we found a wonderland under foot one morning by rowing and poling a small boat far in under the wharf, at the low tide. The water having receded thirteen feet, the piles for that distance were covered with the strangest and most fanciful marine growths. Star fish, pink, yellow, white, and purple, clung to the piles, many of them with eighteen and twenty-one feelers radiating from their thick fleshy bodies, that were twelve inches and more in diameter. There were slender, skeleton-like little starfish of the brightest carmine, and bunches of snow-white and pale yellow anemones (*actinia*) that looked like large cauliflower blossoms when opened fully under the water. Long brown pipes, growing in clusters on the piles, hung out crimson petals and ragged streamers until it seemed as though thousands of carnation pinks had been swept in among the piles. The *serpula*, that lives in this pipe-stem house, is valued for fish bait, and the voyage under the wharf was not wholly for studies in zoology. Huge jelly-fish floated by, opening and shutting their umbrella-like disks of pink and yellow, as if some wind were blowing rudely the petals of these wonderful blossoms of the sea. Shells of the "Spanish dollar" lay on the sands at the bottom, and at the water line little jelly-fish could be seen shimmering like disks of ice in the clear light of the early summer morning. A scientist would have been wild at sight of that natural aquarium, and to any one it would appear as a part of wonderland, a beautifully decorated hall for mermaids' revels, and a model for a transformation fairy scene in some spectacular drama. The woods and drives, the scenes and shores about Port Townsend, excite the admiration of every visitor, and when the aquarium under the wharf is regularly added to its list of attractions, that charming town will have done its whole duty to the travelling public.

CHAPTER XXIII.

SEALSKINS.

I have never been to the Seal Islands myself, and have no desire to cross the twenty-six hundred miles of rough and foggy seas that lie between San Francisco and the Pribyloff Islands, in Bering Sea. Considering that there are so many good people who think that the Seal Islands constitute Alaska, or that all Alaska is one Seal Island, it has been urged that I must include something about the seal fisheries if I mention Alaska at all. In deference to the prejudice which exists against having people write of the regions they have never visited, all apologies are offered for this reprint of a rambling letter about the Seal Islands and sealskins, and containing a few facts for which I am indebted to members of the Alaska Commercial Company of San Francisco, and others who have been to the islands and are interested in the fur trade.

For all that has been written concerning the Seal Islands, many very intelligent people have the vaguest ideas of their position, size, and condition, and few women who own sealskin garments even know that the scientist's name for the animal that first wears that fine pelt is *Callorhinus ursinus*, or are acquainted with any of the other remarkable facts and statistics concerning the sealskin of commerce. Such an absurd misstatement as the following lately appeared in a journal published at the national capital in an article entitled "Our Northern Land," and worse errors are frequently made:—

"The seal fisheries are situated near Sitka, and on the first of July (1884) a railway will be begun between the two points."

When we first started for Alaska we expected to find Sitka the centre of information about everything in the rest of the Territory, but at that ancient capital less was known about the seal fisheries than at San Francisco. The Seal Islands, discovered by the skipper Gerassim Pribyloff in 1788, lie to the north and west of the first of the Aleutian chain of islands. St. Paul, the largest of these four little rocky islets in Bering Sea, is fourteen hundred and ninety-one miles west of Sitka, and between two and three hundred miles from the nearest mainland. All communication with these islands is by way of San Francisco, and the company leasing them permit none but government vessels, outside of their own fleet, to touch at St. Paul and St. George. The Alaska Commercial Company's vessels make four trips a year, their steamers going in ten days generally, but the *Jeannette*, when starting on its Arctic expedition, fell behind all competitors in a slow race by taking twenty-five days to steam from San Francisco to St. Paul.

At the time of the Alaska purchase, in 1867, the most ardent supporters of the measure laid no stress upon the value of these Seal Islands, and Senator Sumner made no reference to them in his great speech which virtually decided the destiny of Alaska, and made it a possession of the United States. Hayward Hutchinson was one of the first of our countrymen to engage in the fur trade after the transfer, and, with a company of San Francisco capitalists, bought the buildings and good-will of the old Russian-American Fur Company. He went from Sitka across to the Pribyloff Islands in 1868, and there encountered Captain Morgan, of New London, Conn., who, like himself, had gone up to look over the possibilities of the new Territory in the interests of home capitalists. They joined forces, and, returning to San Francisco, had long and quiet consultations with their partners. Through their efforts, Congress passed a law in 1869, declaring the Seal Islands a government reservation, and prohibiting any one from killing fur seals, except under certain restrictions. On the first of July, 1870, the islands of St. Paul and St. George were leased for a term of twenty years to the Alaska Commercial Company of San Francisco. The lease was delivered August 31, 1870, and is signed on behalf of the company by its president, John F. Miller, previous to that time collector of the port of San Francisco, and, since his retirement from the presidency of the company, a United States senator from California. Beginning with the first day of May, 1870, they had sole right to the seal fisheries. The annual rent of the islands was fixed at $55,000, the payment to be secured by the deposit of United States bonds to that amount. They were also required to pay a tax of two dollars sixty-two and one-half cents upon each of the one hundred thousand skins of the fur seal permitted to be taken each year. Fifty-five cents was to be paid for each gallon of seal oil obtained, and the company was to furnish the inhabitants of the islands with a certain amount of food and fuel, to maintain schools for the children, and to prevent the use of fire-arms on or near the sealing-grounds. A bond of $500,000 was required of them, and the original firms of Hutchinson, Kohl, & Co., of San Francisco, and Williams, Havens, & Co., of New London, were merged into this Alaska Commercial Company.

Although 269,400 sealskins are said to have been exported from the islands from 1868 to 1869, it is claimed that the company had up-hill work for three years in getting themselves established and introducing their goods to the market. Since that time they have ridden on fortune's topmost wave, and been the envy of all the short-sighted rivals who might have done the same thing had they been shrewd enough. None of the original members have left the company, save by death, and, it being a close corporation, they keep their financial statements, their books, their profits, and affairs to themselves; and the outer world, compelled to guess at things, puts a fabulous estimate upon the sum annually divided among the stockholders. The officers of the company only smile with annoyance, and shrug their shoulders, if one repeats to them the common gossip of San Francisco, about each of the twelve shares of the stock paying an annual dividend of $90,000, and they laugh aloud if one appeals to them for the confirmation of it. There will be a great scramble and competition among rival traders in 1890, when the present lease of the islands terminates, and by the bids and statements made then, more light may be cast upon the value of the franchise, unless fickle woman puts sealskin out of fashion by that time, and the tanners, instead of the furriers, apply for the lease.

By a contract with the Russian government, dating some years later, this same Alaska Commercial Company, in the name of two of its members, has a monopoly of the fur trade on Bering and Copper Islands, and at points on the Kamschatka coast. By the terms of this contract one of the members had to be a Russian, and the ships engaged in this trade on the Asiatic side have to carry the Russian flag. Out of the company's fleet of a dozen vessels, two steamers fly the Muscovite colors, and, on their regular trips up, carry large cargoes of flour and provisions to Petropaulovski, as well as to their own stations.

Besides the Seal Islands, the Alaska Commercial Company has thirty-five other trading posts in the Territory, and its agents are established along the Yukon, and at many points in the interior. The trade in seal skins from the Pribyloff Islands amounts to about one half of the general business transacted by this corporation. At their offices on Sansome Street, in San Francisco, the company has a museum, crowded with specimens and curios. Seal life is represented at all ages, and all the birds and fishes and minerals of the country are shown. There are mummies and petrifactions, reindeer horns, canoes, albino otter skins, stone-age instruments, costumes and household utensils of the natives, and needles, books, pipes, toys, and oddities carved out of bone and ivory, and decorated in black outlines with sketches of men and animals in profile. A ponderous old silver watch is supposed to have belonged to some one of the early Russian governors, and there is a curious bronze cannon, with an inscription in ancient Slavonic lettering that no one has yet read. The company has been very generous in giving specimens and collections to different museums and societies, and its agents are instructed to gather such things and send them to the company's headquarters. In an upper room, where there were sixty thousand fox skins, hanging tail downwards from the rafters, thousands of mink and marten skins, and piles of bear, beaver, lynx, and deer skins, we were shown the skeleton of the extinct sea-cow. The exact number of bones in the sea-cow's body has been a matter of contention and uncertainty to scientists, and there was once a wordy war over it. Prof. Elliott, who made a long and careful study of seal life for the Smithsonian Institution, and whose monograph on that subject has been included in the census reports of 1880, was a leading combatant in the battle over the sea-cow's bones. This fossil skeleton, sent down by one of the company's agents, was presented to the California Academy of Sciences, and the palæontologists' war is over. Captain Niebaum, one of the vice-presidents of the company, is a great authority in matters pertaining to Arctic and polar navigation, and he was consulted about the details of the cruise by Captain De Long of the *Jeannette* expedition, and the Alaska company freely supplied that ship with provisions, clothing, dogs, and other necessaries when it reached St. Michael's Island. For his own use, Captain Niebaum has had made a large map of the polar regions, which is the most complete and unique chart in the country. On it are traced the courses of all the exploring ships, and the dates of their reaching important positions, and the artist, who worked at this circumpolar chart for more than one hundred days, is obliged, for a certain number of years, to add to it each discovery or incident of exploration in the arctic world.

The company's ships usually stop at Unalashka Island on their way to St. Paul, and that chief trading post of the old Russian-American company has become an even more important place under the new régime. Unalashka is one of the largest of the seventy Aleutian islands that stretch out in line towards Japan, and on it was made the earliest Russian settlement on the northwest coast. All of the Aleutian islands are volcanic, and occasionally another peak thrusts its head up out of the water, flames and cinders come from the mountain tops, and earthquakes and tidal waves create disturbances in honor of a new island added to the chain. The climate is rather mild, and the temperature varies little from the average at Sitka. There is almost constant fog and rain during the summer months, and the islands, though treeless, are covered with luxuriant grasses. Cattle were successfully kept by the Russians, and lately there have been several plans laid for raising cattle and sheep on these grassy islands on a large scale; Lieut. Schwatka, the hero of Arctic and Yukon adventures, being a promoter of one of these schemes. At this time, instead of cattle ranches, there are fox ranches on several of the Aleutian Islands; and even from far-away Attu, the most western point in the United States, a shipment of two hundred or more blue-fox skins is regularly made each year, and care taken to protect and increase the numbers of the foxes. Sea otters are hunted all along the Aleutian shores; and in the group of Shumagin Islands, northeast of Unalashka, the cod fisheries have become an important industry. A small fleet of schooners from San Francisco make one or two trips every year to the headquarters on Popoff Island, where from 500,000 to 600,000 fish are dried and salted each season. The Alaska Commercial Company has also a trading station and a salmon cannery on Kadiak Island, beyond the Shumagins, and the sea otter is also hunted around Kadiak, by native hunters in their tight skin canoes or *bidarkas*. Two men from Kadiak acquired a certain fame in 1884 by journeying from that place to San Francisco in one of these canoes, nineteen feet long. They were Danes,—Peter Müller and Nils Petersen by name,—and, following the general line of the shore, they made the sixteen hundred miles to Victoria in one hundred and five days. It is considered quite a feat in these times, but, a century ago, the natives thought nothing of such a journey.

Although Unalashka has a custom house and is a port of delivery, the collector at Sitka only hears from his Unalashka deputy by way of San Francisco, and a prisoner arrested at Unalashka has to be taken first to San Francisco in order to reach the authorities at the capital of the Territory. The culprit travels three thousand nine hundred and ten miles to reach the Sitka jail, while the distance straight across is but twelve hundred and seventy-eight miles. Unalashka is a headquarters for the whaling fleet of the North Pacific, which now numbers thirty-eight vessels. The whalers call there for mail, water, and supplies, and stop on their way up each season to learn how the ice is beyond Bering Straits. They leave word as to the condition of the bergs and floes, the positions of the remaining ships and their catches, as they come down each fall.

At the Pribyloff Islands, two hundred and twenty and two hundred and seventy miles further north, neither whalers nor other trading ships are ever seen. The heaviest fogs rest upon them in summer, and ice floes beleaguer them in winter, stilling the heavy roar of the surf, and putting one and two miles of broken ice between the shores and the open water. The shallow waters, and the upward current through Bering Straits, prevent icebergs from floating down from the Arctic Ocean, and that element of danger does not threaten the navigators in those foggy waters. During the breeding season each summer, United States officers are stationed on the two smaller islands, Copper and Walrus, to prevent any seal pirates from unlawfully killing the animals, and on St. Paul and St. George islands special treasury and revenue agents watch closely that none of the regulations are disregarded.

The three hundred and ninety-eight natives who inhabit the two islands are mostly half breeds of the Aleut tribe. They live now after a certain civilized way, in neat and comfortable houses provided for them by the company, but it was at first difficult to get them to leave their filthy underground hovels. They are nearly all members of the Greek Church, and, with the help of the company, support a chapel on either island. Bishop Nestor used to include these little parishes on his annual visits, and celebrated the mass in his richest vestments before their altars. To prevent the evils of intemperance, the company is careful that no intoxicants are sent up with their stores, and sugar and molasses are sold to the natives, only in the smallest quantities, for fear that they might distil the same *hoochinoo* as the Thlinkets. Failing these luxuries, the poor Aleut satisfies his sweet tooth with other substitutes. The greatest quantities of condensed milk are sold them each year, the seal hunters drinking a can of milk at a time, or spreading it thickly on their daily bread. The large sums they receive during the few weeks of the sealing season enable them to live in idleness and plenty for the rest of the year. They are inveterate gamblers, as well as feasters and idlers, and after the long hibernation and pleasuring of the winter they are anxious and ready for the summer's work.

It has not been learned yet where *Callorhinus ursinus* stays for the rest of the year; but early in June the desolate shores of the Pribyloff Islands become vocal with the hoarse voices of the seal, which have made this their gathering-place during the breeding season for unnumbered years. It is estimated that three million seals congregate on the rookeries of St. Paul Island each summer, and those who have looked down upon these rookeries at the height of the season report it as a most astounding spectacle. Acres of the rocky shore are alive with seals of all sizes and kinds, and the very ground seems to be writhing and squirming as the ungainly creatures drag themselves over the rocks, or pause to fan themselves with their flippers. Great battles are waged between the heads of seal families from June to August, and the harsh chorus of their voices is heard at sea above the roar of the breakers, and is the sailors' guide in making the islands during the heavy summer fogs. Only the male seals from two to four years of age are killed, and the skins of the three-year-olds have the finest and closest fur. The method of killing them has nothing heroic or huntsmanlike about it. The natives start out before dawn, and, running down the shore, get between the sleeping seals and the water, and then drive them, as they would so many sheep, to the killing-ground, a half mile inland. They drive them slowly, giving them frequent rests for cooling, and gradually turning aside and leaving behind all seals that are not up to the requisite age and condition. When the poor, tame things have reached their death-ground, the natives go round with heavy clubs and kill them with one blow on the head. The skins are quickly stripped from them and taken to the salting-house, where they are covered with salt and laid in great piles. The natives receive forty cents for each skin taken in this way. After a few weeks in the salting-house the company's steamer brings them down to San Francisco. The special agent of the United States Treasury at the islands counts the skins before they are shipped, and, accompanying them to San Francisco, they are again counted in his presence by the inspectors at that port. The tax of $2.62-1/2 is paid on each skin, the dirty yellow pelts treated to more salt, rolled into bundles, and packed in tight casks ready to ship to London. Of these one hundred thousand sealskins, eighty thousand come from the island of St. Paul, which is sixteen miles long and from three to six miles wide, and twenty thousand skins come from the island of St. George, which is not even as large. On one trip in 1883, the steamer *St. Paul* brought down sixty-three thousand sealskins, valued at $630,000, and the tax paid to the government on them amounted to $165,375.

When *Callorhinus ursinus* has thus delivered up his skin, and been salted and packed into barrels, he is sent on by railroad and steamship to London, where the Alaska Commercial Company controls the sealskin market of the world. Over seven firms in London are now engaged in the dyeing and dressing of sealskins, although there is a fiction still passed around about the secret of dyeing being held by one family of London furriers. Smiths, Oppenheimers, and other great firms buy the sealskins, dress them, pluck them, and give them the deep velvety brown and black dye that constitutes them such articles of luxury and fashion. A firm of Paris furriers has been setting the fashion of dyes for several years, and in accordance with their behests the color has been made darker and darker, until it is now nearly black. The old London furriers shake their heads at this change, as the strong nut gall and acids used to obtain this rich dark tone are liable to eat and destroy the leather. Cheap labor is the only answer to the question why this dressing and dyeing is done in Europe instead of America. The long, coarse hairs that overlay the fine fur have all to be removed by hand, and is best accomplished by that "pauper labor" at which emigrated demagogues rail. In New York there is one furrier who attempts to rival the London and Paris houses, but the results have so far proved his inability to outdo them in price and quality of work. If well dyed, a sealskin will never fade, spot with rain, nor mat together with dust, and it is even told that one London dyer put one of his sealskins in a tub and washed it with soap as a proof that they would lose neither lustre nor color by such treatment. It takes many handlings to turn the coarse long hair of these skins into a short, velvety, and glossy fur. Hot sand baths and chemicals are used to get the grease and oil out of the skins, and if this process is not thoroughly done at the time, the dull and matted furs have to be put through hot sand again after they have been made up into garments and worn. Six and more coats of dye are necessary, and it is applied to the surface only, so as to leave the roots of the fine hairs a golden yellow. Like the manufacture of gunpowder and so many other things, the art of dyeing sealskin originated with the Chinese, to whom the Russians used to sell nearly all of their furs. It is most probable that it was their intention to imitate the costly, purplish brown fur of the sea otter, which in Russia, as well as China, was formerly a badge of rank, and is still the most expensive fur sold, single skins being shown at the San Francisco warehouse, worth $100 and $300. The otter skins are brought down dried, and require only to be dressed and plucked of the coarser hairs before being ready to use.

After being dressed and dyed, the sealskins pay a duty of 20 per cent when they return to this country, and the cost of sealskin garments may be wondered at when one counts the items. The raw and unsightly skins in their salt are worth from $10 to $18 each, according to quality. There is to be added to this a tax of $2.62-1/2 each to the government; a charge of $6 or $8 for the dyeing and dressing; a duty of 20 per cent when they are returned to this country; and a fair charge for all the transportation the skins undergo, and the insurance on them during this time. This gives a dressed sealskin ready for the furrier to make up into garments, at an average value of from $15 to $30. It takes three skins to make a sacque of medium size, and the furriers always charge well for the making, as the greatest skill and nicety are required in sewing the skins. That furriers reap a profit of one hundred per cent on each sealskin garment is quite evident.

By the wise action of the government in reserving the seal islands and leasing them to a responsible company, the seal fisheries have become more and more valuable. The seals are increasing in number yearly, and more than the regular 100,000 could be killed each season without diminishing them to any extent, although to regulate prices the company has often taken less than the maximum number allowed in a season. Alaska seal is now the only seal in the market, since the rookeries of the Antarctic Sea have been so persistently hunted that the seals have become extinct. The Shetland seals, found on the islands of that name off Cape Horn, for a long time furnished the finest skins in the market, and commanded almost double the price of the Alaska sealskins. Not being protected by any government, the islands were free hunting grounds for every ship that went "round the Horn," and no skipper could resist a venture at such costly pelts. From the Island of South Georgia and the Island of Desolation 2,400,000 sealskins were taken annually from the time of their discovery, in 1771, until within the last twenty years, when the seals gradually became extinct. A San Francisco furrier sent a schooner down to those Antarctic islands a few years ago, and sixty skins were all that were obtained, and in another season only three skins were taken. All along the northwest coast, from Vancouver's Island to Unalashka, where the authority and monopoly of the Alaska Commercial Company begins, a general warfare is waged on the fur seal by independent hunters and traders; but their catch has seemingly no effect upon the millions of seal that annually gather on the Pribyloff shores, and the pelt grows coarser and poorer the further south of those islands it is obtained. The seal's skin is in its best condition during the summer months, when the animals frequent the Pribyloff rookeries, and by wise protection the government has an inexhaustible source of wealth in these two small islands, that have already paid into the Treasury, in rent and taxes, nearly the whole amount that was paid to Russia for the immense territory of Alaska. From the date of the lease in 1870 up to March, 1884, the Alaska Commercial Company has paid into the United States Treasury $4,662,026. Having invested $7,200,000 in the purchase of the Territory, comprising an area of 580,107 square miles, the government has derived an annual income ranging from $262,500 to $317,000 from two of the smallest islands off its coast.

CHAPTER XXIV.

THE TREATY AND CONGRESSIONAL PAPERS.

The following is the official text of the "Treaty concerning the cession of the Russian Possessions in North America by His Majesty the Emperor of all the Russias to the United States of America; concluded March 30, 1867; ratified by the United States May 28, 1867; exchanged June 20, 1867; proclaimed by the United States June 20, 1867:"—

By the President of the United States of America.

A PROCLAMATION.

Whereas a treaty between the United States of America and his Majesty the Emperor of all the Russias was concluded and signed by their respective plenipotentiaries at the city of Washington on the thirtieth day of March last, which treaty, being in the English and French languages, is, word for word, as follows:—

The United States of America and His Majesty the Emperor of all the Russias, being desirous of strengthening, if possible, the good understanding which exists between them, have, for that purpose, appointed as their Plenipotentiaries: the President of the United States, William H. Seward, Secretary of State; and His Majesty the Emperor of all the Russias, the Privy Counsellor Edward de Stoeckl, his Envoy Extraordinary and Minister Plenipotentiary to the United States.

And the said Plenipotentiaries, having exchanged their full powers, which were found to be in due form, have agreed upon and signed the following articles:—

ARTICLE I.

His Majesty the Emperor of all the Russias agrees to cede to the United States, by this convention, immediately upon the exchange of the ratifications thereof, all the territory and dominion now possessed by his said Majesty on the continent of America and in the adjacent islands, the same being contained within the geographical limits herein set forth, to wit: The eastern limit is the line of demarcation between the Russian and the British possessions in North America, as established by the convention between Russia and Great Britain, of February 28-16, 1825, and described in Articles III and IV of said convention, in the following terms:

"Commencing from the southernmost point of the island called Prince of Wales Island, which point lies in the parallel of 54 degrees 40 minutes north latitude, and between the 131st and the 133d degree of west longitude (meridian of Greenwich), the said line shall ascend to the north along the channel called Portland channel, as far as the point of the continent where it strikes the 56th degree of north latitude; from this last-mentioned point, the line of demarcation shall follow the summit of the mountains situated parallel to the coast as far as the point of intersection of the 141st degree of west longitude (of the same meridian); and finally, from the said point of intersection, the said meridian line of the 141st degree, in its prolongation as far as the Frozen ocean.

"IV. With reference to the line of demarcation laid down in the preceding article, it is understood —

"1st. That the island called Prince of Wales Island shall belong wholly to Russia" (now, by this cession, to the United States).

"2d. That whenever the summit of the mountains which extend in a direction parallel to the coast from the 56th degree of north latitude to the point of intersection of the 141st degree of west longitude shall prove to be at the distance of more than ten marine leagues from the ocean, the limit between the British possessions and the line of coast which is to belong to Russia as above mentioned (that is to say, the limit to the possessions ceded by this convention) shall be formed by a line parallel to the winding of the coast, and which shall never exceed the distance of ten marine leagues therefrom."

The western limit within which the territories and dominion conveyed are contained, passes through a point in Behring's straits on the parallel of sixty-five degrees thirty minutes north latitude, at its intersection by the meridian which passes midway between the islands of Krusenstern, or Ignalook, and the island of Ratmanoff, or Noonarbook, and proceeds due north, without limitation, into the same Frozen ocean. The same western limit, beginning at the same initial point, proceeds thence in a course nearly southwest, through Behring's straits and Behring's sea, so as to pass midway between the northwest point of the island of St. Lawrence and the southeast point of Cape Choukotski, to the meridian of one hundred and seventy-two west longitude; thence, from the intersection of that meridian, in a south-westerly direction, so as to pass midway between the island of Attou and the Copper island of the Kormandorski couplet or group in the North Pacific ocean, to the meridian of one hundred and ninety-three degrees west longitude, so as to include in the territory conveyed the whole of the Aleutian islands east of that meridian.

ARTICLE II.

In the cession of territory and dominion made by the preceding article are included the right of property in all public lots and squares, vacant lands, and all public buildings, fortifications, barracks, and other edifices which are not private individual property. It is, however, understood and agreed, that the churches which have been built in the ceded territory by the Russian government shall remain the property of such members of the Greek Oriental Church resident in the territory, as may choose to worship therein. Any government archives, papers, and documents relative to the territory and dominion aforesaid, which may be now existing there, will be left in the possession of the agent of the United States; but an authenticated copy of such of them as may be required will be, at all times, given by the United States to the Russian government, or to such Russian officers or subjects as they may apply for.

ARTICLE III.

The inhabitants of the ceded territory, according to their choice, reserving their natural allegiance, may return to Russia within three years; but if they should prefer to remain in the ceded territory, they, with the exception of uncivilized native tribes, shall be admitted to the enjoyment of all the rights, advantages, and immunities of citizens of the United States, and shall be maintained and protected in the free enjoyment of their liberty, property, and religion. The uncivilized tribes will be subject to such laws and regulations as the United States may, from time to time, adopt in regard to aboriginal tribes of that country.

ARTICLE IV.

His Majesty the Emperor of all the Russias shall appoint, with convenient despatch, an agent or agents for the purpose of formally delivering to a similar agent or agents appointed on behalf of the United States, the territory, dominion, property, dependencies and appurtenances which are ceded as above, and for doing any other act which may be necessary in regard thereto. But the cession, with the right of immediate possession, is nevertheless to be deemed complete and absolute on the exchange of ratifications, without waiting for such formal delivery.

ARTICLE V.

Immediately after the exchange of the ratifications of this convention, any fortifications or military posts which may be in the ceded territory shall be delivered to the agent of the United States, and any Russian troops which may be in the territory shall be withdrawn as soon as may be reasonably and conveniently practicable.

ARTICLE VI.

In consideration of the cession aforesaid, the United States agree to pay at the treasury in Washington, within ten months after the exchange of the ratifications of this convention, to the diplomatic representative or other agent of his Majesty the Emperor of all the Russias, duly authorized to receive the same, seven million two hundred thousand dollars in gold. The cession of territory and dominion herein made is hereby declared to be free and unincumbered by any reservations, privileges, franchises, grants, or possessions, by any associated companies, whether corporate or incorporate, Russian or any other, or by any parties, except merely private individual property holders; and the cession hereby made conveys all the rights, franchises, and privileges now belonging to Russia in the said territory or dominion, and appurtenances thereto.

ARTICLE VII.

When this convention shall have been duly ratified by the President of the United States, by and with the advice and consent of the Senate, on the one part, and on the other by his Majesty the Emperor of all the Russias, the ratifications shall be exchanged at Washington within three months from the date hereof, or sooner, if possible.

In faith whereof, the respective plenipotentiaries have signed this convention, and thereto affixed the seals of their arms.

Done at Washington, the thirtieth day of March, in the year of our Lord one thousand eight hundred and sixty-seven.

[L. S.]	WILLIAM H. SEWARD.
[L. S.]	EDOUARD DE STOECKL.

And whereas the said Treaty has been duly ratified on both parts, and the respective ratifications of the same were exchanged at Washington on this twentieth day of June, by William H. Seward, Secretary of State of the United States, and the Privy Counsellor Edward de Stoeckl, the Envoy Extraordinary of His Majesty the Emperor of all the Russias, on the part of their respective governments,—

Now, therefore, be it known that I, ANDREW JOHNSON, President of the United States of America, have caused the said Treaty to be made public, to the end that the same and every clause and article thereof may be observed and fulfilled with good faith by the United States and the citizens thereof.

In witness whereof, I have hereunto set my hand, and caused the seal of the United States to be affixed.

Done at the city of Washington, this twentieth day of June, in the year of our Lord one thousand eight hundred and sixty-seven, and of the Independence of the United States the ninety-first.

[L. S.]	ANDREW JOHNSON.

By the President:
WILLIAM H. SEWARD, *Secretary of State.*

From the Revised Statutes of the United States for the Second Session of the Fortieth Congress is taken the following:—

An Act making an Appropriation of Money to carry into Effect the Treaty
with Russia of March thirtieth, eighteen hundred and sixty-seven.

WHEREAS the President of the United States, on the thirtieth of March, eighteen hundred and sixty-seven, entered into a treaty with the Emperor of Russia, and the Senate thereafter gave its advice and consent to said treaty, by the terms of which it was stipulated that, in consideration of the cession by the Emperor of Russia to the United States of certain territory therein described, the United States should pay to the Emperor of Russia the sum of seven million two hundred thousand dollars in coin; and whereas it was further stipulated in said treaty that the United States shall accept of such cession, and that certain inhabitants of said territory shall be admitted to the enjoyment of all the rights and immunities of citizens of the United States; and whereas said stipulations cannot be carried into full force and effect except by legislation to which the consent of both houses of Congress is necessary: Therefore, *Be it enacted by the Senate and House of Representatives of the United States of America in Congress assembled*, That there be, and hereby is, appropriated, from any money in the treasury not otherwise appropriated, seven million and two hundred thousand dollars in coin, to fulfil stipulations contained in the sixth article of the treaty with Russia, concluded at Washington on the thirtieth day of March, eighteen hundred and sixty-seven.

Approved, July 27, 1868.

During the First Session of the Forty-eighth Congress, the following bill, originating in the Senate, became a law:

AN ACT PROVIDING A CIVIL GOVERNMENT FOR ALASKA.

Be it enacted by the Senate and House of Representatives of the United States of America in Congress assembled, That the territory ceded to the United States by Russia by the treaty of March thirtieth, eighteen hundred and sixty-seven, and known as Alaska, shall constitute a civil and judicial district, the government of which shall be organized and administered as hereinafter provided. The temporary seat of government of said district is hereby established at Sitka.

Sec. 2. That there shall be appointed for the said district a governor, who shall reside therein during his term of office and be charged with the interests of the United States Government that may arise within said district. To the end aforesaid he shall have authority to see that the laws enacted for said district are enforced, and to require the faithful discharge of their duties by the officials appointed to administer the same. He may also grant reprieves for offences committed against the laws of the district or of the United States until the decision of the President thereon shall be made known. He shall be ex officio commander-in-chief of the militia of said district, and shall have power to call out the same when necessary to the due execution of the laws and to preserve the peace, and to cause all able-bodied citizens of the United States in said district to enroll and serve as such when the public exigency demands; and he shall perform generally in and over said district such acts as pertain to the office of governor of a territory, so far as the same may be made or become applicable thereto. He shall make an annual report, on the first day of October in each year, to the President of the United States, of his official acts and doings, and of the condition of said district, with reference to its resources, industries, population, and the administration of the civil government thereof. And the President of the United States shall have power to review and to confirm or annul any reprieves granted or other acts done by him.

Sec. 3. That there shall be, and hereby is, established a district court for said district, with the civil and criminal jurisdiction of district courts of the United States exercising the jurisdiction of circuit courts, and such other jurisdiction, not inconsistent with this act, as may be established by law; and a district judge shall be appointed for said district, who shall during his term of office reside therein and hold at least two terms of said court therein in each year, one at Sitka, beginning on the first Monday in May, and the other at Wrangel, beginning on the first Monday in November. He is also authorized and directed to hold such special sessions as may be necessary for the dispatch of the business of said court, at such times and places in said district as he may deem expedient, and may adjourn such special session to any other time previous to a regular session. He shall have authority to employ interpreters, and to make allowances for the necessary expenses of his court.

Sec. 4. That a clerk shall be appointed for said court, who shall be ex officio secretary and treasurer of said district, a district attorney, and a marshal, all of whom shall during their terms of office reside therein. The clerk shall record and preserve copies of all the laws, proceedings, and official acts applicable to said district. He shall also receive all moneys collected from fines, forfeitures, or in any other manner except from violations of the custom laws, and shall apply the same to the incidental expenses of the said district court and the allowances thereof as directed by the judge of said court, and shall account for the same in detail, and for any balances on account thereof, quarterly, to and under the direction of the Secretary of the Treasury. He shall be ex officio recorder of deeds and mortgages and certificates of location of mining claims and other contracts relating to real estate and register of wills for said district, and shall establish secure offices in the towns of Sitka and Wrangel, in said district, for the safekeeping of all his official records, and of records concerning the reformation and establishment of the present status of titles to lands, as hereinafter directed: *Provided*, That the district court hereby created may direct, if it shall deem it expedient, the establishment of separate offices at the settlements of Wrangel, Oonalashka, and Juneau City, respectively, for the recording of such instruments as may pertain to the several natural divisions of said district most convenient to said settlements, the limits of which shall, in the event of such direction, be defined by said court; and said offices shall be in charge of the commissioners respectively as hereinafter provided.

Sec. 5. That there shall be appointed by the President four commissioners in and for the said district, who shall have the jurisdiction and powers of commissioners of the United States circuit courts in any part of said district, but who shall reside, one at Sitka, one at Wrangel, one at Oonalashka, and one at Juneau City. Such commissioners shall exercise all the duties and powers, civil and criminal, now conferred on justices of the peace under the general laws of the State of Oregon, so far as the same may be applicable in said district, and may not be in conflict with this act or the laws of the United States. They shall also have jurisdiction, subject to the supervision of the district judge, in all testamentary and probate matters, and for this purpose their courts shall be opened at stated terms and be courts of record, and be provided with a seal for the authentication of their official acts. They shall also have power to grant writs of habeas corpus for the purpose of inquiring into the cause of restraint of liberty, which writs shall be made returnable before the said district judge for said district; and like proceedings shall be had thereon as if the same had been granted by said judge under the general laws of the United States in such cases. Said commissioners shall also have the powers of notaries public, and shall keep a record of all deeds and other instruments of writing acknowledged before them and relating to the title to or transfer of property within said district, which record shall be subject to public inspection. Said commissioners shall also keep a record of all fines and forfeitures received by them, and shall pay over the same quarterly to the clerk of said district court. The governor appointed under the provisions of this act shall, from time to time, inquire into the operations of the Alaska Seal and Fur Company, and shall annually report to Congress the result of such inquiries and any and all violations by said company of the agreement existing between the United States and said company.

Sec. 6. That the marshal for said district shall have the general authority and powers of the United States marshals of the States and Territories. He shall be the executive officer of said court, and charged with the execution of all process of said court and with the transportation and custody of prisoners, and he shall be ex officio keeper of the jail or penitentiary of said district. He shall appoint four deputies, who shall reside severally at the towns of Sitka, Wrangel, Oonalashka, and Juneau City, and they shall respectively be ex officio constables and executive officers of the commissioners' courts herein provided, and shall have the powers and discharge the duties of United States deputy marshals, and those of constables under the laws of the State of Oregon now in force.

Sec. 7. That the general laws of the State of Oregon now in force are hereby declared to be the law in said district, so far as the same may be applicable and not in conflict with the provisions of this act or the laws of the United States; and the sentence of imprisonment in any criminal case shall be carried out by confinement in the jail or penitentiary hereinafter provided for. But the said district court shall have exclusive jurisdiction in all cases in equity or those involving a question of title to land, or mining rights, or the constitutionality of a law, and in all criminal offences which are capital. In all civil cases, at common law, any issue of fact shall be determined by a jury, at the instance of either party; and an appeal shall lie in any case, civil or criminal, from the judgment of said commissioners to the said district court where the amount involved in any civil case is two hundred dollars or more, and in any criminal case where a fine of more than one hundred dollars or imprisonment is imposed, upon the filing of a sufficient appeal bond by the party appealing, to be approved by the court or commissioner. Writs of error in criminal cases shall issue to the said district court from the United States circuit court for the district of Oregon in the cases provided in chapter one hundred and seventy-six of the laws of eighteen hundred and seventy-nine; and the jurisdiction thereby conferred upon circuit courts is hereby given to the circuit court of Oregon. And the final judgments or decrees of said circuit and district court may be reviewed by the Supreme Court of the United States as in other cases.

Sec. 8. That the said district of Alaska is hereby created a land district, and a United States land-office for said district is hereby located at Sitka. The commissioner provided for by this act to reside at Sitka shall be ex officio register of said land-office, and the clerk provided for by this act shall be ex officio receiver of public moneys, and the marshal provided for by this act shall be ex officio surveyor-general of said district, and the laws of the United States relating to mining claims, and the rights incident thereto, shall, from and after the passage of this act, be in full force and effect in said district, under the administration thereof herein provided for, subject to such regulations as may be made by the Secretary of the Interior, approved by the President: *Provided*, That the Indians or other persons in said district shall not be disturbed in the possession of any lands actually in their use or occupation or now claimed by them, but the terms under which such persons may acquire title to such lands is reserved for future legislation by Congress: *And provided further*, That parties who have located mines or mineral privileges therein under the laws of the United States applicable to the public domain, or who have occupied and improved or exercised acts of ownership over such claims, shall not be disturbed therein, but shall be allowed to perfect their title to such claims by payment as aforesaid: *And provided also*, That the land not exceeding six hundred and forty acres at any station now occupied as missionary stations among the Indian tribes in said section, with the improvements thereon erected by or for such societies, shall be continued in the occupancy of the several religious societies to which said missionary stations respectively belong until action by Congress. But nothing contained in this act shall be construed to put in force in said district the general land laws of the United States.

Sec. 9. That the governor, attorney, judge, marshal, clerk, and commissioners provided for in this act shall be appointed by the President of the United States, by and with the advice and consent of the Senate, and shall hold their respective offices for the term of four years, and until their successors are appointed and qualified. They shall severally receive the fees of office established by law for the several offices the duties of which have been hereby conferred upon them, as the same are determined and allowed in respect of similar offices under the laws of the United States, which fees shall be reported to the Attorney General and paid into the Treasury of the United States. They shall receive respectively the following annual salaries. The governor, the sum of three thousand dollars; the attorney, the sum of two thousand five hundred dollars; the marshal, the sum of two thousand five hundred dollars; the judge, the sum of three thousand dollars; and the clerk, the sum of two thousand five hundred dollars, payable to them quarterly from the Treasury of the United States. The district judge, marshal, and district attorney shall be paid their actual, necessary expenses when travelling in the discharge of their official duties. A detailed account shall be rendered of such expenses under oath and as to the marshal and district attorney such account shall be approved by the judge, and as to his expenses by the Attorney General. The commissioners shall receive the usual fees of United States commissioners and of justices of the peace for Oregon, and such fees for recording instruments as are allowed by the laws of Oregon for similar services, and in addition a salary of one thousand dollars each. The deputy marshals, in addition to the usual fees of constables in Oregon, shall receive each a salary of seven hundred and fifty dollars, which salaries shall also be payable quarterly out of the Treasury of the United States. Each of said officials shall, before entering on the duties of his office, take and subscribe an oath that he will faithfully execute the same, which said oath may be taken before the judge of said district or any United States district or circuit judge. That all officers appointed for said district, before entering upon the duties of their offices, shall take the oaths required by law, and the laws of the United States, not locally inapplicable to said district and not inconsistent with the provisions of this act are hereby extended thereto; but there shall be no legislative assembly in said district, nor shall any delegate be sent to Congress therefrom. And the said clerk shall execute a bond, with sufficient sureties, in the penalty of ten thousand dollars, for the faithful performance of his duties, and file the same with the Secretary of the Treasury before entering on the duties of his office; and the commissioners shall each execute a bond, with sufficient sureties, in the penalty of three thousand dollars, for the faithful performance of their duties, and file the same with the clerk before entering on the duties of their office.

SEC. 10. That any of the public buildings in said district not required for the customs service or military purposes shall be used for court-rooms and offices of the civil government; and the Secretary of the Treasury is hereby directed to instruct and authorize the custodian of said buildings forthwith to make such repairs to the jail in the town of Sitka, in said district, as will render it suitable for a jail and penitentiary for the purposes of the civil government hereby provided, and to surrender to the marshal the custody of said jail and the other public buildings, or such parts of said buildings as may be selected for court-rooms, offices, and officials.

SEC. 11. That the Attorney-General is directed forthwith to compile and cause to be printed, in the English language, in pamphlet form, so much of the general laws of the United States as is applicable to the duties of the governor, attorney, judge, clerk, marshals, and commissioners appointed for said district, and shall furnish for the use of the officers of said Territory so many copies as may be needed of the laws of Oregon applicable to said district.

SEC. 12. That the Secretary of the Interior shall select two of the officers to be appointed under this act, who, together with the governor, shall constitute a commission to examine into and report upon the condition of the Indians residing in said Territory, what lands, if any, should be reserved for their use, what provision shall be made for their education, what rights by occupation of settlers should be recognized, and all other facts that may be necessary to enable Congress to determine what limitations or conditions should be imposed when the land laws of the United States shall be extended to said district; and to defray the expenses of said commission the sum of two thousand dollars is hereby appropriated out of any moneys in the Treasury not otherwise appropriated.

SEC. 13. That the Secretary of the Interior shall make needful and proper provision for the education of the children of school age in the Territory of Alaska, without reference to race, until such time as permanent provision shall be made for the same, and the sum of twenty-five thousand dollars, or so much thereof as may be necessary, is hereby appropriated for this purpose.

SEC. 14. That the provisions of chapter three, title twenty-three, of the Revised Statutes of the United States, relating to the unorganized Territory of Alaska, shall remain in full force, except as herein specially otherwise provided; and the importation, manufacture, and sale of intoxicating liquors in said district except for medicinal, mechanical, and scientific purposes, is hereby prohibited under the penalties which are provided in section nineteen hundred and fifty-five of the Revised Statutes for the wrongful importation of distilled spirits. And the President of the United States shall make such regulations as are necessary to carry out the provisions of this section.

Approved, May 17, 1884.

Lector House believes that a society develops through a two-fold approach of continuous learning and adaptation, which is derived from the study of classic literary works spread across the historic timeline of literature records. Therefore, we aim at reviving, repairing and redeveloping all those inaccessible or damaged but historically as well as culturally important literature across subjects so that the future generations may have an opportunity to study and learn from past works to embark upon a journey of creating a better future.

This book is a result of an effort made by Lector House towards making a contribution to the preservation and repair of original ancient works which might hold historical significance to the approach of continuous learning across subjects.

HAPPY READING & LEARNING!

LECTOR HOUSE LLP
E-MAIL: lectorpublishing@gmail.com